Power
SPELLCRAFT
FOR LIFE

The Art of Crafting and Casting
for Positive Change

ARIN MURPHY-HISCOCK

PROVENANCE
PRESS

Avon, Massachusetts

Published by
Provenance Press, an imprint of Adams Media,
an F+W Publications Company
57 Littlefield Street, Avon, MA 02322. U.S.A.
www.adamsmedia.com

ISBN 13: 978-1-59337-272-9
ISBN 10: 1-59337-272-8

Printed in Canada.

J I H G F E D C

Library of Congress Cataloging-in-Publication Data
Murphy-Hiscock, Arin.
Power spellcraft for life / Arin Murphy-Hiscock.
p.   cm.
ISBN 1-59337-272-8
1. Charms. 2. Magic. I. Title.
BF1611.M78 2005
133.4'4—dc22
2004026846

This publication is designed to provide accurate and authoritative information with regard to the subject matter covered. It is sold with the understanding that the publisher is not engaged in rendering legal, accounting, or other professional advice. If legal advice or other expert assistance is required, the services of a competent professional person should be sought.
　　　　　—From a *Declaration of Principles* jointly adopted by a Committee of the American Bar Association and a Committee of Publishers and Associations

Many of the designations used by manufacturers and sellers to distinguish their products are claimed as trademarks. Where those designations appear in this book and Adams Media was aware of a trademark claim, the designations have been printed with initial capital letters.

This book is available at quantity discounts for bulk purchases.
For information, please call 1-800-289-0963.

Mike:
You were right.
Thank you.
1970–1990

contents

acknowledgments

No work is ever created in a vacuum. There are several people who helped me reach where I am today:

To everyone at Le Melange Magique, and Debra in particular, without whom I wouldn't be working with Adams Media;

To everyone at Provenance Press and Adams Media, especially Danielle and Courtney, who have encouraged and supported me;

To t! and the Tough-Love Muse of Montreal, who have kept me creatively honest and writing for a combined total of eighteen years.

To my Black Forest family, including my wonderful Coven of the Silver Deer, and Triskelene Crow Moon;

To all my students, past and present, who were the original participants in various courses on spellcrafting and cultural magic, through the Crescent Moon program and independent workshops;

To my fellow Daughters of the Flame, whose light and love warm my life and heart in service of our Lady Brid;

To all the friends who have told me that I should play to my strengths, especially MLG, who, as part of his informal career-path therapy, told me to write a book;

To my beloved parents, who supported my choice of pursuing a B.A. and M.A. in English Lit, and then my paradoxical insistence on working for minimum wage in a bookstore;

And to my wonderful husband, partner in life, love, and magic, who makes me dinner, washes dishes, and helps me understand how fine I am to him.

introduction

Spellcraft.

The very word suggests a mystical art with secrets hidden from ordinary men and women. You already know that you want to learn more about this art. Otherwise, you wouldn't be here. *Power Spellcraft for Life* is a manual designed to help intermediate practitioners learn more about the art of crafting and casting spells, and how those spells can be used for positive change within their lives. Spellcraft isn't about hidden secrets; it's about learning to use the knowledge you already possess and the information you will acquire through experience for the betterment of your life.

Perhaps you've read a couple of spellbooks already, and you want to know why and how spells are crafted. How does one determine a problem, craft a spell to address it, include correspondences to fine-tune the energy to power it, cast it at a favorable time, and enjoy the benefits of success?

It may be that you're dissatisfied with the spellbooks that you've read, and you're not quite certain why. As a result, you might be looking for more information to help you develop your own spells, tailored to you and to your unique situation.

You might have cast a spell from a book in the past that didn't have the effect you were hoping for, and you want to know *why* it didn't work. Or, maybe that spell *did* work, and you want to know *how*. *Power Spellcraft for Life* addresses all these topics, and more.

The majority of spellbooks on the market give you pages of spells for all sorts of purposes, with lists of ingredients, directions, and words to say. I call this "cookbook craft." A spell isn't like a recipe for lasagna. A spell is more than a list of ingredients, directions on how to mix them, and a sure outcome. It isn't as simple as adding A to B to obtain C. That's chemistry, not spellcraft. What differentiates spells from chemistry and cooking is the inclusion of *you*, your *will*, and your *intention*. All these things have an important influence over spellcrafting and spellcasting. You have an enormous amount of control throughout the process, and over the outcome. This fact is probably why you've chosen to read a book on spellcraft, and not a chemistry text: you're looking for some sort of control over your life.

Of course, there are random and unknown factors in spellcasting, just as in cooking and chemistry, which affect the outcome. The personal factor of spellcasting is unique, however, and this factor is what classifies spellcraft as an art more than a science.

There's something else that the "cookbook craft" crowd is missing. This is the factor of spiritual and personal evolution. In order for your situation to change, the common element over which you have the most control is yourself. Magic often transforms the caster instead of the environment around the caster. Spellcraft isn't just about bringing home a bigger paycheck or finding the love of your life; it's about growth and evolution, making the career choices that lead to that bigger paycheck, accepting that the love of your life will have a few flaws and accept your flaws, too. Spellcrafting is about reassessing your life, isolating the obstacles, and striking a new balance.

Spell*crafting* is the process of creating a spell. Spell*casting* is the act of putting it into motion. Casting is, in fact, one of the final steps of spellcrafting, for the moment you begin to craft your spell is the moment you begin an active process.

Make no mistake: as a spellcaster, you are a part of the active process of change. You cannot interact with the energy of the world on a daily basis, at the depth required by spellcrafting, and not be changed by it. As you read through this book and deepen your understanding of the adaptability and benefits of spellcasting, you will see your entire life begin to reflect your inner changes.

Onward! Explore the wonderfully flexible and enriching world of spellcrafting!

1

spellcasting defined

An introduction to the concept of spells by looking at what a spell is—and what it isn't. In examining the basic steps involved, you can begin to understand the function and purpose of a spell. The popular areas usually addressed by spellcasting are introduced, as are suggestions for various and creative uses of spells. Also explored are the many benefits and opportunities for growth and positive change within your life by crafting and casting spells.

ॐ

WHAT IS A SPELL?

Simply put, a spell is something you do with intent and awareness to create change. It consists of a set of symbolic actions performed in the physical world to initialize change on a higher level. A spell seeks to redress the balance of a situation by introducing new energy or redistributing the energy already present.

A spell is *not* a religious act. Spellcasting is a method of using energy to power some sort of change. Many religions use spells or a form of energy transfer or energy management as part of worship. However, spells aren't unique to any one religion. They are often described as a form of prayer, but there are subtle differences between prayer and spellcraft. First of all, prayer to a higher power implies that you honor that higher power, and that an established relationship exists between you, which enables you to call on that higher power for aid. It also implies that the higher power possesses the wherewithal to fix the situation. On the other hand, spells use the abundance of energy around us in the world to catalyze change. It's a more active process than prayer. In a spell, you are the agent of change: you call upon your own resources to gather and direct energy instead of employing a separate agent such as a higher power to accomplish the task. Don't misunderstand the phrase "more active process"—heartfelt prayer raises a lot of energy on the part of the practitioner. In fact, partnering a spell with some form of prayer is a very popular practice in several cultures. What it comes down to, though, is that prayer is a religious act, whereas spellcraft is secular. When you cast a spell, you acknowledge that your actions are the ones responsible for creating change.

Power Spellcraft for Life focuses solely on the art of spellcrafting. What you learn here can have spiritual applications, but on the whole, spellcrafting is a practical art. Be aware that other books sometimes use the words *spell* and *ritual* interchangeably. These are two very different things. A spell is the use of natural energies to bring about internal or external change. A ritual is a set of spiritual actions, often performed with the intent to honor or celebrate, but sometimes also to initialize spiritual change. To make matters even more confusing, a spell can be a *part* of a ritual. The two should never be confused, however. At its most basic, the use of the word "ritual" suggests something performed with awareness and set apart from the everyday action for symbolic reasons. A spell does possess ritual elements, but ritual more correctly indicates an act of honoring or worship.

Why Use Spells?

There are a variety of reasons why people choose to perform spells. Crafting and casting a spell gives you a sense of control over a situation;

you no longer have to sit and wait for life to sort itself out. Spellcraft is an active method of dealing with life, instead of being a passive method. Engaging in spellwork can very often boost your confidence, as well, reinforcing your sense of "I matter" in the world. There's nothing quite like the feeling of realizing that one of your spells has worked. Your self-esteem rises a few notches, and the happiness catches.

Spellcraft also exercises your creativity. You might not be able to play the saxophone, or paint a masterpiece, or win a flamenco dance competition, but you can sit down and craft a web of energy from a variety of objects and words, linked together by intent and desire, and cast that web out into the cosmos to draw your goal to you. Spellcraft combines the use of imagination, language, and action in a variety of ways, and the way you put it all together will be unique to you.

Spells aren't only about getting what you want, either; they can also be about giving back. You can raise positive energy and send it out into the world, as a way to say "thank you" for all the joy you feel in your own life. Affirming your blessings is one way to draw more blessings to you.

Spellcraft also serves to actively create and maintain a sense of balance in your life.

Finally, you probably already cast spells without knowing it. If you want something badly enough, and you think about it constantly, you're sending out energy to that new reality, helping it to come into being. Be aware, however, that obsessing over a want or need can also impede the energy required to obtain it: A healthy balance is necessary for successful manifestation.

The Benefits of Spellcasting

By crafting and casting spells, you learn the ins and outs of the flow of energy through your life. You don't need to know how a car works in order to drive one, but the more you know, the better the car works for you.

Spellwork teaches you about how energy moves, how you can handle it, and how you can direct it into various areas of your life. Once you understand how energy behaves, you can fine-tune your use of it, and experiment tapping into it via different methods.

Spellwork is designed to make our lives easier, not harder. However, if you're looking to use spells to avoid work, forget it. Spellcraft

3

requires work and focus, particularly at the beginning of your study as you acquire new information and explore various techniques. There's no snapping of the fingers to achieve instant change. Spellcraft is a deeply transformative process, which touches the spellcaster as well as the goal and the environment containing them both. Energy must be put into the equation in order for the outcome to manifest. A spell acts as a catalyst for change. Yes, you still do work in order to achieve your goal, but you're more in control of what happens, and how it happens.

A spell creates the added benefit of knowing exactly what you want. Part of the spellcrafting process involves determining a precise goal. Often in our lives, we think we know what we want, but we rarely take the time to sit down and seriously think about how deeply we desire something. If we did, we'd likely discover that much of the time our desires are superficial, or that they mask another desire. You have to be completely honest with yourself in order to cast a successful spell. It's easier to work toward a clearly defined target or goal. If you do not have a defined goal, you end up throwing energy at a vague objective, wasting most of it. The result is a spell that doesn't succeed, or succeeds only partially. Knowing your target and being able to aim at it is one of the keys of spellcasting expertise. It benefits the rest of your life; being able to sift through the superficial desires clarifies your areas of strength and areas for you to work on.

How Do Spells Work?

Everything in the world possesses an energy signature of some kind. Organic objects possess more energy than inorganic objects. The closer to an organic object's natural state, the higher its energy. The more removed from nature an organic object is, the more processed and refined it is, and the less energy it has. For example, a tree rooted in the wild has more energy than a stack of lumber created from that tree, and a varnished table built from that lumber has even less energy. The energy of a plastic chair drawn up to that table will be even lower.

A piece of cotton or silk fabric will have more energy than a piece of polyester. A natural undyed piece of cotton will have more energy than a dyed piece of cotton.

All the energy possessed by these objects reaches out to connect with other energies. Essentially, a web of energy connects and interconnects the physical and nonphysical worlds. When we seek to influence a situation, we tweak the energy in one location, and that tweak sends shivers all over the web, and every energy field ripples a bit.

A common metaphor is that of a spider's web. No matter where a spider is on her web when an insect strikes it, the tiny shocks travel through all the strands of the web to alert her that she has a visitor for tea.

The world is covered with a spider's web of energy, connecting all the organic and inorganic glows. Strands of energy connect everyone and everything, and enable us to send and receive input from our surroundings.

People have varying levels of sensitivity to this incoming information. The more sensitive you are, the more capable you can become at managing and influencing your environment.

A common phrase in occult work is "as above, so below," which originates from a work called the Emerald Tablet, a record of the Hermetic principles (named for Hermes Trismegistus, who is referred to as the father of the occult study known as Hermeticism). J. F. Ruska's modern translation of this principle (called, appropriately enough, The Law of Correspondence) states that, "In truth certainly and without doubt whatever is below is like that which is above, and whatever is above is like that which is below, to accomplish the miracles of one thing" (as quoted by Silver RavenWolf in *Solitary Witch: The Ultimate Book of Shadows for the New Generation*, 2003). The concept of a microcosm reflecting a macrocosm is a common worldview. This concept is, in part, what allows a spellcaster to perform a symbolic action in the physical dimension, and to create change on another level such as mental, emotional, or astral, which then manifests again on the physical level, thus changing reality to some degree.

What Is the Purpose of a Spell?

A spell is designed to initiate change on some level by shifting the balance of energy within a situation. The shift doesn't simply occur in response to your wish for a change; there are certain stages through which you must pass. Let's take a look at them.

The Basic Steps

While every spell is different, most steps can be classified somewhere in the following:

1. **Establish your need or desire.** There's no point in doing a spell for the sake of doing a spell. That's simply a waste of time and energy.
2. **Compose your spell.** Take the time to think about your desired outcome, and what energies you wish to harness to help you achieve this outcome.
3. **Shift consciousness.** In order to maximize your spellwork, you should ideally be in a spellcasting frame of mind. Author Lilith McLelland calls this being in "magic mode." Our everyday, scattered, and busy brains aren't very efficient at gathering energies, melding them into a sleek, powerful spell, and releasing them toward a goal. Shifting consciousness allows you to attain a different state of mind, filtering out the surface noise and distractions in order to concentrate and focus on what you're doing.
4. **Raise energy and release it toward your goal.** This is the moment where spell*crafting* becomes spell*casting*. Spells are powered by the energies held by the components or ingredients you choose to use, and by your own personal energy as well. Chapter 6 and Chapter 7 explore the use of various energies in detail.
5. **Manifestation.** Ideally, the final step is the achievement of your goal.

Common Areas in Which Spellcraft Is Applied

While spells can be and are used in every sort of situation in life, there are certain areas that attract a lot more focus in spellbooks. Not surprisingly, these areas address basic human comforts such as prosperity, love, and safety.

A major stumbling block to successfully creating abundance and happiness within your life is often a feeling caused by guilt or greed. Let's set something straight right now: crafting and casting spells for the basic necessities of life isn't selfish, or greedy, or bad. Fulfilling those basic needs enables us to explore the higher potential of our lives and spirits. Abraham Maslow created a theory called the Hierarchy of Needs; it's specifically a hierarchy because Maslow argued that every subsequent need is rooted in the previous one. If a basic need such as food or shelter isn't met, then an individual isn't going to feel secure enough to address higher needs such as self-actualization. Examining the Hierarchy of Needs will help you understand that worrying about financial security isn't selfish; it's a valid need, which must be addressed before needs such as creating an aesthetically pleasing environment. While Maslow's theory isn't irrefutable, it does provide a useful guide to understanding why certain varieties of spells are immensely popular, and have been popular throughout the ages.

WHEN TO CAST A SPELL—AND WHEN NOT TO

You can pretty much cast a spell any time you feel comfortable doing so. However, there are a few things to keep in mind. You must:

- Have a valid need or desire, clearly delineated
- Be in the correct frame of mind
- Be in the proper state of health

If you cannot aim your spell at a clearly defined goal, then you have no concept of what you truly wish to manifest as a result of that spell. Apart from being a waste of energy, this can create more problems as the energy your spell casts out into the world bounces randomly like a pinball around and through the issues in your life. With no clear goal or need, a spell becomes dangerously unpredictable.

Your mental state is crucial to your success. Being distracted or worried will weaken your focus and your subsequent effects. States of high emotion can also be dangerous. Emotion is one of the energy sources that fuels spells. This might sound ideal to you, and in one respect, it is: the ability to feel intense emotion during the casting process can help you a lot. However, that intense emotion should be summoned and accessed *during* the process. If you fire off a spell as an emotional reaction to something, you are guilty of not thinking the situation through. You are not in proper command of yourself, which you need to be in order to cast a focused and well-aimed spell. Spells are a method of controlling yourself and your life, and to cast like this is not only irresponsible, it undermines the whole principle of creating positive change in your life.

Your state of health is also vitally important. When you are ill, your personal energies are unbalanced, and your handling of outside energies will be affected. Every spell, no matter how many other power sources you pull in such as components and correspondences (see Chapter 6), uses your own personal energy to guide it. Casting while ill can worsen your physical health, leaving you low on vital energy. Raising energy is a crucial step within the spellcasting process, and it takes energy to raise energy. Remember, spells don't *replace* work; they *are* work. Many practitioners feel like they've run a marathon after casting a spell. If you had the choice, would you run a marathon if you were sick? Probably not; in fact, most of us want to stay home from work as soon as we experience the first warning signs of a cold. Casting while ill is irresponsible, as it counters the principle of creating beneficial change. It is somewhat hypocritical to attempt to create beneficial change in your life when you're making yourself more ill by doing so.

What about casting a spell to regain your health? This is the one and only exception to the rule about performing spells while ill. However, make sure the spell you craft or use isn't too taxing, and choose a gentler method of raising energy. (For more on the subject of raising energy, see Chapter 7.)

Spellcraft and the Divine

In *Power Spellcraft for Life* I have chosen to guide you through a denomination-free exploration of spellcrafting and casting. The art of spellcraft can be used by anyone following any spiritual path, within any religious structure.

Some modern religions use spellcraft regularly as part of their worship. Neo-Pagan religions such as Wicca, Druidry, Asatru, and other established paths such as Santeria, Voudoun, and Candomblé all use spellwork as part of their worship process. Spellwork can certainly be done within a religious context, whether the religion is one of those mentioned or not. Within a spell, the inclusion of a deity or a higher power of some kind immediately transforms the spell into a spiritual act. However, the deity you appeal to in a spell should be a deity to whom you have at least introduced yourself, and have obtained their permission to work with them, otherwise you're not going to get much out of it. Several spells in the "cookbook craft" category toss around invocations to Hecate as the Queen of Witches, or invoke Aphrodite to help out in a love spell. These are ancient deities, now often thought relegated to mythology books. You can't just harness their energies; there has to be more to it than that. If your spell knocks at their door, they're likely to take a look through the spyhole, not recognize you, and won't answer. Even ancient deities understand what dangers lie with inviting just anyone into their home. Conversely, why invoke a deity associated with another culture or religion just because a spell in a book tells you to do it? What do you know about them? Who knows what kind of energy you might be inviting into your spell?

If you function within an established faith, your best bet is to appeal to the deity or aspect of the Divine that you already work with. You have an established relationship with this deity. When your spell comes knocking, the deity will recognize your energy, and your spell will have the added boost of love and energy freely given.

If you involve a spiritual entity such as a deity or an angel in a spell does it become a ritual? Not necessarily. It depends on your goal. Is your goal to achieve nirvana, or to become spiritually balanced within your religious path? Then you're performing a ritual. Is it to obtain a new car, or to release anger or stress? Then it's a spell. When you're not precisely sure if your goal is spiritual or practical, then it's probably still a spell.

White Magic, Black Magic

Magic is, in essence, the use of energy for a variety of purposes. Energy is neutral. What isn't neutral, however, is the intent of the person casting the spell, and this is where the misunderstanding of calling magic "black" or "white" arises. Generally, if the spellcaster seeks to cause damage or perform a malicious act, then it's referred to as "black magic." If the spellcaster seeks to do good work and benefit themselves or others, this is seen as "white magic." In reality, it's a lot more complex than this simple dichotomy, but I'll talk about good versus bad and the importance of employing an ethical system in conjunction with spellcasting in Chapter 4. For now, the point is that magic is neutral. A common illustration is the use of a tool such as a knife. The knife itself is a neutral object. However, it may be used to cut someone's throat, to cut up vegetables to feed a family, or to slice through the bonds holding someone prisoner. The knife isn't good or bad; what you choose to do with it determines its value within the context of a situation.

As a rule, the energy you will use in spellcraft is neutral. It is true, however, that if it has at some time been programmed with a strong intent, energy can sometimes retain the echo of that original purpose. People visiting various monuments or historical sites often comment on a certain feeling that seems to be perpetuated or generated by the location itself. Energy in the form of strong emotion has soaked into the area, creating a permanent echo of the original event. Take, for example, the islands used as quarantine containment areas off the coast of Australia. As each ship of settlers arrived, a doctor inspected the passengers, and if anyone was deemed a health threat, then the entire load of passengers was exported to one of these islands. Close quarters ensured that whoever wasn't sick would become ill through contact with those who were, resulting in a pervasive feeling of dread and despondency throughout the quarantined community. Visitors to these islands today remark on the feelings of despair, fear, and resignation that the islands possess, even though their original purpose of isolating immigrants has long passed.

These echoes of strong energy can remain for years, and sometimes give rise to the belief that a place or an object is "haunted." However, the majority of energy that a spellcaster will encounter and work with throughout his or her practice is neutral, and safe to use in spells to improve one's life.

Spellcasting Is a Natural Act

Magic is the art of creating change in accordance with your will. It's also the transfer of energy that creates change. I don't use the word often in this book, because it usually suggests that there's something supernatural about the process of spellcasting.

Let me stress that there is nothing *more* natural than a spell. In essence, wishing for something really hard is a form of spell: you have a goal, and you have emotion, and you want it so badly you can almost feel it in your hands. Vivid daydreams wherein you are awarded Employee of the Month, or receive a job offer, are also forms of spells. They are unrecognized spells, however, because these acts are not performed with intent.

Intent indicates performing an action with awareness, which in turn indicates that you are consciously channeling energy and emotion into the action. Intent is what makes a wish or simple daydream a spell. If you deliberately put yourself in the correct frame of mind and use your imagination to create a situation wherein you are offered the job for which you applied, concentrating upon the event, then that's a simple spell.

Spellcraft uses natural objects infused with natural energy, and combines them with your intent to create a catalyst for change. If casting a spell was an unnatural act, success would be impossible.

There is a long tradition of spellcrafting in most cultures, including Western culture. People from all walks of life have engaged in it, both men and women, for a variety of purposes, including religious purposes. An examination of spellcrafting and casting throughout history will help situate it in modern society, and help you understand the broad applications of spells.

2

spellcasting in history

A look at the perception of magic and the use of spells in various religious paths, Western cultures, and time periods, culminating in modern day usage.

⤳

When examining the position occupied by spellcraft in history, remember that the occult is rarely documented in the way that politics or science is. Occult advances or developments are usually accomplished in an atmosphere of intolerance or mistrust. In addition to this, spellcrafters often work alone, and thus developments are not shared within a larger community, as scientific discoveries are today. Finally, the dissemination of information throughout history was a much slower process than we have come to know and expect in our contemporary world.

We frequently assume that something newer is an improvement over the older method. However, this is an example of historical bias. What is older is not necessarily outdated. In fact, looking at an older approach to a problem or situation offers an alternate view of reality as we now know it. Modern science replaced many mystical and metaphysical practices and beliefs. When Mary Shelley's Victor Frankenstein is depicted reading the works of such men as Paracelsus, Cornelius Agrippa, and Albertus Magnus in his youth, scholars of his time deride him for turning to the "chimerical powers" of "exploded systems and useless names." Instead, they encourage him to turn to the wonders of modern science, which is based in powers "real and practical." As the world experiences progress, older valuable techniques and systems are often thrown out without further thought as to their potential philosophical benefit.

Science and magic are not two extremes, one real and the other delusional. They are simply two different methods of exploring the world, and affecting or controlling an environment. In fact, early practitioners of science were as mistrusted as spellcasters, and viewed as dangerous individuals who dared to work against the will of God as expressed by the Church. Galileo (1564–1642), for instance, was arrested as a heretic for publishing works examining scientific explorations of the heavens and planetary motion, exploring Copernican theory, and hypothesizing that the planets orbited the sun, not the earth.

Anything that could not be easily explained had the potential to be perceived as magic. Sickness could be explained as ill-wishing in the form of "someone who doesn't like me has cast a spell on me," since the concept of a virus was centuries away. Magic was a means by which certain occurrences could be rationalized. It was also a convenient method of denying responsibility for actions.

While it served as a useful scapegoat in certain situations, magic and spellcraft were also often practiced in conjunction with a particular religious path in which spells called upon the power of God, or the spell itself was designed to improve the soul, in order to seek further harmony with God.

Magic and spellcraft are frequently separated into two specific categories in several cultures. In the Western occult tradition, these categories are referred to as "high magic," which revolves around spiritual improvement, ceremony, and structure, and "low magic," which involves spellcraft designed to divine the future, heal, ensure fertility or prosperity, and other basic needs. This might have contributed to the emphasis placed by the Church upon the evil nature of spells: low magic and spellcasting for material and practical needs suggested an emphasis on this life and the mundane world. By contrast, high magic looked toward

Heaven and the creation of spiritual wealth. High magic can be contrasted with low magic in several ways, but the most obvious comparison lies between the level of education of those who practiced each path. High magic users (sometimes referred to as ceremonial magicians) were generally educated, literate people of higher classes (for example, clergy in the Middle Ages), whereas low magic users were people of little or no formal education who were closer to the natural world. Those spellcrafters who lacked the benefit of education practiced as wise women, cunning men, and faith healers in villages and towns. They specialized in folk healing and remedies, and various forms of spells useful to village life and citizens.

A spell would likely not be done by the wise woman or cunning man. Instead, the supplies would be carefully measured out and mixed, then given to the petitioner or client who asked for help, along with specific directions regarding the application or execution of the components. In such a case, the components and directions were supplied by the individual with the practical knowledge of how to deal with the situation, but the execution was deliberately left to the individual in need, ensuring that the pertinent will, emotion, and intent were applied to the spell by that individual.

Much surviving spellcraft has come down to us as superstition, folk tradition, and old wives' remedies. The action or words of the spell still exist, but the original purpose or intent has been lost over time.

In high magic, spells were frequently used as spiritual aids in religious settings. In fact, most major grimoires, or collections of spells and lore in manuscript form, were created by churchmen.

Alchemy

Alchemy is the basis of modern chemistry. In the Middle Ages, alchemy was the study of how lead or other base metals could be transformed into gold, both theoretically and practically. Throughout Europe, alchemists were maintained by monarchs and courts.

Alchemy was practiced by educated men and philosophers seeking to secure the key to the secrets of the natural world. By learning the secrets of nature, an alchemist would not only possess the wisdom and knowledge of how to modify substances and create new substances, but he would also possess information concerning the secrets of life and death. Alchemy was simultaneously an exploration of the material world, and the philosophical world.

On a basic level, alchemy can be seen as a cash grab, an attempt to satisfy a need or desire for an unlimited source of money. Alchemy is also an allegory for the transcendence of mundane existence, the transformation of crude matter into spiritual gold. It's a metaphor for spiritual development and improvement, a method of self-actualization leading to what Maslow calls transcendence or peak experience. Alchemy is a form of spellcasting in which the alchemist seeks to penetrate and possess the secrets of nature, which in turn will provide a concrete method by which the alchemist can transform and improve the self.

Grimoires

A grimoire is a French word meaning a collection of magical lore and information. The word is probably derived from the word "grammaire," a French term meaning a book of lessons upon the use of syntax and grammar, which teaches correct usage of a language. It's important to remember that a grimoire isn't a complete training manual; it's a collection of bits of information, with fragments of spells and rituals.

At various points in history, what we call *spells* would variously be seen as superstition, or maintenance of the Divinely ordained order, the latter being the responsibility of high-ranking clergy. In fact, a lot of the grimoires which rest in various European library archives as precious pieces of history were developed by, and maintained as the property of, clergy.

The use of spellwork within a religious context can be described as self-improvement by the grace of God. Much of religious practice throughout the ages can be interpreted as spells and energy manipulation to achieve a particular goal; however, these practices are accepted as they are performed to develop the individual's personal moral and spiritual worth, as opposed to spells that affect the outside environment. Spiritual magic exercises power over the self, not necessarily power over others. Although many clerical grimoires included spells to banish and control demons, this was done in the name of God to protect the world and mankind.

The grimoires that have survived the trials of time hold high magic, not low. The truth of the matter is that throughout the ages folk practitioners were mostly illiterate, and paper was unavailable to the masses for a large part of the last two millennia. Collections of spells for purposes such as healing, prosperity, love, and such goals did not exist. Those books which are found in museums and archives collect rituals and diagrams used in high magic spells and rituals, developed and performed by those who had the time, the education, and the money.

Examples still exist of grimoires collected by various key figures within the evolution of the occult art and science; modern magicians still study them in order to gain as much insight as possible. Working magic from a grimoire is not recommended. First, the terminology can be confusing; the grimoires date from the late Middle Ages and the Renaissance; languages have evolved over the centuries. Second, grimoires are incomplete records of magical acts. They are fragmentary, and presume that the practitioner already possesses other information that should be applied in various places. This is one of the reasons why attempting to perform spells from older grimoires can be risky; the material is incomplete.

However, the grimoires still serve as valuable insights into how spellcraft was used and formulated. Various grimoires have been translated and annotated by occultists of the nineteenth and twentieth century. These are some of the seminal works, which have become available to the modern spellcrafter for research:

- *Grimoire of the Honorius*: A collection of Christian magic said to have been discovered in Rome in 1670 (although some sources say 1629). This grimoire is attributed to Pope Honorius, although it is unclear if the author was Honorius II (d. 1130) or Honorius III (d. 1227). All the conjurations and all the symbolism within it are based on Christian doctrine, with influence from the Qabala as well. The basic theme of this grimoire revolves around fallen angels and how to raise them. It was considered an essential handbook for advanced clergy in order to conjure and control spirits as part of their spiritual work.
- *The Key of Solomon the King*: Attributed to the wise King Solomon, this grimoire is basically a collection of invocations, rituals, and spirit-summoning spells. *The Key of Solomon* (also known as *Clavicula*

Solomonis) typifies the Judeo-Christian magic of the Middle Ages. Much of the work of the Hermetic Order of the Golden Dawn (a late nineteenth-century occult order) and the original rituals of Wicca as codified in the Gardnerian practice were based on information derived from the *Key of Solomon*, translated and transcribed from various versions in the late nineteenth century by Golden Dawn co-founder Samuel Mathers. Roger Bacon (approximately 1190–1289), alchemist and traveler, was the first person to record the *Clavicula Salomonis*.

- *Grimoire of Armadel*: Translated by Mathers in the early twentieth century, this seventeenth-century French grimoire is a collection of Christian magic. It contains seals and sigils of demons and planetary spirits, as well as instruction for their various uses.

WITCHCRAFT

The idea of witchcraft being used to manipulate others is a concept that usually ensures a reaction of either disdain for simple-minded superstition, or deep-seated fear and suspicion. The idea of losing free will and the ability to control one's own actions strikes at the very heart of what humanity considers sacred. Spellcraft, then, became an excellent accusation to level at those who were disliked, successful, or simply different.

As an example, let's look at Joan of Arc (1412–1431). As a teenager, she claimed to hear the voices of Saint Catherine, Saint Michael, and Saint Margaret. These voices instructed her to work with Charles VII of France in his ongoing conflict with the Burgundians and their allies the British, to help him retake his throne in order that he could be crowned and confirmed the king of France. Obeying the voices, Joan did all this in the name of God. She led troops of men on the battlefield, wore armor, and inspired phenomenal loyalty.

Eventually, Joan of Arc was captured by the British in 1430, and for these things she was brought to trial and accused of heresy and witchcraft. She possessed at times information that she could in no way have obtained personally, and this apparently supernatural knowledge, which had served her and the French so well during their conflict, eventually also served as her undoing. Joan did not use obvious spells, but there was no way her society could explain how a young woman could accomplish the things that she did. Witchcraft was the obvious conclusion. As no one could naturally do what she had done, she must have used unnatural means. Hence her actions were evil, and against the will of God. Her voices and visions were declared false and diabolical, as God would never instruct a girl to dress as a man and take up arms; it was against the natural order (which of course would have developed according to God's plan).

Apart from a short period in which Joan confessed to witchcraft simply to be pardoned, she never deviated from her story: God and the saints had given her a task, and she had accomplished it, to His glory. The British burned her at the stake, and the French, as thanks for all she had done in securing the throne for Charles VII, did nothing to help her. Centuries later, the Catholic Church officially declared Joan of Arc a saint, thereby endorsing her claim that God had indeed directed her actions.

As illustrated by Joan's story, and by the stories of thousands of unfortunate and innocent men and women all over Europe, spells and witchcraft are useful catch-all terms for explaining and exploiting the weakness, suspicion, and jealousy found in every community.

The Words

There are several words associated with spellcraft that have evolved throughout history, and in various languages.

The word "witch" is often applied to a woman who uses spellcraft. Illustrations depicting a witch as an unattractive older woman began to circulate as early as the 1700s. Interestingly enough, illustrations showed beautiful young women engaging in spellcraft as well, suggesting that the feminine nature was easily swayed by the evil temptations offered by the use of witchcraft. Between approximately 1450 and 1750, during the European witch trials, both men and women of all ages were accused and convicted of witchcraft, and put to death in the name of God. The word "witch" is associated with many other Indo-European words. Words and etymological roots such as *wick, wic, vik, wise, weave,* and *wisdom* are usually associated with the idea of possessing some sort of knowledge of the natural world, or the ability to bend or shape something. Both concepts are embodied in the art of spellcraft, which uses energies derived from the natural world, and which intends to shape a new reality.

If you work with spells, are you automatically a witch? Of course not. It's simply a word that has in the past been used to describe a type of spellcaster. If you like it, then go ahead and use it. Many people are more comfortable with the term "spellcrafter." Men in particular are uncomfortable with the word "witch," due to the feminine association of low magic over the years. (Avoid the word "warlock," however; there are a couple of different etymological interpretations, but more often than not it is interpreted to mean an oath-breaker, which is not the sort of energy you want associated with your spellwork. A male spellcaster is technically still a witch. Some prefer the term "wizard" as an alternative, meaning "wise one.")

"Magic," on the other hand, comes from the word *magus* or *magii*, a Persian practitioner of occult arts. The three wise men who came to honor Christ at his birth were Magi, wise men from the east who studied such arts as astrology and astronomy. The word "magician" is derived from this Persian root. Today we often associate stage illusionists with the word "magicians." In the late nineteenth and early twentieth centuries, ceremonial magicians Eliphas Levi and Aleister Crowley began spelling the word with an additional "k"; "magick," then, was the spiritual use of spellcraft, as differentiated from stage magic. Although the need for such differentiation is past, many modern authors still employ this alternate spelling.

The use of magic is often perceived as exotic and dangerous due to its unknown influences and sources. A common theme found in most cultures is the belief that foreigners practice some sort of magic, which reflects the perception of the "other" as barbarian, as compared to the civilized practice of religion. Meyer and Smith (1999) state that " . . . magic puts a label on those invasive threats to traditional civic piety and cultural cohesiveness . . . A 'magician' was either a criminal or a quack, condemned by law and ridiculed. . . . "

CULTURAL EXPRESSIONS OF SPELLCRAFT

Every culture has used some form of spellcraft, or has employed the manipulation of energy in the pursuit of knowledge or worship. Let's look at some brief examples of spellcraft in a selection of major civilizations in Western history.

Magic in Ancient Egypt

The use of magic in ancient Egypt followed the same division of high and low magic according to the purpose: low magic was applied to immediately beneficial goals; high magic took the form of priestly rites and rituals designed to provide guidance to the people, as well as to maintain life on its regular daily course. The most well-known text from Ancient Egypt, *The Egyptian Book of the Dead*, is basically a grimoire of highly complex spells and rituals which served as a training manual for Egyptian priests. These priests, as part of their duties, were charged with speaking certain words and performing certain actions in order to maintain cosmic order.

What many people consider superstitions today, the priests and temple communities of ancient Egypt saw as their duty. If certain words were not spoken, and certain rituals not enacted, the rhythm of the universe would be interrupted, and harmony would collapse. Much of Egyptian magic was based on the belief that words were holy, and that they possessed immense power and energy. Another form of magic used frequently throughout the ages in Egypt is that of amulets. An amulet is an object charged with protective energy. The word itself is derived from "hamala," the Arabic word meaning "to carry." Everyone in Egypt wore amulets. Semiprecious stones were used, such as lapis lazuli or carnelian, and precious metals. Amulets were often carved in the forms of animals, or rectangles with magical words inscribed upon them. Such amulets were also used in the process of wrapping embalmed and mummified bodies, in order to protect the individual in the journey through the afterlife.

If you are interested in how magic was practiced and spells were used in Ancient Egypt, I recommend reading Egyptologist E. A. Wallis Budge's *Egyptian Magic*.

Magic in Classical Greece and Rome

Egyptian magic and spiritual practices migrated through Greek colonies to Athens, carried by traders and travelers. Over time the Egyptian magic blended with native Greek practices, as well as those of neighboring cultures such as Zoroastrian, Chaldean, Jewish, Indian, and Arabic cultures.

Greco-Roman magic also used amulets, written invocations inscribed upon metal disks or semi-precious stones, worn on the body for healing or protection.

Grimoires, or collections of spells and rituals, have been found for practical purposes such as love charms, divination, healing, protection, and cursing. Curse tablets, a form of written curse, are one of the most frequently found magical artifacts within Roman areas, from Italy to Britain, dating from the fifth century B.C.E. All levels of society used these for various reasons, including legal issues, business, gambling, love affairs, and so forth. The earliest examples were simply a name inscribed on a tablet and left in a grave, pit, or well: these locales were literally closer to the underworld, and hence a petition left there was closer to the spirits who would act upon it. Lead was frequently used as the material for the tablet, as it too was associated with the underworld, and was soft enough to carve easily. Wood, clay, other metals, stones, gems, and papyrus were also used. Curse tablets could become quite elaborate, with long directions written out up to three times. Poppets, dolls, or human forms in a variety of materials such as wax or wood, were also used as focal points for spells.

The intelligentsia of Rome (among them philosophers such as Plotinus) made certain that their practices weren't misinterpreted as vulgar, common magic by creating a new name for it. "[H]ighbrow philosophers who practiced invocation of divine powers tried to disengage themselves from the magical tradition by rewriting the vocabulary. They called what they did *theurgy*, divine work, as opposed to *goeteia*, howling out barbaric words. From this came the enduring debate, which has continued into the modern period, over high . . . magic versus low . . . magic" (Meyer and Smith, 1999). Here we see a clear, early example of high magic differentiating itself from low magic by setting itself apart as philosophical and intellectual, as opposed to addressing basic material needs.

For an interesting look at surviving classical magic, read Charles Leland's *Etruscan Roman Remains,* which documents rituals, invocations, spoken charms, and practices from the Romagna region of Italy as preserved in the late nineteenth century.

Magic in Northern Europe

In the Scandinavian and Teutonic areas of Northern Europe, two very particular forms of magic were practiced. *Galdr* was a more intellectual form of magic, which employed symbols and mysteries, and was practiced by men. *Seithr* was a more shamanic, intuition- and instinct-based magic, performed by women.

Galdr magic is based on the runes, a set of symbols that are sometimes called an alphabet, although they are in reality much more. Each rune is associated with a mystery, an experience, or an abstract that the rune-master (or *galdrman*) must have internalized and meditated on. A rune is a compilation of knowledge and meditations, not merely a shape or letter. Runes have three aspects: the sound, the shape, and the mystery itself. These three aspects cannot be separated; they are inextricably linked. A rune-master possesses the knowledge of how to combine or apply these runes in various combinations to create spells and move energy in a desired fashion.

Seith magic is associated with soothsaying and prophecy. The practitioner, called a *seidkona*, achieves an altered state through one of several methods, such as sleep deprivation, chanting, drumming, sensory overload, or drugs, and receives messages from the other world. Traditionally a seidkona was a wanderer.

For more information on Scandinavian magic, I recommend Freya Aswynn's *Northern Mysteries and Magic* (previously *Leaves of Yggdrasil*), and Edred Thorsson's *Northern Magic*.

Magic in the Celtic Tribes

The Druids of the Celtic tribes and lands had a practice similar to the seidkona, through which they sought counsel from the otherworld. When seeking counsel from the spirit realm, one of the techniques a Druid might use involved wrapping himself in the hide of a white bull, which had been sacrificed with honor for the purpose, and sequestering himself in a small, dark hut for a specific period of time, such as three days and nights. The Druid would then emerge with insights gained through visions, incurred by fasting, sleep deprivation, and other shamanic methods of contacting the otherworld to access information.

The use of language was very important to the Celts. Indeed, the use of spoken charms to create some sort of change has been used all over Europe, and most countries possess a strong oral tradition based in song and verse. Bards still exist in the modern Druidic hierarchy. Bards enjoyed a very honorable place within Celtic culture, as the words a bard wrote and recited could influence a kingdom. This respect for language and its power has remained as one of the defining aspects of Celtic culture to this day. In nineteenth-century Scotland, Alexander Carmichael collected such charms in a book called *Carmina Gadelica* (songs or chants of the Gaels), which encodes chants and prayers from the Highlands, and serves as an important historical record of Scottish invocations, praise of the Divine, and charms passed down throughout the ages. Many of these spoken charms accompany daily tasks, such as lighting the fire, or caring for crops and animals.

For information on modern Druidic practice, read books on Druidry by Philip Carr-Gomm, or take a look at Ross Nichol's *Book of Druidry*.

Judeo-Christian Magic

Judeo-Christian magic also used spoken invocations and protective amulets. Through the Middle Ages, talismans were often copper or bronze and inscribed with psalms or prayers. Sacramental magic formed an essential element within the practice of Christianity, which is based upon the belief that Christ's body was resurrected and assumed into Heaven after his death. Transubstantiation, or the belief that an object, body, or spirit changes into something else, is performed every time communion takes place, as the priest blesses the Host and the wine, which change into the body and blood of Christ. The use of sacred oils and holy water to anoint and purify is also a common example of religious magic.

Christian magic focuses frequently on the use of psalms, holy recitations designed to invoke a certain power of God to surround the practitioner. Appealing to the saints as intercessors, each saint having an area or realm of specialty (what we term correspondence), is also a very popular practice. As mentioned before, *The Key of Solomon* has been one of the central texts used in Judeo-Christian magic.

Another valuable body of knowledge, which has influenced Judeo-Christian magic (and, indeed, most Western occult practice), is the Judaic Qabala. The Qabala is the essential core of Jewish mysticism.

The *Sepher Yetzirah* (or the Book of Formation) and the *Zohar* are the two fundamental texts, apart from the Torah. Qabala is a mystical and philosophical system of thought, not a system of magic per se, which is not to say that it does not have practical application. Like other philosophies, Qabala has evolved in various directions according to the needs of the people. One of the greatest symbols of meditation, the Tree of Life, is founded in Qabalistic mysticism. The Tree of Life describes both a map of the cosmos and a process by which energy flows from the Divine to the material plane and back again to the Divine.

If the Qabala interests you, take a look at Dion Fortune's *The Mystical Qabalah*. Meyer and Smith's *Ancient Christian Magic* is an excellent record of early Christian magical texts which addresses spells for protection, curses, and various magical recipes dating from the first through the twelfth centuries. *Candle Burning Magic with the Psalms* by William A. Oribello instructs a practitioner when specific psalms may be used for certain purposes. Ray Malbrough's *Magical Power of the Saints* provides spells and rituals by which saints may be invoked for magical help.

Magic in Europe: The Middle Ages

While many of the magical practices in these cultures seem far away and long ago, within the past two thousand years there have been remarkable men and women who have done work within the area of metaphysics. Much of their work has served as the foundation for modern sciences such as chemistry, physics, and astronomy.

Spellcasters in the Middle Ages and the Renaissance were often respected academics. As Lars Lindholm, in *Pilgrims of the Night*, explains it:

[A] magician was always welcome by the gentry. He was generally a learned man, a gentleman, and a scholar. In many cases, he was a fugitive monk from one of the orders, and the orders were respected for their high ideals and compassionate practices. . . . A squire would always welcome such men. They had many uses. They took care of the sick. They tutored the squire's children. They helped develop and cultivate the land. [Monks possessed such skills because their monastic communities were independent, with] the freedom to experiment, and great things happened in a creative environment like that and had a tremendously beneficial impact upon the whole age. (Lindholm, 1993, pp. 16–17)

Subjects such as astronomy, astrology, mathematics, and alchemy were still controversial enough in Western Europe to be considered occult. In fact, the idea that man could measure or attempt to predict God's creation was considered dreadfully presumptuous in some circles.

Magic in Europe: The Renaissance

Men who studied natural philosophy sought to understand the connections between man and the natural world, and to gain wisdom regarding the function of the universe. The Humanism movement and the fascination for all things classical revived interest in ancient texts and provided the impetus for translations into English. These translations, and the creation of the printing press, made such information more readily available.

Nicholas Flamel (1330–1418) was a well-known alchemist of the time, and was said to be the only man who found the Philosopher's Stone, the ultimate goal of the alchemical process. The Philosopher's Stone was a concept indicating the key to understanding all of nature's secrets, enabling not only the transformation of dross into gold, but also the possession of wisdom and knowledge of how to become immortal.

Henry Cornelius Agrippa (1486–1534) wrote the valuable *Three Books of Occult Philosophy* which address numerology, Qabala, divination, demonology, astrology, elemental energy, and other fascinating subjects. Published in 1431, these books outline magical lore and Neo-Platonic observation on the writings and thoughts of other natural philosophers such as Cicero, Ptolemy, Plato, and Pythagoras.

Paracelsus (1493–1541) was an alchemist and physician who worked with the spirits of chemical substances. He believed that every element contained its own spirit, and that one could capture and influence them to bring about certain changes. Paracelsus was one of the first men to systemize medical symptoms and cures, and although his writings and theories were not well known during his lifetime, they had significant impact in the years following his death.

Dr. John Dee (approximately 1527–1608) was court astrologer, herbalist, alchemist, and magician to Queen Elizabeth I of England, known for his channeling and scrying work. Dee was also a cartographer, a mathematician, and was said to have been the inspiration for Shakespeare's magician character Prospero in *The Tempest*. Together with his assistant Edward Kelley, Dee transcribed messages from entities he claimed were angels, using an angelic alphabet they termed "Enochian."

The Nineteenth-Century Occult Revival

The nineteenth century saw an increase in various forms of cultural research, including anthropology and archaeology. Remains of older civilizations were unearthed, artifacts were brought to light, and the cultures of non-European locales were observed and documented. Among the conclusions made by scholars of the time was the conclusion that only primitive peoples practiced magic, because they had not yet developed a worldly experience, which would logically lead them to the development of religion, and eventually to science. This viewpoint presumes that individuals who believe in magic are in some way less culturally evolved than those who hold a scientific view.

In reality, science and magic are two different methods of interpreting the laws of nature. Both methods observe cause and effect, and seek to work with those laws in order to control them.

Even in the so-called modern Western cultures, vestiges of magical practice still existed. Families continued to enact old folk customs or beliefs, even in North America, brought over from the Old World when millions emigrated from their homelands in the nineteenth and twentieth centuries. The Pennsylvania Dutch practice of Pow-Wow is an example of this. Now a magical system of healing, blessing, and protection, Pow-Wow has its roots in German high magic and Christian prayer magic. Many older spells from several European cultures similarly devolved into simple sayings or apparently superstitious practices, with the form preserved but the original meaning lost.

The nineteenth century also saw a revival of interest in occult matters. The Theosophical Society and Spiritualism, for example, developed as the outcome of a keen interest in the afterlife and spiritual expression. Occult orders such as the Rosicrucians and the Freemasons continued to develop. One of the most influential occult orders of the last two centuries was founded upon such principles in the 1880s: the Hermetic Order of the Golden Dawn was created by three men of Masonic and

Rosicrucian background to serve as spiritual and occult training and refinement. The Golden Dawn still exists in various forms, and much modern magical practice owes some sort of debt to the body of lore collected and encoded by the Golden Dawn.

For a look into examples of American folk magic, read *American Folk Magic: Charms, Spells, and Herbals* by Silver RavenWolf, or *Hex and Spellwork: The Magical Practices of the Pennsylvania Dutch* by Karl Herr.

African-Catholic Syncretism

When people from the African cultures were brought to the shores of the New World as slaves, they brought with them their native beliefs and practices. When the slave owners disallowed the practice of the native system of religion, however, a curious synthesis of Catholicism and African belief evolved into what would become known as Voudoun, Candomblé, Palo, or Santeria, depending on the original culture of the slave community. Syncretic religions such as these took Catholic concepts and saints and overlaid them on the native god-forms to disguise them, thus protecting the native belief from persecution. Thus, the Haitian Legba, god of the crossroads, became referred to as Saint Peter; the African Yemonja, goddess of the ocean, became Mary, Star of the Sea; the Cuban Shango was referred to as Santa Barbara; and so forth. In the modern day, practitioners of these syncretic religions are free to once again call their gods by their original names.

Techniques found in these magico-religious practices include spiritual baths, the use of *gris-gris* or mojo bag talismans, candle magic, and others. Voudoun is nothing at all like the sensational pop culture portrayals of the practices in various movies. It is an intensely personal religious practice, and very emotional. There is a nonreligious American derivative called Hoodoo, which uses the techniques without requiring the practitioners to completely immerse themselves in the spiritual system of Voudoun.

For a look into modern syncretic religious practices, read Luisah Teish's *Jambalaya,* or Ray T. Malbrough's *Magical Power of the Saints.* If you are interested in the practice of Hoodoo, the Americanized magical system based on Voudoun, read Ray Malbrough's *Hoodoo Mysteries.*

Modern Practice

In the twentieth century, spellcraft became even more revitalized as the findings of anthropologists and researchers of ancient civilizations were further released into the mainstream. The writings of the nineteenth century scholars were also reinterpreted.

New material examining cultural magical practices was continually released, and perhaps to the surprise of Western society, it wasn't all based in foreign cultures. Margaret Murray, an Egyptologist, shifted the focus of her research to Scotland and Britain in the early twentieth century, and in 1921 she published a book entitled *The Witch Cult in Western Europe*, which postulated the continued existence of small pockets of spellcasters who honored fertility deities. In the wake of this publication, interest in the indigenous practice of spellcraft and magic grew.

Spellcraft was indeed still being practiced in the twentieth century in Britain, as revealed by Gerald Brosseau Gardner in the 1950s with the publication of the seminal texts *Witchcraft Today* (1954) and *The Meaning of Witchcraft* (1959). Practiced in private, spellcraft was still used to address basic needs such as money and affection, and other such needs encountered in daily life.

Today's approach to spellcrafting is very eclectic. With the explosion of New Age texts made available within the past twenty years, the art of spellcrafting has attracted the attention of millions who have learned to use it for positive change in their lives. While some are drawn to specific cultural practices, often related to their ancestry, others borrow freely from techniques found in several cultures and from various time periods. Indeed, modern metaphysical practice can still be found in orders such as The Golden Dawn and other magical lodges, but the art of spellcraft descends from the "low magic" found in most cultures. Magic for dealing with daily life is still what spellcraft is used for, although it is now recognized that by dealing with the practical issues and basic needs, spellcraft is also a nurturing, spiritual advancement.

3

crafting a spell

This chapter covers detailed step-by-step instructions on constructing a spell. Each step is separated from the others and examined in depth. The steps are also analyzed in relation to each other by how they affect you in the spellcasting process, and by how they initialize change.

※

You've probably already performed spells, either from books or spontaneously, so you have a vague idea of what a spell is. It's a series of symbolic actions performed with intent, which channel power and will toward a specific goal. To understand what a spell is takes time, however, and it helps to walk through the steps from start to finish.

To cast a spell means that you have to trust yourself, trust your intuition and your ability to sense and handle energy. It means that you have to have confidence in yourself. It means that you have to deeply, truly *desire* something.

That last necessity is more of a stumbling block than you may realize. We very often want things for superficial reasons: either the want is artificially created by the media, or we convince ourselves that, with the attainment of a certain goal, happiness will be ours. This type of desire can be identified by how you react when your goal is attained. Do you lose interest in it soon afterwards?

An opposite problem exists as well. When I began spellcasting I talked myself out of more spells than I actually cast, because I didn't think that I wanted anything badly enough. Spells exist to help us attain goals, whatever those goals might be: a new car, a mortgage, a promotion, less stress, more creativity. I rationalized most of my desires as petty or unimportant.

This had a twofold result: one, I now rarely cast spells to acquire something, choosing instead to focus my spellcraft upon my own evolution and spiritual development; and two, I succeeded in being pretty miserable and stressed out for half a dozen years because I felt that spells were somehow a form of cheating life.

Crafting the Spell

Unless you intend to perform a spontaneous spell (and there's nothing wrong with that), you'll need to create one. In order to do that, here are the steps you'll need to work through.

A Need or Desire

A need or desire has every right to be met, whether it's a need for a scholarship to enable you to study at the postgraduate level, or a desire for the traffic light to change so that you can cross the intersection to walk on the sunny side of the street. That need or desire is the first requirement in order for a spell to exist. If you don't have a need or a desire, don't waste your time. Spellcraft isn't something to pass the hours, or an art to practice on a whim. It's a powerful force for transformation and change, requiring your dedication and involvement. Crafting and casting a spell requires time, focus, great concentration, and energy, and if you're doing it on a whim, you're going to a lot of trouble for nothing. Emotion is one of the key concepts that powers a spell, and a whim just doesn't have the depth of emotion required. In addition, there's the issue of responsibility: if you ask for it, you're responsible for it. (For more on the idea of responsibility, see Chapter 4.)

Laying the Groundwork

Spells function best when some sort of context exists for them in which to manifest. Have you acted in the physical world to work on the situation you intend to address with a spell? Spells will not solve your problems for you. They will help, but leaving them to function without putting any other effort in on your end reduces the chances of the spell coming to successful fruition. Would you cast a spell to pass an exam for an area of study with which you had no experience? What would be the point of that?

Evaluate the Potential Repercussions

The subject of ethics has a whole chapter to itself later on in this book, but it's worth a mention here. Will granting this wish or desire infringe on anyone else's life or personal rights? Bear in mind that the reason you are able to perform spellwork is because everything is connected by energy, and if you harm someone else, intentionally or otherwise, you'll taste the effects of that act as well.

It's simply impossible not to harm anyone or anything. Every breath you take involves inhalation of microorganisms. Walking down the street crushes ants. Driving along the highway kills bugs. The point of this step is to make you seriously evaluate the impact of your actions and choices upon your environment and community. If you conclude that the desire or need does not merit the resulting impact, then think about how you could rework the wish or desire so that the impact is lessened or altered.

Write Down Your Need or Desire

Write down your need or desire, including as many details as you can. For example, if you need a scholarship to attend graduate school, write, "I need a full scholarship to pay for tuition and supplies and living expenses for the three years of my art history degree."

Use as many words as you need to in order to explain the situation clearly. Imagine that you're explaining the situation to someone who has no idea of what you want. The more precise you are, the more likely it is that you will achieve the result you desire.

It's entirely likely that during this step you will realize that you don't actually want what you thought you wanted; in fact, you desire something entirely different. That's okay. This step is essential for pinpointing your true desire. You might have to think and write for a while, and pour out a whole slew of feelings in order to sift through them, then ponder what they all mean. In the end, though, you'll have a better idea of what your goal actually is. If you end up with pages of material, read them carefully and reduce your goal to a single statement that is clear, succinct, and precise. Now you have a specific aim.

So often we're so overwhelmed by daily life that we can't put our finger on individual needs, which must be addressed one by one. This exercise will help you work out the areas of your life that require attention.

Exercise: Determining your Need

Sit down with a hot drink, some paper, and a pen or pencil. Relax, clear your mind, then write "Dear [your name]" at the top of the paper.

Then allow your mind to write you a letter. Don't think about it, don't search for the right words, and don't force it. Look at yourself from your life's point of view, and imagine what it would say to you if it used words. Don't censor; no one will ever see this but you.

Reread the letter when you are done. Isolate the areas that obviously need work, but also look for areas and issues indirectly suggested by the letter. Did your life tell you that you don't pay enough attention to it? Did it say that it worries about you because you take on too many tasks and responsibilities? These are areas you can focus on to improve your spells.

Did your life tell you that you're not worth anything? That's not your life talking; that is the voice of what author and creative coach Jill Badonsky calls your "inner critic," chipping away at your self-confidence and drowning out the true voice of your life. One of the things you need to work on is supporting and encouraging yourself. This, then, could be an area you could begin to develop with spellwork.

Perform this exercise frequently, especially when you feel as if nothing will ever go right again.

Once you have identified a goal or a need, you will likely have to simplify it. A spell to get a new job doesn't just get you a new job offer; it also includes several smaller goals such as deciding what kind of job you would like, researching open positions, creating your resume and cover letters, and applying for the job.

Exercise: Simplifying Your Goal

This exercise helps you break down your goal into manageable steps. You can apply a spell to one step, several steps, or every step.

1. Name a goal.
2. Break that goal down into three separate steps.

Yes, the exercise is that simple. If any one of those three steps still seem too vague, why not try breaking it down into an additional three steps? Alternately, break your original goal down into five or seven steps.

One of the keys to successful spellcasting rests in the language you use. Once you have a clearly defined goal, make sure you phrase it positively and in the present tense. For example, if you are seeking to ensure the safe final weeks of your pregnancy, you might phrase your goal as, "I am the content and healthy mother of a healthy, happy infant." This tells your subconscious and the energy you will use to fuel the spell that the spell is already succeeding. Your goal is to give birth to a baby, and for both of you to be happy and healthy. If you view your goal as "I am a healthy pregnant woman with no obstacles before me" you're creating the opportunity for those obstacles to arise. You're also focusing on the pregnancy, not the result.

Exercise: Stating Your Goal in the Present Tense

Examine the following goal statements and rephrase them so that they are in the present tense, and the language is as positive as possible.

1. I will no longer have financial trouble.
2. I will be happy and successful.
3. We will sign for the perfect house, for below their asking price.

Decide on a Time

When will you do this spell? There are two major factors in determining your spell's timing.

The first factor is the theme of your goal. Does it have to do with business, health, love? When you've determined the subject of your goal, you can select the appropriate season, month, moon phase, day of week, or time of day that will enhance the success of your spell. For an in-depth look at learning about timing, read Chapter 5.

The second factor is your own personal schedule. The ideal metaphysical time for your spell is often incompatible with real life. Look at the times you have free, the times when you'll have access to a certain place, the times you will be alone, the times you can fit spellcasting in between the mundane details of daily life, such as working, cooking, or chores. If the spell is important enough, you'll find a way to do it. Otherwise, the ideal metaphysical timing might not be a top priority. Don't stress about it. The method and materials you choose will still carry energy corresponding to your spell's goal.

Select a Method and Materials

Will you use a candle? Will you create an herbal sachet? Chapter 8 explores several methods of spellcasting. This is where you choose your technique, and decide on specifics such as colors, components, and ingredients, and the correspondences you'll employ throughout. For example, if you've chosen to do a spell to improve your finances, you might decide to perform a candle spell. You can go on to decide on what size and shape of candle to burn; what color; if you want to carve anything on the candle, and what symbols or words to carve if you do; if you want to anoint the candle, and what oil you will use to anoint it. To determine the correspondences, you would check your notes or references to see what other items possess similar energy associated with money, such as the colors green, gold, and brown; herbs such as Irish Moss and bay; symbols from various cultures or designed by you; and stones such as aventurine and jade.

Create a Symbolic Action

This will be the symbolic action that will represent the larger change in the world you wish to make. Essentially, this is the heart of your spell.

Performing this action, in conjunction with the raising and release of energy toward your goal, is what triggers the change you desire.

For example, I led a celebration of Earth Day a few years ago. Participants were told to bring a small bag or container of soil from their own gardens, or their houseplants if they had no garden. The symbolic action we performed was to pour everyone's earth into a large cauldron along with a wish for the coming year. A bag of rich new potting soil was added to, and blended with, the cauldron's contents. Energy was raised and released into the earth, and everyone divided up the positively charged soil to bring home to use, in order to return energy to the earth upon which we live.

Blending the personal earth with the new soil and empowering it was the symbolic action of this spell. It represented the energy we wanted to give back to the earth in thanks for all that the earth provides for us on a daily basis.

Another example of a symbolic action might be found in a spell to cut ties with someone who won't release you after a relationship is over. Two candles are set up side by side, about two inches apart, one representing each person. A black thread is tied around first one candle, then the other, linking them together. The symbolic action is in using a pair of scissors to cut that thread linking the candles together, reflecting the physical act of severing the energy link.

A symbolic action can be as simple as lighting a candle, or tying a knot; it may be as complex as dancing a complicated pattern of steps for a certain period of time, or writing a concerto.

Compose Your Spell

Yes, write it out. In point form, note down every action you will perform. Completely write out anything you intend to say; don't trust your memory, especially if you think of a wonderful invocation that flows well, because you won't remember it perfectly. It can be quite disappointing and frustrating when you reach that point and the words that come out aren't as evocative as the ones you originally created. Of course, if you prefer the spirit to move you to speak from your heart when you get there, you can just make a couple of notes here as well. If you're even a bit uncertain, though, do yourself a favor and write it out.

Make a complete list of everything you will need, from start to finish: the tools you will use (knife, burin, cup), accessories (lighter, candleholder, water), ingredients (herbs, salt, cloth, cord), and so forth. If your symbolic action requires special tools or supplies, make sure to include them in the list as well. This list will be invaluable later on, as you will see. Write down the items that seem obvious, because when you begin setting up your mind will be on casting the spell, not the preparation.

If you're not pressed for time, put the spell away for a bit and go back to it later. Reread it and change it if it isn't to your liking. If the spell is for something important, I recommend crafting it in advance and rereading it to make any alterations you think necessary. Does the spell still appeal to you? Are the words right? Is the goal or purpose stated correctly, or can you refine it to make it even more precise? Remember, precision is another method of ensuring successful manifestation.

Don't be concerned with creating art, or deep, meaningful poetry. No one will ever see your spells but yourself, unless you choose to share them with others.

Gather Your Materials

Preparation is just as important as performing the actual spell itself. Make sure you have everything you require before you begin the spell itself. Use the written copy of your spell to check everything off as you assemble it. Nothing kills a spell faster than realizing that you haven't got a match or a lighter when the time comes to light the candle in a candle spell. (In fact, make sure you have both on hand, so that if the matches are damp you have a backup, and vice-versa.)

CASTING THE SPELL

Now that you have a spell, you can cast it. Casting the spell does not have to happen right after the crafting process; in fact, crafting a spell can often take more than one session, especially if it's an important spell.

Set Up

Lay out your tools and components in your chosen work area and get everything ready to go. Double-check your written list to ensure that you have everything there, laid out in an easily accessible place or in the correct pattern indicated in your spell. Remember, a spell is a set of symbolic actions, and how you set up your workspace can be a significant part of that symbolism. You might choose to place specific things out in relation to one another. Be precise and be neat. You don't want to dig through a pile of components for something important. Put premeasured ingredients in bowls instead of measuring them out during the spell. This step ensures that things will run as smoothly as possible during the casting of the spell itself, eliminating obstacles and extraneous actions that slow down or distract from the process of raising and managing energy.

Purify

This is a step often overlooked, but it's extremely important. This is the first step toward preparing your mind and body for the energy you will be using in the spell itself. To purify means to remove the negative energy from something. Think of purification as taking off your work clothes after a day at the office and changing into your relaxed at-home gear. Along with that change of clothing comes a shift of mental space as well: you are indicating that you are prepared to address different issues in a different environment. By purifying your body and your workspace, you are indicating that you are putting aside the everyday distractions in order to focus upon your spellwork.

In this step you may take a bath or shower, meditate, do a bit of yoga, or simply sit with your eyes closed and breathe deeply for a couple of minutes. Let the noise and bustle of your everyday world fade away, and focus only on the here and now, and your goal. Purifying your space is equally important. You can light a candle to signify the presence of light banishing darkness, or you might burn some incense to bring sympathetic energies to your work. Some spellcasters use a broom to symbolically sweep their workspace clean of distracting energy, or they sprinkle salt, salt water, or holy water to neutralize any negativity.

Dedicate the Space

Set apart the space in which you will be working by creating some sort of delineation that will prove it is a space and time apart, dedicated to working your will. If you choose to use a circle, this is where you would cast it (more on circles later).

For some practitioners, the act of purifying the space serves as a dedication. Others choose to surround themselves with a physical reminder of a sacred place: they place a cord or ribbon around them on the floor, or sprinkle salt, or unfold a special blanket or scarf upon which they work. This step sets your working area aside as a place of transformation.

State Your Purpose

This is another simple step that is often dropped or overlooked by practitioners, but including it can make all the difference. It's a signal that you are beginning the spell. It's also a statement of will and of intent. "I cast this spell this day to secure my scholarship" is a confident announcement of purpose that has you off and running. It anchors your energy right away and provides a springboard for your subsequent words and actions. Note that it is phrased in a positive fashion.

Raise and Release Energy

This is one of those mysterious steps that is often glossed over in spellbooks. To "raise energy" refers to gathering energy and building or stockpiling it in preparation for launching it toward your goal. Think of the process as pulling or drawing the energy in, filling a deep well or container until it almost overflows, then casting it out when you are ready. To release that energy describes the act of sending it out into the universe to attain your goal. This is accomplished in part by performing the focal action you created in your spellcrafting process, the action that symbolizes the transformation required to fill your need.

If you've ever tried archery or drawn a bow, you know the tension, strength, and control required to grasp the bowstring, draw it back, and hold it, all while aiming at your target. Raising and releasing energy requires a similar control. Holding the energy as you draw more and more to you is a challenging action, and it takes practice. Like drawing a bowstring a bit further each time, though, each time you cast a spell you'll be able to hold a little more energy before releasing it.

A phrase you might have encountered refers to this process as "raising a cone of power." Energy isn't static; it's always in motion, and it's often described as flowing. When a spellcaster gathers energy, it tends to flow in a circular, usually clockwise motion around him or her. The term cone of power refers to the shape created by the energy as it flows around the person drawing it in, spiraling slightly upward and inward with every circle it travels. When the cone is released, people often envision the tip leading the rest of the cone out into the universe toward your goal.

When is the right time to release your energy? There's no clearcut rule; you just have to feel it and make your own judgment call. Trust your intuition. The first few times, you'll probably release it early because you're nervous or inexperienced. Experiment with holding onto it as long as you can, and see what happens. Sometimes if you hold it too long, the energy begins to die down because you begin to lose focus. If you feel the energy crest and begin to dissipate, force yourself to concentrate and release it right away. If you don't, you'll end up absorbing a whole lot of energy that you shouldn't absorb, which may cause physical discomfort. After a few spells you'll be able to better judge the moment when the tension is high and the energy is cresting; you'll be able to release it more easily.

Chapter 7 is entirely devoted to techniques of raising energy, and of adding that energy to your spell.

Sealing Your Spell

Other spellbooks have probably directed you to say something along the lines of "So mote it be" at the end of a spell. This particular phrase is something popularized by Wicca, one of the modern religious paths which uses spellcraft as part of its practice. "So mote it be" is basically a fancy way of saying, "it must be so" or "it is so." This statement reinforces your will, and your intent of success. Saying "it must be so" doesn't give any room for disagreement. This is what you want, and this is what you get.

The use of the word "amen" at the end of a Christian prayer serves much the same purpose, as does the Hebrew word "selah." You might want to develop your own punchy end-of-spell phrase to say when you release all the energy you've gathered and spun together toward your goal. Regular use of a sentence like this signals to your conscious and unconscious mind that you're finished working, and that it's time to relax and rebalance. Even saying something as simple as "it is done" will serve to seal your work.

Grounding

This is another important step which, like your statement of purpose at the beginning of the spellcasting process, anchors you. When you've raised and released energy, you might feel shaky, or as if you could leap tall buildings in a single leap. Grounding connects you to the energy of the earth, allowing you to rebalance your own personal energy that flows through you all the time. Spellwork often knocks your personal energy out of whack since you've just been channeling and drawing on other energy to blend and cast them out toward your goal. Sometimes you get a bit over-enthusiastic and send too much of your personal energy along with it, or traces of the other energies remain clinging to you after you've sent the bulk of them on their path. Either way, it's more or less energy than you're used to. In order to achieve balance once again, you can use a technique called grounding that allows you to pour out the excess or drink up replacement energy. If you have too much extra energy, place your hands on the floor and visualize the excess draining away. If you prefer, you can drain the extra energy into a tool of your choice instead, or a stone, or something you wish to use as a battery in the future. There isn't any sense in wasting the energy, after all. If you need energy to replace what you've lost, place your hands on the floor and visualize the calm cool energy of the earth flowing up your arms as if they were straws. Drink up as much of that cool energy as you need. If touching your hands to the floor isn't enough, sit down, kneel, or lie flat on the ground. It doesn't matter if you're in a basement or on the forty-fifth floor; you can ground anywhere, anytime. Try this basic exercise to get used to the method, and use it frequently.

Exercise: Basic Grounding Visualization

This is a terrific grounding exercise that has several different versions, used by a lot of people. The earth is a wonderful resource: you can download energy to it if you have too much, and upload energy from it if you require it. This technique allows you to do both.

Close your eyes and imagine a small seed of light within your chest. Visualize it extending a small tendril of light downwards through your body, splitting into two as it reaches your legs, and continuing down to your feet. See those two tendrils continuing down through your feet into the floor, past the floor into the ground. Visualize those tendrils strengthening into thick and strong roots, growing further into the ground. When they are anchored securely, allow your energy to equalize with that of the earth. If you need energy after your spell, draw it up, using those roots like straws; if you have excess energy, allow it to flow down those roots into the earth.

~·~

Release the Dedicated Space

Just as you set your work area apart as somewhere special for spell-casting, you should return it to its everyday use. An excellent way to do this is with another statement of intent, such as, "I now return this space to the physical world with thanks and blessings." If you like, you can snuff out a candle if you lit one to signify purification by light, or burn more incense to rebalance the energy of the area. The simple act of cleaning up and putting away your tools and items helps return the space to its everyday energy. You might run the vacuum or sweep the area when you're finished, too; nothing grounds a practitioner or a space like good, old-fashioned housework.

Reinforce the Spell with Action

Once the spell is cast, don't just sit on your hands or blithely wait for the universe to place the solution in your lap. Go out and do work in the physical world to reinforce your spell. Wiccan author Amber K calls this "acting in accord." Magic helps, but it can't do the work on its own. I might sound like a broken record, but consider this: a spell is a form of energy. You can cast a spell for a glass to levitate off the table and hover in mid-air, but it will take less energy to reach out and pick it up with your hand. Acting in the physical world reinforces the energy you gathered and directed toward your goal with your spell. A man once came back to the metaphysical shop where I worked and told the staff that the spell they'd given him to get a job hadn't worked. The staff went over the spell step by step with him. Yes, he'd done it all just as they'd recommended, during the correct moon phase; he'd done it a month ago, but nothing was happening. This went on for a while, the man insisting that the spell had been useless and demanding a better one, until someone thought to ask him how many jobs he had applied for. He hadn't even sent out a resumé.

Just as we create our own reality by how we perceive the world around us, so too do we create our own opportunities for magic. If you take the time and energy to craft and cast a spell, then you owe it to yourself to expend a little more in order to help it flow smoothly toward successful manifestation. Magic takes the path of least resistance to create a change, and if you have the means to create that path, then do it. Energy is energy. If you've cast a spell to pass a challenging exam, study for it, too. Support the spell. And remember to think positively. Thoughts are energy as well, and there's no point in sabotaging your spell by doubting the outcome after all of your hard work.

What Should I Do with All This Stuff?

What you do after the spell with all of your ingredients and tools is as crucial to your success as the spell itself. This is one of those things that the average spellbook doesn't cover, possibly because the question doesn't occur to you until you've just finished physically performing the spell and are faced with bowls of herbs and water and bits of candle wax, and yet it's one of the most common questions asked.

What you do with your ingredients depends on what kind of spell you've cast. If you have created an herb pouch, then the pouch should be placed where it will have the most effect. If it's to aid conception, for example, it should be hung over the bed, or tucked under the mattress. If it's to keep negative energy away from your home, you might bury it under the front porch or hang it on your front door.

If your spell is for banishing something, then dispose of the remains off your property. Put the candle ends, the herbs, and the ashes, if you burned something, into a paper bag. Go for a walk and drop it in the trash bin at your local park. If it is to sever yourself from an old relationship or something similar, take the bits and pieces and bury them in rich earth, again, off your property, and allow nature to recycle them.

If you have ingredients left over, you can do one of two things. You can label them carefully and store them for future use, or you can dispose of them by releasing them into running water, or bury them in the earth. The former may be done if you have not empowered or charged the ingredients in any way; the latter should be done if you misjudged the amount of ingredients you would need, and have coded them for a specific purpose.

Things like oils can be tightly capped and stored, clearly labeled, for future use. Stones, once their purpose has been accomplished, can be cleansed and cleared to prepare them for another spell.

Keeping Records

If you think I sound like a broken record about acting in the physical world, just wait until you hear me harp on about keeping records.

Successful spellcrafting depends on keeping clear and detailed records. If you have ever taken a class in physics or chemistry, then you understand the need for clear lab reports. Spellcrafting is very similar to working in a lab: you have to keep track of everything you use, how you use it and in what proportions, how you combine it, and the results, in order to be able to replicate the experiment at a later date. Record keeping is crucial: it allows you to go back and do a postmortem of sorts on your spell to understand why it succeeded, or why it didn't. If you haphazardly toss stuff together, and something goes dreadfully wrong, then you won't be able to refer back to the spell in order to undo it.

Records allow you to analyze data in order to ascertain times of personal power for you, to change small things in order to understand how each component influences the outcome, to use a proven successful spell again, and to rewrite a faulty spell, among other things. Records also document a very personal journey through the world of enchantment and transformation. By referring back to older spells you can easily see how you acquired new techniques, sharpened spells, and experimented with new methods. You will also be able to see how your life has improved and changed for the better.

A well-rounded record sheet ought to include the date and time you performed the spell, the weather, the location in which the spell was performed, the complete text of the spell, a list of required components, a record of your immediate feelings, short-term results, and long-term results. Go ahead and include the worksheet where you wrote out all the pertinent information while crafting your spell: it will have most of this information already. The more details, the better: you can include your health, astrological information such as the moon phase and sign, the sun sign, any major planetary positions or activity, and just about any other information that you consider important. If you think of a way you could have performed the spell better, make note of it. If there was something you forgot, write that down too. If you changed something mid-spell, add the new parts. If you stopped the spell in the middle for any reason, mark down where you stopped, why, and what happened when you did. Appendix 1 contains a sample template for a spell record sheet that you can copy and use as a guide for creating your own spell records.

This collection of notes and records will become a valuable reference as you evolve as a spellcaster. Records such as these were known as grimoires or spellbooks, and, in the twentieth century, gained the term Book of Shadows, referring to the solitary and mysterious pursuit of weaving magic to improve one's life. You may call it whatever you wish. Some call their records their Book of Illumination, for the light it sheds on the workings of energy. Perhaps it will be your Book of the Art, so named for the art of combining components and energies to produce a manifestation of your will. Or perhaps it will simply be your spell journal.

A binder may be the most practical place to keep your notes, for you can add to it without difficulty and move pages around. I prefer a thick blank hardcover book of the sketchbook variety, easily found at art supply shops. You will fill more than one of these journals throughout your spellcasting career, so don't worry too much about finding a large enough book or binder to last you forever. I actually have three different spell journals simultaneously in use: a book in which I write my correspondences and invocations; a book in which I make notes as I read, or when I brainstorm for a spell; and a book in which I record my meditations, the texts of spells, and their results. I also keep an herbal grimoire with samples and pressings of herbs, sketches, and correspondences both mundane and magical, although some of that information is replicated in my book of correspondences as well. You may choose to separate your information however you please. Make sure you date all the information you take down; this will facilitate connecting the dots later on, especially if you keep notes in more than one book. If you copy any information from a book you've read for future reference, make note of the source, both the book's title and author. This not only enables you to go back to the source later on, but it also ensures that you give proper credit where it is due if you ever share the information with others.

Whatever you call it, and however you choose to record all your information, treat it with respect. Your spell journal is the tangible record of your experiments and your thoughts. Some practitioners wrap it in a cloth between uses, both to protect its energy and to keep it from curious eyes. You may decorate it as you please, and record the information in whatever fashion you prefer. My working notebook and my meditation record book are handwritten, as is my herbal grimoire, whereas my book of correspondences and invocations is a collection of typed and printed pages, trimmed and glued into a blank book. It's neater, easier for me to read, and I find I can fit more information to a page this way. Some people are nervous about keeping a handwritten record neat, and keep all their information on a computer, printing out whatever pages are necessary. I have seen beautiful binders with personalized spell record sheets and printouts of meditations and correspondences. I have seen beautifully handwritten texts. I have also seen wonderfully messy spell journals, which are true reflections of the crafting process. Some practitioners consider their collection of notes and records to be a gift to their heirs, the sum total of their research and positive energy. Others never share their knowledge. What you do with your information, and how you record it, is up to you.

Spontaneous Spells

What about the magic of the moment? What about those times where you're swept up by emotion and you perform a spontaneous spell right then and there?

Spontaneous spells can be lovely, deep, and very meaningful. There's no rule anywhere insisting that every spell has to be thought and planned out to the last detail. If you're standing on the seashore under a full moon and your heart swells, then by all means, do what you feel inspired to do.

Just write it down when you get back home. Scribble down as best you can what you said and what you did. You can use a spell record sheet, or you can record it in a journal reserved for spellcrafting. A journal like this can also record meditations, questions, dreams, and bits of research, and over time can become a beautiful and personal record of your evolution as a spellcrafter. Knowledge is power, and the more knowledge you acquire from studying your successes and failures, the more power you have over your abilities and your life.

Reduce the Risk of Fear

Many spellcrafters are paralyzed by the idea of making a mistake. They have some vague conception of their lives imploding if they add the oregano before the deer's tongue grass, or if the candle is lit before the incense.

Part of the spellcrafting process involves having the courage to take your life into your hands and commit yourself to making a difference. There's no way around that. In fact, it's one of the greatest truths of spellcasting that people rarely talk about: a successful spellcaster has accepted that *he or she can make a difference in his or her life.* As a spellcrafter, you possess the power to initiate change. If you're petrified of doing something wrong, though, you're not even giving yourself the opportunity to make a difference, let alone the chance to make a mistake—or to succeed.

Resolve right now to allow yourself to make mistakes. Mistakes are how we learn. "Be willing to look like a beginner in order to be an expert," says creative coach Jill Badonksy, and she's right: everyone has to start somewhere. When you learned to ride a bicycle, you fell off and skinned your knees over and over until you finally mastered the trick of balancing on two narrow, moving tires. Spellcrafting can be a much less painful experience, as long as you remember to come up with a clearly defined goal, to think through your spell carefully, and to consider the consequences. Practice gives you experience to apply to your future spells. Note, however, that practice does not make perfect in the subjective area of spellcraft. Life is a work in progress, after all. Things are rarely perfect.

Experimenting

If you ever had a chemistry set as a child, or you knew someone with a chemistry set, you might know the chaos that can arise from the simple decision to "see what happens if you do this and this." I want to reassure you right now that experimenting in spellcraft does not mean fooling around. Spells are serious. Experiment all you like; in fact, I encourage it. Experimentation leads to experience, which leads to wiser spellcrafting. Push your boundaries. Always assume that you can do whatever you're setting out to do. Experiment by all means, but never cast spells for frivolous or dangerous things. Spellcraft is a very real power with repercussions. The price of getting what you think you want is getting what you asked for. If you haven't thought your spell through, you can end up encountering a nasty surprise.

The Spellcasting Paradox

On one hand, you have to have a clear need and feel strongly about it, but on the other, you sort of have to forget it once you've done the spell.

This is one of those paradoxes you have to encompass and accept in spellcrafting, like the idea that your intent is what makes a component resonate with love instead of peace for one spell. Of course it's hard to let go of a process when you care deeply about the goal. You can't hold the spell's hand while it works, though: it has to be completely released to move, develop, mature, and produce a result. The adage "a watched pot never boils" is very true in spellcasting terms. Do the spell, and *let it go.* Don't obsess about it, don't fret about it, don't do the spell again "just in case." If you do, you're telling yourself that you doubt the outcome, and that you don't believe the spell will work. If you find yourself anxious about the spell, channel that emotion and energy into working in the everyday world to achieve your goal instead.

Have faith in yourself. You possess that power to make a difference, to change your life for the better. Believe.

4

the ethics of spellcasting

What's to stop you from taking over the world? Your own ethical code, that's what! Every decision you make has effects and consequences for yourself and others. This chapter talks about how to evaluate a situation in order to fine-tune a spell, and how to take appropriate action.

Spellcasting is really no different from living your everyday life. You make decisions, you act on them, and you live with the consequences. For some reason, however, the use of spells sometimes tempts people to throw their established ethical systems out the window. Perhaps it's connected to the realization that spellwork creates a different point of view, and empowers the caster to work "behind the scenes" in secrecy. Perhaps it derives from the bad press spellcasters have suffered over the ages, or the accusations of manipulation, or misuse of power.

Wherever it comes from, it's a serious issue. Knowing that you can use energy for pretty much any goal you choose can be empowering, but it can also tempt you to use it for less ethical goals. Imagine if you discovered you had superpowers. Would you use your powers to protect others and preserve peace, or would you be tempted to loot a bank?

Trust me, it crosses everyone's mind at some point. Thinking about it doesn't make you a bad person. In Victor Hugo's *Les Miserables*, the protagonist Jean Valjean steals a loaf of bread to feed his sister's starving family. In a desperate situation, you're often forced to choose between the various values that you uphold. How you choose to proceed is a result of your values operating within your system of ethics.

A value is a quality that you cherish, such as honesty, freedom, peace, charity, justice, and so forth. A cultural ethical system is a structure of common values within which a community operates in order to maintain some sort of civilized society. Within that cultural system, every individual also has a slightly different system of personal ethics, because everyone has a slightly different point of view regarding how the world works, and what constitutes right and wrong. A choice is rarely purely right, or purely wrong. Instead, we're forced to choose between what is more right or less wrong. Sometimes it seems as if there is no correct answer, only answers which differ in their degree of incorrectness.

Every religion has some sort of moral structure guiding its adherents, although ethics function independently of religion as well. The basic guideline found in most religions is some version of what is known as the Golden Rule: *do unto others, as you would have them do unto you.* This rule functions on the basic belief that what goes around comes around, and that we reap what we sow. If we put goodness and positive energy out into the world, goodness and positive energy is what will come back to us. Remember the analogy of the spider web that I used in the first chapter? That web of energy is one of the ways in which spells function. If that web is how we can affect our lives and environments by use of willpower and spellcraft, then everything and everyone connected by it are affected by what we do. If we perform a thoughtless action, then everything connected by that web suffers, including ourselves. If we perform an unethical action, then the repercussions travel throughout the web as well.

Don't mistake "goodness and positive energy" for weakness. Love and light can be expressed with a good sharp wake-up call, or a colossal life-changing event. If you're angry, or seeking to harm others because it makes you feel better or justified in your own actions, then what you're doing is *reacting* instead of *acting*. You're striking back at someone or something because you feel hurt or wronged. If you're looking to intentionally hurt someone, then your ethical system had better support it in spades, and you'd better not come crying when someone intentionally harms you. You'll still have to deal with all the harm coming back to you in some way, shape, or form, thanks to that cosmic web of energy.

What it comes down to is that ethics determine what you consider morally right and wrong. An ethical system has to have consistency; otherwise it isn't reliable. If you oppose murder one day and condone it the next, that's an inconsistency that weakens your system of ethics. An unreliable or fluctuating system of ethics isn't a system; it's convenience. Hypocrisy is introduced when you are morally angered if someone else performs the same actions that you yourself perform. Make sure your ethical system is consistent; otherwise you're adrift without a rudder upon the sea of life.

Situational ethics are unavoidable due to the fact that sometimes you're choosing what's less wrong. Sometimes the needs of the many outweigh the needs of the few.

Ultimately, however, your ethical system exists in order to make you think about your actions, and to take responsibility for them.

How does this relate to working with spells? It can be tempting to use spellcasting to obtain goals that aren't very ethical. An example used to illustrate this point is casting love spells. If Michaela has a crush on Jake, crafting a spell to make him fall in love with her is considered unethical, whereas crafting a spell to increase her attractiveness or draw a new love to her is ethically acceptable. Why?

In life, everyone has free will. Sometimes we are given the responsibility of making decisions for others, such as children or someone who has assigned us power of attorney. When we make decisions in those cases, we attempt to make the best decision for the individual in our care, to the best of our ability. If someone has not granted us that right, then ethically we have no right to interfere in how they choose to live their life. Michaela might believe that Jake would be happy with her, but using a spell to cause him to fall in love with her robs him of his free will. And, honestly, do you think you'd be happy with someone who loved you simply because you'd forced them to? Frankly, love is more magical when it happens without being forced. On the other hand, if Michaela works spells to increase her attractiveness and to draw new love into her life, the only person she is directly influencing is herself. She's creating the opportunity for Jake to notice her and think about her in a romantic fashion.

As I've discussed previously, acting in the physical world to reinforce your spells is the best way to help things along. If you do as Michaela does and craft a spell to enhance your attractiveness, then ask the object of your affection out for coffee or dinner. Spells work best when you give them the opportunity to function.

A good rule of thumb is to not use spells for anything that you wouldn't try for in person in the physical world. Spellcasting isn't a way to cut down on work, or to avoid responsibility; that's far from the truth. By now you've discovered that spellwork is as successful as you allow it to be, and that spells work with the natural order, not against it. Now, you're probably already living an ethical life; you presumably value concepts such as honesty, freedom, and compassion, so the ethics applied to your spells aren't likely to be very different. Just be sure that you take the time to consider what you're doing so that you can make the best moral judgment possible under the circumstances.

The ethics of spellcrafting involve two very basic ideas: the use of common sense, and pausing to think twice. Both these concepts exist to reduce the possibility of error, or bad judgment.

It's said that common sense is remarkably uncommon. This stems from an inability or reluctance to consider the needs or positions of others around you in your environment. Common sense involves understanding that there are consequences to every decision and action. If you are secure in your own position, you have the confidence to accept that other people may have a different stance, and you agree to disagree.

It is essential to take the time to discover as much information as possible regarding the situation in order to know your true feelings regarding it, and to understand your motives before you begin to draft a spell to deal with a particular situation. Pausing to think twice ensures that you don't make a snap decision based on an emotional reaction or incomplete data. If it is a time-sensitive matter, then do your best to look at the situation fairly and invoke your common sense to guide you as you draft your spell. If the issue isn't time-sensitive, then take some notes, and give yourself time to cool off. Come back to your notes later and reread them. Do you still feel the same way? Have any new insights or possibilities occurred to you in the meantime? Has any new information come into your possession?

The concept of responsibility is key within spellcrafting. Responsibility is a natural partner of power. In our society, most people seek to hold and exert power while passing the responsibility to someone else, so that "it's someone else's problem." Every action has consequences, and if you choose to undertake the action, ethically you should accept the consequences as well. When you choose to use spells, you are acknowledging that you accept the responsibility that comes with the ability to change your life. It's not "someone else's problem." Responsibility is another important aspect that functions within the ethical system. You can't dismiss responsibility, because it isn't morally right to do so.

Exercise: Ethics and Morals

Ethical perspectives vary from person to person. Your basic sense of right and wrong will depend on your past experiences, your cultural background, and your upbringing. Define the following words for yourself:

• Truth	• Freedom	• Respect
• Right	• Justice	• Ethics
• Wrong	• Responsibility	• Values

ETHICAL OUTS

Lots of spellbooks tell you to add a codicil of sorts to your spell to absolve you from any repercussions. Astrologer and witch Sybil Leek's "may this spell not reverse or place upon me any curse" is a common one. So is adding the phrase "by the free will of all, to the harm of none." In some instances, using such phrases may be an attempt to avoid taking responsibility. However, there are times when they reinforce the purity of your intent or cover areas you inadvertently omit. Only you know for sure.

Ask yourself if the spell itself without one such codicil actually empowers you in a positive fashion. Have you enhanced your spiritual growth through this spell? Are you a better person because of it? Have you improved the world in any way? Your goal, your intent, and your motive count for a lot more than adding a few words at the end of your spell as a means of avoiding responsibility to yourself and others.

Trust Yourself

There's only so much guidance an employee in an occult shop or an author's book can offer you.

When spellcasting, complete confidence in your actions is a necessity. If something in a ritual or a spell doesn't feel right to you, change it! This doesn't mean you should wander through a spell or ritual changing things for the sake of changing them; often, correspondences have been carefully thought out, angels or deities chosen for their associations with the spell's intent, and so forth. If you alter one part of a spell without understanding its place within the spell, often you can unbalance it.

Take the time to research the different aspects of the ritual; thoroughly understand why each component has been selected, and with this new knowledge you might conclude that perhaps the ritual doesn't require altering after all.

If you still do not feel comfortable after your research, give serious thought to the aspects of the spell you wish to change. If you wish to substitute another entity or deity, make sure they govern similar interests. Again, careful research will give you the knowledge necessary to substitute appropriate correspondences or components. If you already work with an aspect of the Divine, consider asking its blessing upon the spell instead of invoking an angel or deity with whom you have no personal connection. You might have to rewrite the words a bit. Just be sure not to lose the original thrust of the spell. If you read through a spell and on the surface it appears to be fine, but you feel that there is something niggling in the back of your brain, which makes you slightly uneasy, either find another spell or write a new one.

The Importance of Instinct

Trust your gut instinct at all times. You might not be able to find the proof in a book, but if you're strongly pulled to it, use it. Your own ethical system exists as a form of barometer to warn you when something's not quite right. Rely on it.

The human mind and body are an astonishing set of partners. They take in information and act upon it without our conscious mind being aware of it. The rapidity with which we evaluate a situation and navigate through it, while multitasking on the phone, driving in a car, or walking down the street while listening to music, is simply amazing. We pick up information through the standard five physical senses of touch, sight, smell, hearing, and taste. We also have what is often referred to as a sixth sense, an undefined sense, which accesses information the other physical senses cannot. It is this sense that alerts us to knowledge we cannot possibly have acquired through standard acceptable methods.

Your intuition is part of that sixth sense. Although your conscious mind might not be able to put its metaphorical finger on the necessary knowledge at the time, your intuition turns you in the correct direction and guides you to the information you require, all without you quite understanding how or why. It can be remarkably disconcerting to discover that you "knew" the correct answer without knowing it in a traditional fashion. You might ask yourself how you knew. It's not important. The point is, your intuition is a valuable tool in the art of spellcraft.

Intuition is what tells you to add a pinch of a certain herb to an herbal blend designed for something, even though you have no recorded correspondence anywhere connecting that herb and that goal. What happens is that your intuition grasps the bigger picture and somehow understands that adding this herb will have a beneficial action.

Intuition can be annoying, especially if you are used to working by the book. You can draft an entire spell to heal a broken heart, including flowers and soft music, only to discover, when you actually get to the moment of performing the spell, that your intuition is insisting on loud rock and roll and ice cream. It can be quite a struggle. Trusting your intuition means that you roll with it. At first it might feel awkward. I suggest a compromise: meet your intuition halfway. Stick with your original draft, but allow your intuition to toss in a couple of suggestions. Just because you can't prove it doesn't mean that it's wrong.

Trusting your intuition means allowing yourself to believe that you know what you're doing. Think back to the concept of the web of energy covering the planet. If you believe in that web, then you can also believe that information can travel to you from a variety of directions in a variety of ways.

Living the Magic

One of the hardest things to do is to walk your talk. As you develop your ability to use spells for positive change in your life, your ethical system will hit some bumpy areas along the path. Every situation is a learning experience. As your ethical system is refined, you will notice that you become more sensitive to the ethical choices of others. There will probably come a time when you'll want to stand up for what you believe.

Defending what you believe to be ethically correct is your right. There are other ways to promote your ethical viewpoint, however, and the simplest, most direct way of doing so is to allow your ethical and moral choices to inform your everyday actions. Let your everyday life reflect your magical ethics. The energy flowing in your daily life supports your spellwork, just as your spellwork supports your everyday life.

Fine-Tuning an Ethical Spell

When you encounter a situation that you wish to improve with a spell, there are a few things to ask yourself first in order to keep your spell ethical.

1. Who is involved in this situation?
2. Who is affected by this situation?
3. How do I wish to change it?
4. What are the potential repercussions?

These questions will probably remind you of the first steps in crafting a spell. These four questions, however, pinpoint the ethical aspects of spellcrafting. Let's look at them one by one.

Who Is Involved in This Situation?

This question helps you remember that there are real people with their own lives, hopes, fears, and goals involved in the situation. Every situation is a tangle of energy strands connecting people, emotions, places, and objects. For example, if your significant other is being hassled by his or her boss at work, then the people involved are your significant other and the boss. Some judicious questioning or investigation will reveal the presence of others about which you might not know.

Who Is Affected by This Situation?

Each of the people directly involved in the situation are also connected to other people. What affects the people directly involved can also indirectly affect people not involved. Taking the example from the previous paragraph, the boss's family is also affected by the situation, as well as the other members of the work environment, and yourself.

How Do I Wish to Change It?

There are several different methods with which to address a problem. You could do a spell to have the boss fired; to have the boss transferred and replaced by someone else; to have the boss hassled by his or her own superiors; to have your significant other transferred; to have your significant other offered another, better job at another company; to improve communication between the boss and your significant other; to win the lottery so that your significant other no longer has to work; to charm the boss into adoring your significant other; the list is endless.

What Are the Potential Repercussions?

When you decide upon a goal, think abut what the repercussions will be. What you *can* do to address a problem is not necessarily what you *should* do. If you're being drawn to casting a spell for something less than ethical, such as having the boss fired, then look back to the second question. Who will be affected by that solution? The family of the boss.

Look at it in terms of what it might do for your significant other, as well. If the boss is fired, then someone has to temporarily take up the slack, and that's likely to be your significant other's team or department. Stress will mount; people will start to hassle one another; your own relationship with your partner might become strained. The person eventually brought in to replace the boss will need time to learn the dynamics of the department, and until that replacement has become completely comfortable, things will be awkward. Perhaps the replacement will be even worse than the original boss was.

Do your best to develop a solution that is for the best for everyone involved. Remember that energy travels out along those strands of the energy web. You also will be affected by the web's vibration.

Fine-Tuning an Unethical Spell

As I've stated above, there will be times when you choose the "less wrong" action. Reality doesn't exist in black and white terms. Everything is painted in shades of gray. In addition, the concept of working a spell to change someone else's situation without their knowledge and consent is perceived as being unethical in itself in the spellcasting community. However, you've already established that doing nothing is unethical. Which unethical action do you choose? Remember too that sometimes the correct way to deal with a situation is to do nothing at all, as you may not have all the facts, and your interference may further degenerate the issue.

When you cast spells for or upon yourself, this question of ethics rarely comes up. When you decide to use spellwork to deal with a situation beyond your immediate control, however, the question of ethics immediately arises. In spellcrafting workshops, I often ask students if they would cast a spell to limit someone else's freedom. They are usually horrified, and protest that they would never do such a thing. Then I suggest a situation such as a serial rapist on the loose in their neighborhood. Would they not do a spell to limit the rapist's freedom by being caught by the police? Some students say that they would do spells to protect the neighborhood. Wouldn't it be easier to arrest one individual than attempt to protect thousands? And doesn't that arrest accomplish the same goal: ensuring the safety of the neighborhood? Sometimes, spellwork for the needs of the many outweighs preserving the needs or rights of the few.

This, however, is a decision only you can make, and only you can draw the line separating ethical from unethical spellcasting. If you decide to act, then commit yourself completely to your decision. Don't halve your efforts just to cover your bases. If you're going to do it, do it, and accept the responsibility.

5

timing is everything

Correctly timing a spell can reward you with quicker, deeper change. This chapter looks at how to fine-tune spellcasting using moon phases, days of the week, the daily solar phase, the seasons of the year, and planetary energies. The mystery of calculating planetary hours is also explained in simple terms.

⟋⟍

A spell is designed to meet a need, and if your need is immediate, your spell should be, too. Technically, a spell may be performed at any time; don't let the fact that the moon is dark stop you from casting a spell for protection if there have been a rash of break-ins in your neighborhood.

There are traditional associations with days, moon phases, and other times, which practitioners can use in order to rev up the power of the spell. If you perform a spell at a time sympathetic to your goal, then your spell will encounter less opposition in the flow of energy. For example, Friday is a day traditionally associated with attraction and romance, and is often the day of choice for spells associated with love. However, if you make a date on Tuesday to go out on Wednesday, there's nothing wrong with casting a spell on the Tuesday night or the Wednesday to help things along. Just because Thursday is the ideal day for financial matters doesn't mean that you can't cast spells to attract money at any other time.

Timing isn't absolute, but it can be helpful in fine-tuning your spell-work. There are several different methods by which you can determine an optimal time for casting your spell. You can use one, some, or none of the methods; the choice is yours.

Lunar Phases

The moon is the most common guide for spellcasting. Books will often instruct you to perform your spell when the moon is full, waxing, or waning. Traditionally, the moon is associated with mystery and feminine energy. Feminine energy does not mean that it may only be used by women; rather, it is a descriptive term indicating that the energy is receptive as opposed to projective.

Full and Dark

The moon itself does not emit light; it only appears to shine when sunlight strikes it and the light is reflected. We call the moon "full" when we can see the moon lit up in its entirety. The dark moon is when the last crescent vanishes and there appears to be no moon in the sky. I deliberately use the term "appears to be" because the moon is actually there; you often just can't see it because you're squinting directly into the sunlight. The dark moon occurs when the moon is directly in front of the sun, between the sun and the earth. We can't see the sunlight reflecting off the moon because the sunlight is bouncing directly back to the sun. With no light being reflected back to us, the moon is effectively rendered invisible to our eyes for approximately three days. People who don't cast spells often refer to the dark moon as the new moon, as it signifies the beginning of a new lunar cycle. However, I'm going to refer to the new moon as the first visible slim crescent in the evening sky, about three days into the lunar cycle.

As you might expect, the full and dark moons traditionally represent the extremes of lunar energy. This doesn't mean extremes of quantity of energy—the moon doesn't have more or less power at any time during its cycle—but the extremes of creative and destructive quality associated with that lunar energy. Traditionally, most Western cultures associate the sight of the moon waxing with creative power, and the dark moon with destructive power. The terms "creative" and "destructive" do not refer to a positive and negative value to the energy; they refer instead to two natural functions of the life process, growth and decay.

Blue Moons and Black Moons

There are thirteen moons in one calendar year, owing to the fact that a complete lunar cycle takes twenty-eight and a half days. This means that you'll usually see one full moon per month. Approximately every few years, however, in one calendar month you will see two full moons, one at the very beginning of the month and one at the end. The second full moon in a calendar month is referred to as a Blue Moon. As they are uncommon, Blue Moons are considered to be very special times for spellwork, with plenty of extra power on tap. Blue Moons are excellent times for making wishes, or to fill spell ingredients with this special lunar energy.

Less frequently, one month in a year will also have two dark moons; the second dark moon in that month is referred to as a Black Moon. Like Blue Moons, Black Moons are considered very powerful occurrences, and excellent for meditation, introspective magic, or powerful protection spells.

Waxing and Waning

"Waxing" is a term that describes growth or increase. "Waning" is a term indicating to lessen or decrease. The moon is said to wax between the dark and full moons, as it appears to grow larger in the sky. The moon is said to wane between the full and the dark moons, as it appears to decrease in size. Of course, the moon doesn't actually change size or shape in the sky; what we see changing is the amount of the moon's surface hidden by the shadow of the earth. The moon's shape changes as it moves in and out of that shadow.

The waxing and waning process is tied to the perception of the full and dark moons. Traditionally, Western culture tends to associate the sight of the moon waxing with an increase of creative and nurturing energy. Conversely, the waning moon is associated with banishing and/or destructive energy.

Four Quarters

Your average wall calendar divides the moon's cycle into four equal phases called the first quarter, second quarter, third quarter, and fourth quarter. It would be remarkably nifty if these four quarters matched the waxing-full-waning-dark classification that the layperson observes by looking up into the night sky, but it isn't so. The four quarters are each seven days long, and as you probably know by observation, the full moon doesn't last a week long, nor does the dark moon.

The first quarter begins with the dark moon. The sun, moon, and the earth are all lined up during the beginning of the lunar cycle. This is a terrific time to launch new projects or undertakings, because the sun's energy is traveling along the same energy paths as the moon's energy, giving you a two-for-one zip to your magic. The moon rises in the early morning and sets around sunset, rising and setting a bit later each day. This is why you don't see the moon for about three days; it's keeping the same hours and position that the sun is keeping. When the moon reaches a point where it's setting slightly later than the sun, it can be seen as a luminous slim crescent hanging low in the western sky for a few minutes after the sun goes down. The first quarter is a good time to work on issues involving children, animals, plants, and motivation.

The second quarter begins halfway between the dark moon and the full moon. The moon is seen as a half-circle, which rises around midday and sets around twelve at night. The second quarter is excellent for expansion, patience, peace, family, and harmony.

The third quarter begins with the full moon, rising at sunset and setting at dawn. The full moon is ideal for powering those ventures you started at the dark moon, and for almost everything: knowledge, love, money, protection, dreams, and psychic powers. Two days after a full moon is when the moon appears to begin waning. This begins a time of decrease, where you can prune away old and outgrown thoughts and habits, and discard what is no longer benefiting you. Use this energy for health and healing (as in banishing illness), protection, difficult decisions, and easing stress.

The fourth quarter begins halfway between the full moon and the dark moon. The moon rises just after midnight and sets around noon. This energy is good for justice, endings, separations, and limiting action or expansion.

These quarters aren't absolute, of course; the moon moves through them all sequentially, occupying a slightly different position each day.

Moon Signs

Just as the sun does, the moon travels through the constellations of stars that we call the zodiac, or astrological signs. Whereas the sun takes a year to travel through them all, spending approximately thirty days in each sign, the moon usually spends two and a half days in a sign, thus passing through the whole zodiac in approximately one lunar month. Does the moon actually travel through these signs? No, of course not. It appears to do so from our vantage point on Earth, however.

Each sign has a different personality that affects the lunar (or solar) energy when the luminary is passing through it. For example, if your spell is to help you meet new people, then you might choose to cast it when the moon is in the sign of Libra, the sign associated with social issues. The lunar energy you use to power your spell will be enhanced with Libran energy. Here's a list of correspondences for the signs of the Zodiac. The correspondences are applicable to the moon, and of course to the sun as well.

- **Aries** energy is good for new beginnings and action
- **Taurus** energy is good for manifestation
- **Gemini** energy is excellent for communication and intellectual pursuits
- **Cancer** energy is associated with family and the home
- **Leo** energy is good for success
- **Virgo** energy is organized and practical
- **Libra** energy is terrific for social issues
- **Scorpio** energy is passionate and just
- **Sagittarius** energy is associated with study
- **Capricorn** energy is stable and good for business issues
- **Aquarius** energy is excellent for issues involving groups of people
- **Pisces** energy is associated with mysticism and spiritual evolution

Moon Void of Course

This term does not mean that the moon is invalid and everyone knows it but you. Void of course refers to the time the moon spends between the astrological signs. The term "void" refers to empty, and "course" refers to the path the moon travels. Technically, when the moon is void of course it means it has left the last aspect of one sign, and has not yet achieved the first aspect of the next sign. When you're attempting to use lunar energy and the moon is between signs in this way, clearly defined lunar energy isn't accessible.

Think of it as someone going through a tunnel when you're trying to talk to them on a cell phone: their signal cuts out and you can't communicate until they're back on the open road again. It's the same with the moon.

A void can be anywhere between a few minutes to nearly two days long. The best thing to do is check an astrological calendar for lunar positions. A regular wall calendar or agenda usually tells you the moon phase, but nothing more. Pick up a copy of Jim Maynard's *Pocket Astrologer* or *Celestial Influences*, and you'll be able to plot out spells requiring lunar energy without a hitch.

Can you perform a spell when the moon is void of course? Of course you can. You'd be better to draw on something other than lunar energy to power it, because otherwise your efforts are likely to fizzle.

Night and Day

The majority of spellbooks instruct you to perform spells according to the phase of the moon. This would seem to indicate that the spell itself ought to be done after the sun sets. If I only cast spells at night, I'd lose fifty percent of my potential spellcasting time. Since I like to sleep at night too, I lose more spellcasting opportunity. I go to my orchestra rehearsal every Wednesday night; that means I lose a night for spellcasting associated with communication.

The moon is always present, whether it's on the other side of the earth, obscured by the earth's shadow, or covered by clouds, so of course you can use lunar energy during the day. Line of sight has no effect on using lunar energy in spellwork, nor does the color of the sky surrounding the moon. Admittedly, it does have quite an effect on the ambiance;

there's nothing quite like kneeling under a full moon in the night sky, surrounded by your spell components.

Solar Phases

The immediate assumption of most people is that a spell must be cast at night, as spells are usually scheduled according to the moon's phase. However, there's no need for a modern spellcaster to work solely by the light of the moon when there's an equally powerful luminary at hand during the day.

Using solar energy to power spells might take a bit of rearranging your mental approach to spellwork, but I assure you that it's more than worth it. The traditional association of magic with the moon derives from centuries of lore linking lunar deities with magic. The concept of secrecy and the cover of nightfall probably have something to do with it, too. The popular romantic vision of women and the occasional man creeping from their cottages by moonlight, swathed in cloaks against the chill of the night air as they hasten to a secret meeting place to chant spells, is too ingrained to shed completely.

The sun nourishes the plant life of the planetary ecological system, is essential to the water cycle, regulates our biorhythms, and regulates our moods. It also controls the seasonal cycle, which in turn dictates sowing and harvesting patterns depending on where you live. Our bodies depend on a balance of sunlight and darkness in order to maintain a regular cycle essential to mental, physical, and emotional health. To ignore such an important factor in your spellcasting is a waste of precious and valuable energy.

On a practical level, the best time for you to perform spellwork might be at six in the morning before the rest of your household is up and running. If you're tied to the spells-at-night mentality that will be fine for about half the year, but you'll be casting to the sound of chipper morning birds singing in the light of the rising sun for the other six months. On a slightly more esoteric level, some people just don't work well with lunar energy, and that's nothing to be anxious about. If spells seem to fizzle or don't succeed as well as you'd like when you cast according to the phases of the moon, try using solar energy to power them instead.

Solar energy is different from lunar energy in that it has a warmer, stronger, more active aspect. Some spells naturally work well with solar energy, such as spells for health and activity.

There are a variety of ways to work with solar phases.

Day

The day begins with the dawn, moves to midday, through sunset, and then to midnight. Each of these four phases is associated with a general energy that you can use to add extra power to your spell:

- *Dawn:* origins, new beginnings, illumination, children
- *Midday:* energy, growth, creation, increase
- *Sunset:* decrease, banishment, resolution, maturation
- *Midnight:* endings, gestation, stability

From these four points you can extrapolate other times during the day, such as midmorning or midafternoon.

Seasons

The seasons have inspired more poetry and art than possibly any other natural event. Spellcasting by the seasons means you'll likely be planning your spell far ahead of when you'll be casting it. Chances are good that if you schedule a spell according to a season, you're taking the time to think about it and it will likely be a slow-evolving spell with long-reaching effects.

Like the daily solar phase, the seasonal solar phase is associated with basic energies, which you can use to refine your spells:

- *Spring:* origins, new beginnings, birth
- *Summer:* passion, activity, creation/destruction
- *Autumn:* transformation, farewells, nostalgia
- *Winter:* introspection, planning

Remember that if you work with solar energy, your probable date of manifestation will be calculated by the appropriate solar phase. If you work a spell for new beginnings in spring, then look for slow growth in summer, and the first harvested rewards of the project in the fall.

Answer the following questions. Remember, there are no correct answers, only answers that work for you. Check Appendix 4 for suggested answers.

1. When would you work a spell for a pregnant cat to have a successful delivery?
2. When would you work a spell to bless a baby?
3. In what season would you choose to cast a spell for academic success?
4. What moon phase would you choose to cast a spell to honor a newly deceased elderly relative? What moon sign? What season?
5. When would you choose to cast a spell to deepen spiritual awareness?

Planetary Energy

Apart from the moon and the sun, there are plenty of heavenly bodies that you can draw upon to power your spells with various energies.

The days of the week are each associated with certain energies and concepts. Choosing to perform a healing spell on a Sunday, for example, will draw upon the powers of the sun to cleanse and invigorate an invalid. Casting a prosperity spell on a Thursday will help build up your finances. The following list gives you an idea as to which day is associated with what energies:

- **Sunday** is ruled by the Sun and is associated with active, male energy, power, leadership, authority, success, and sports.
- **Monday** is ruled by the Moon and is associated with female, receptive energy, travel, sea, hunting, cycles, reproduction, dreams, and psychic work.
- **Tuesday** is ruled by Mars and is associated with active energy, aggression, destruction, conquest, violence, animals, and male sexuality.
- **Wednesday** is ruled by Mercury and is associated with learning, intellectual pursuits, communication, gambling, medicine and healing, commerce, deception, and theft.

- **Thursday** is ruled by Jupiter and is associated with good fortune, growth, rites of passage, expansion, finances, career, and bureaucracy.
- **Friday** is ruled by Venus and is associated with music, dance, all arts, social occasions, love, emotion, and female sexuality.
- **Saturday** is ruled by Saturn and is associated with the past, aging, death, abstract thought, higher study, and agriculture.

If you're wondering how these associations came about, take a look at the days of the week in various languages, and the deities they encompass. Friday, for example, is named for Freyja, the Norse goddess of love; in French, the day is known as *Vendredi*, derived from the Roman goddess of love and attraction, Venus. Wednesday derives from Wotan or Odhinn, the travelling Norse god of wisdom; in French, it is *Mercredi*, named for the Roman god Mercury, lord of medicine, commerce, and, ironically, of theft.

PLANETARY HOURS

Most basic spellbooks don't go into any sort of detail regarding calculations of any kind, which might be at odds with engravings showing magicians poring over books and working out the most accurate time for a spell to be cast. Basic spellbooks often tell you simply to cast a spell on a full moon. You've already learned a couple of techniques to further pinpoint a beneficial time to work a spell. Here's a more advanced technique that might be a bit tricky to master, but is worth it in the end.

Calculating planetary hours is a skill that is best to learn by heart, simply because unlike checking to see what day of the week is best suited for a spell to increase your psychic sensitivity, planetary hours must be calculated anew for every single day. That's right; it's a technique that you have to learn and implement. Why? Because calculating planetary hours is based on the time of sunrise and sunset in your time zone, and that time changes daily thanks to that pesky orbit our planet follows around the sun.

There's more. If you have an entire twenty-four hours, and you want to work out the planetary hours for that twenty-four hour period, you have to do the calculations twice, because the length of the daytime "hour" will be different from the length of the nighttime "hour." Unless, of course, you happen to be calculating the planetary hours for the Spring Equinox or the Fall Equinox, as there are equal hours of day and night on those two days. Confused yet?

If so, you're in good company. Planetary hours are tricky, I agree, but once you know how to calculate them, your spell scheduling will become much more flexible.

Here's how to work out planetary hours:

1. Check your local newspaper, newscast, almanac, or the Internet for sunrise and sunset times.
2. Calculate the difference in minutes between the time of sunrise and the time of sunset. Divide this number by twelve. Your result is how long a single planetary hour will be *for that day only*. The result can range from around thirty minutes to almost seventy minutes. Repeat the procedure for the time between sunset and sunrise the next morning. Be aware that the hour length *will not* be the same for the daytime planetary hours and the nighttime planetary hours!
3. What day of the week is it? Depending on the day, a different planet begins the schedule of hours: Sunday: Sun; Monday: Moon; Tuesday: Mars; Wednesday: Mercury; Thursday: Jupiter; Friday: Venus; Saturday: Saturn.
4. Once you have your beginning planet, assign a planetary ruler to the hours in the following order: Saturn; Jupiter; Mars; Sun; Venus; Mercury; Moon. For example, if it were Sunday, the first planetary hour would be ruled by the Sun, the second planetary hour would be ruled by Venus, and so on. *(Note: This is a different order than the days of the week!)* When you get to the seventh hour, start at the first planet again, until you reach the twelfth hour. Do the same for the night planetary hours.

Let's work through an example. I use the twenty-four hour clock to do these calculations, as it facilitates the math. In my time zone, the sun rises at 5:18 A.M. on Monday, July 12, 2004, and sets at 8:42 P.M., or 20:42. It rises again at 5:19 A.M. on July 13. To work out how much time there is between 5:18 and 20:42, convert each time to minutes in the following way:

12:00 to 5:18 A.M. = 5 hours 18 minutes

5 hours x 60 minutes = 300 minutes

300 minutes + 18 minutes = 318 minutes between midnight and 5:18 A.M.

5:18 = 318 minutes

12:00 midnight to 8:42 P.M. = 20 hours 42 minutes

20 hours x 60 minutes = 1200 minutes

1200 minutes + 42 minutes = 1242 minutes between midnight and 8:42 P.M.

20:42 = 1242 minutes

If I subtract 318 minutes from 1242 minutes, I get 924 minutes of daylight. If I wanted to know how many *conventional* hours this makes, I would divide by sixty (the number of minutes in a conventional hour), which yields 15 hours and 24 minutes. Instead, to figure out how many minutes will be in a *planetary* hour on this day, I divide my 924 minutes of daylight by twelve, and I discover that my planetary hour unit works out to be 77 minutes long, or 1h 17m. As it's a Monday, my planetary hours would begin with the Moon. If I construct a table to refer to, it would look like this:

Hour	Duration	Associated Planet
Hour 1	5:18 – 6:35	Moon
Hour 2	6:35 – 7:52	Saturn
Hour 3	7:52 – 9:09	Jupiter
Hour 4	9:09 – 10:26	Mars
Hour 5	10:26 – 11:43	Sun
Hour 6	11:43 – 13:00	Venus
Hour 7	13:00 – 14:17	Mercury
Hour 8	14:17 – 15:34	Moon
Hour 9	15:34 – 16:51	Saturn
Hour 10	16:51 – 18:08	Jupiter
Hour 11	18:08 – 19:25	Mars
Hour 12	19:25 – 20:42	Sun

The sun sets at 20:42.

If I wanted to do spellwork on the night of July 12, 2004, I know that the sun sets at 20:42, and I can verify that the sun rises again the next morning of July 13 at 5:19 A.M. There are 517 minutes of night between the time when the sun sets and rises again the following morning (that's 8h 37m of night). Dividing that duration of night by twelve, I discover that a planetary hour for the night of July 12 is 43.1 minutes long, which I'll round down to 43 minutes for ease of calculation. Continuing the sequence of planetary rulership for the hours, the daylight sequence of which ended with the Sun, I construct a reference table, which looks like this:

Hour	Duration	Associated Planet
Hour 1	20:42 – 21:25	Venus
Hour 2	21:25 – 22:08	Mercury
Hour 3	22:08 – 22:51	Moon
Hour 4	22:51 – 23:34	Saturn
Hour 5	23:34 – 00:17	Jupiter
Hour 6	00:17 – 01:00	Mars
Hour 7	01:00 – 01:43	Sun
Hour 8	01:43 – 02:26	Venus
Hour 9	02:26 – 03:09	Mercury
Hour 10	03:09 – 03:52	Moon
Hour 11	03:52 – 04:35	Saturn
Hour 12	04:35 – 05:18	Jupiter

The sun rises at 05:19 A.M.

You'll notice that the end of the twelfth planetary hour falls one minute short of when the sun rises. This sometimes happens. Remember, I rounded down from 43.1 minutes to 43 minutes, and if each hour is losing just a few seconds, a shortage of one minute is created, give or take a few seconds. If you want to be extremely precise, you can add the extra seconds to each planetary hour unit, but if the math daunts you, just make sure to schedule your spell in the middle of your planetary hour, rather than at the beginning or the end. That way you'll ensure you're operating within the correct planetary association.

Planetary hours are a challenge to work out, but when you've accomplished it you'll feel remarkably smug and understandably proud of yourself. You'll also have acquired an invaluable skill, which will enable you to time your spellcasting with remarkable precision. Planetary hours allow you the flexibility of using the corresponding planetary energy even if you can't cast your spell on the ideal day of the week.

If you work with computers, there is a wonderful resource called the Lunabar created by Clysmic software (shareware which is free to try, and inexpensive to purchase; you can find it at *www.clysmic.com*). It's a small program, available for downloading, which places a small moon and planetary sign in your system tray, to the right of your status bar at the base of your monitor's screen, to indicate the moon phase and the sign the moon is currently transiting. The program is adjustable to your latitude and longitude, ensuring accuracy, and also includes seasonal information, tables of the moon phases, sunrise and sunset, and yes—planetary hours. A moon void of course table can be downloaded every three months to further fine-tune the Lunabar information.

Exercise: Planetary Hours

Answer the following questions. As always, there is no right answer. Check Appendix 4 for suggested answers.

1. What kind of spell could be cast on a Monday in the hour of the sun?
2. You've decided to study for an M.B.A. What planetary hour on what day would be a good time to cast a spell to support this?
3. Your relationship with a hopeful new significant other just isn't working out. What planetary hour on what day of the week would be best to break the news that you think you should just be friends? (Okay, there's never a good time for something like this, but what time might minimize the potential fallout, maximize understanding, and a cordial return to being single?)
4. Your daughter is being pestered by someone at school. What planetary hour on what day would be a good time to create a talisman for her to carry to help keep her safe?
5. You and your partner have just planned your first vacation in years. You've made reservations, bought tickets, and now your partner's boss is threatening to cancel the vacation time in order to keep your partner working on a project. What planetary hour on what day would you choose to work a spell to protect your vacation plans from being ruined?

Timing of Manifestation

A common question associated with timing concerns how long you'll have to wait until you see the results of your efforts. There is no hard and fast rule about when success will manifest, and this is due to a number of variables such as the degree of concentration and focus, the amount of energy that went into the spell, the kinds of obstacles and challenges you are working against, and what your goal is.

As a general rule, however, your evaluation ought to be connected to the method of timing you employed in your spell. As I mentioned above, if you choose to cast a spell timed to a season, look for the manifestation of results to be reflected in that temporal process. One of the reasons why spellcrafters tend to use moon cycles more frequently than solar cycles is because the moon goes through a full cycle in approximately twenty-eight days, as opposed to the sun's 365-day cycle. A standard practice is to wait one full lunar cycle before you evaluate the spell's progress; that means if you haven't seen any movement whatsoever concerning your problem within about twenty-eight days, note it down in your records and think about what to do next. Do you want to do a small spell to raise energy to support the original spell?

By the second lunar cycle after your spell (that's just under two months), if you still haven't seen any movement concerning your situation, it's time to evaluate again. Do you want to recast the spell? Do you want to do another spell to remove obstacles?

In your first and second monthly evaluations, you'll have to make a personal choice between leaving the original spell to do the work you sent it out to do, undisturbed; supporting the original spell by raising and sending it more energy; or redoing the spell completely. Have patience, and have faith. Even though you may not see significant changes, the energy of a spell has a lot of little things to shift and nudge in order to rebalance a situation. It can take a while for any kind of result to become obvious.

If, by the time the moon has cycled three times after your original spell (that's just under three months), you still haven't felt or seen any change, then abandon the spell and approach the situation differently, perhaps with a different spell, a rephrased need, or a simplified goal.

A common error on the part of spellcasters is to assume that their spell isn't working and to cast it again soon after the original spell. Ours is a society which functions on instant gratification, and patience is not one of our strong points; we forget that life moves in cycles, and that nature is not about to jump the tracks just to hand us our hearts' desires. Scrapping your spell simply because it hasn't demonstrated dramatic change is like throwing the proverbial baby out with the bath water. There's a bunch of your energy out there, patiently toiling away to slowly reform reality in accordance to your will. If you recast the spell, or create a new spell to do the same thing, you're not only telling your subconscious that you don't trust it, you're ordering the energy out there to stop in its tracks.

Remember, more often is not necessarily better. If you keep stirring those energies, you can stir them right off course.

Repeating a Spell

People often want to cast a spell again to increase the effect. For the most part, spells aren't cumulative. There's a danger that in drawing energy toward you as you raise power, you might very well pull the energy you've already sent out right back to you.

However, if you plan it ahead of time, you can structure your spell to maintain a sustained flow of energy by spreading it out over a specific number of days.

There are two ways of approaching this. First, you can plan to repeat a spell according to a determined cycle of time such as lunar or solar phase. For example, every third day after the new moon you might do a house cleansing spell, or a spell for inspiration at dawn for nine days, or a spell to increase your courage every Tuesday for a month. Second, you can do a single spell over a series of consecutive days. A spell like this might involve marking seven equal sections on a green candle with your fingernail, then burning one section each night for seven nights, while meditating on improved finances.

The difference between performing spells this way, and just doing it again to increase the effect, is how you think of it. These sequenced spells are deliberately performed one after the other *as a unit*. The spell is technically not finished until you have performed the specified actions on the last day. In spells such as this, if the sequence is broken, you have to start all over again at the beginning.

Your Time of Personal Power

By keeping records of your spellwork, you should be able to figure out which days of the week or time of day your spells tend to work. Perhaps there's a particular time of day or time during the moon cycle when you feel as if you could do anything, when raising energy is easy, when you can focus easily and tune out distractions with no problem. This, then, would be a power time for you.

Your power time is an alternate timing bonus for you. It's like a secret weapon: you can default to casting a spell during your power time and know that it will have just as much impact as scheduling the spell for 7:38 on a Thursday evening during the waning moon might have.

To pinpoint your power time, look through your spell journal. Your notes concerning the immediate results will be important: how did you feel during the actual casting of the spell itself? Conscientious maintenance of short-term and long-term results will be important as well. Look at the time, moon phase, or moon sign of the successful spells. Is there a pattern? Are you particularly on the ball when the moon is in Pisces, or in Virgo? Perhaps casting during the hour of Mars is the key to your success. Take a look at the weather as well. It may be that clear sunny days or cool evenings are your power times.

Everyone's power time is different. You also might have more than one power time, which might make it difficult to narrow down. Don't worry; the more often you cast spells, the clearer it will become.

Final Words on Timing

Remember when your parents used to warn you about waiting an hour after eating before jumping into the pool? The reason, they told us, was to avoid cramps. Simply put, if you eat and then try to do any sort of strenuous activity too soon afterwards, your body can't handle it.

I'm issuing you a similar warning concerning spellcraft. Don't eat directly prior to spellcasting; wait at least one to one and a half hours before beginning. Why? Well, food is energy, but your body also uses up energy while digesting and transforming the food into different forms of energy. Fundamentally, your body shuts down to a certain extent while digesting. Give yourself time to restore your energy levels. In the same vein, don't spellcraft after working out, a stressful day at work, or a night of insomnia. You've depleted your energy resources, and they must be rebalanced before spellcasting.

There will always be times when we absolutely have to do a spell right away—for example, a protection spell—and we can't wait for the best possible time. When that's the case, do the spell anyway at whatever time it might be. But for the most part, take the time to relax and reconnect with yourself before starting in on your spellcasting. You and your spell will be more likely to succeed.

6

correspondences

Add extra power to your spellwork with the use of correspondences. Elemental energy, herbs, stones, deity energy, specific tools, and other components can increase the power and precision of your spell. This chapter examines how to determine what correspondences you can use, and how to combine them for maximum energy and benefit.

⤳

A spell can technically be cast with three things: a goal, stemming from a need or desire; focus and visualization; and a gathering and release of energy toward that goal. However, just as the use of props facilitates drama and theater, spellcasting benefits from the addition of energy-rich ingredients to enhance the effects and results. These ingredients are also called components, and they possess specific corresponding energies that you can use to help achieve your goal.

The system of correspondences is a classification of objects, entities, and energies, which affect one another or evoke certain outcomes. The system of correspondences arises from a *sympathetic* association:

by using components or ingredients that demonstrate a certain kind of energy, you can attract more of the same energy, thus illustrating the "like attracts like" principle.

Conversely, by using components possessing one kind of energy, you can push away the antithetical energy, like using a magnet to repel another magnet with the same polarity, for example. (For more examinations of magical methods, see Chapter 8.) A correspondence is an identification of what an object's energy represents: for example, a correspondence for sandalwood is purification. Thus, if you were creating an incense to help power a purification spell, you might choose to use sandalwood in it. Using sandalwood enables you to draw on the energy of the wood to help power your spell; since sandalwood is associated with purification, it also employs the sympathetic magic principle and draws your goal closer to you.

Components are the elements you use in the act of spellcasting to help gather energies associated with your goal. Looking through other spellbooks, you've likely noticed spells calling for a variety of components such as herbs, flowers, stones, incense, oils, candles, dolls (also called poppets), cords, and other objects. Some spells have elaborate lists of ingredients. However, a perfectly good, powerful spell can be performed with a comparatively short list of components. More components are not necessarily better. Remember, it's *how* you use the energy of your correspondences that increases the power of your spellcasting, not how many correspondences and associated energies you can plug into it. It's definitely an issue of quality over quantity.

Charging and Empowering Components

There are a few basic steps you can take in order to ensure quality, and to fine-tune how you handle the energy of your components. Whatever ingredients or components you use in a spell, make sure to cleanse or clear them of any previous influence or energy hanging around, then empower them with your desire or purpose. It is called empowering or charging. If you don't do this, you're not energizing the components to act in accordance with your spell; it's like a badly plugged-in electrical cord. You're not being energy-efficient, and your spell won't be using the power as well as it could.

There are several different methods to empower or activate the energy of your ingredients. Words used in spellbooks include enchant, empower, program, bless, charge, and consecrate. Different practitioners have different techniques to empower components, but it can be quite simple. Here are two methods by which you can charge spell ingredients.

Charging Technique #1

Hold the ingredient in your hand, or hold your hands over the ingredient. Close your eyes and take three deep breaths, releasing tension or stress with each exhalation. Reach deep inside yourself to the core of your heart and feel your need or desire. Allow your emotion concerning this desire to flow up from your heart and down your arms to your hands, and from there into the ingredient. Continue until you feel that the energy of the ingredient resonates with your desire.

Charging Technique #2

This technique clears any previous energy hanging around your components which might interfere with your new purpose. Hold your hands over your ingredients. Take three deep breaths, releasing tension and stress with each exhalation. Say:

> I ask the great love of the cosmos,
> The light of the universe,
> To cleanse and charge these components
> That they may be prepared and consecrated
> To ensure my success.
> Bless these ingredients, and bless my goal.
> These are my words, this is my will.

By empowering your components, you are programming them to act in accord with your intent and goal.

When you charge an ingredient, use only as much as you need in the spell. If the component is an herb, this is likely to be a pinch or a spoonful, no more. Empowering your entire jar of mint for prosperity means that you can't use it for healing later on. In other words, it's a waste. Take only as much out as you intend to use, and keep the rest in an airtight jar. The only components you can really cleanse and reuse are objects such as stones, statues, boxes, and so forth, and even then it depends on your chosen method of spell disposal once your goal has been met. Sometimes it's more appropriate to bury the object, or burn it, or some similar action.

Working with Correspondences

The system of correspondences has been developed over time by thousands of practitioners experimenting and researching. If you examine your correspondences of your chosen components carefully, you will likely notice that most items have more than one association attributed to them. This comes as a result of different people experimenting with the same object and discovering new uses for it.

Don't take any list of correspondences as truth set in stone. Spellcraft is an intensely personal art, and even though people have retested and reinforced the system of correspondences over time, you may discover that although other people have experienced success with using roses for love, your personal energy might not mesh well with the energy of a rose. If such is the case, regardless of the number of experts telling you that a rose is essential for a love spell, you know that if you use a rose, your spell will fall flat. This isn't a sign of being a bad spellcaster; far from it. It simply indicates that as an individual, your success lies in using another component. This is where testing and keeping records comes into the creation of your system of correspondences. If you perform a spell for romance with a rose and it fizzles, make note of it. The next time you try the spell, you might choose to use a jasmine flower and discover to your delight that it works very well. Note this down in your records. Now you have a reference to which you can return, and the beginning of a personal system of correspondences in which roses don't work for love, but jasmine does. Just because you don't agree with everyone else's correspondences, published or not, doesn't mean you're the odd one out. On the contrary, it indicates that you're a canny spellcaster who knows that to power a spell, you need to have a personal relationship with your supplies. You can't just run down a list and see that roses are associated with love, and toss a rose into the mix. You have to understand that a rose isn't just a symbol for love; it possesses a certain energy that will have a certain influence on your spell, which is driven by your personal desire and bound together by your energy.

Due to the fact that most components have an aggregate of various correspondences, it pays to do your research. If you use a number of components, double check to make sure that none of the listed corresponding energies contradict one another, or cancel each other out. For example, camphor is often used to banish negativity, but it also has associations with chastity. If you're attempting to banish negative energy from your bedroom in order to free up your sexual energies, and you choose to use camphor and lavender, then using camphor in your spell might cancel out the lavender, which is also associated with purification and love. Using another component with the correspondence of purification instead of camphor, such as salt, would be a better choice.

If all you have is camphor, though, or you really feel strongly drawn to using it, then here's a technique to strengthen the banishing aspect. When you empower the component, call on the specific associated energy that you want to use. For example, when you empower the camphor, you would hold it between your palms, and say something like, "I call upon the energy of purification in this camphor to banish the negative energy in this room." In this way, you specifically code the act of empowerment to activate only one of the component's associated energies.

If you don't cleanse or empower your components before you use them in a spell, the energy they contain is still present, but it's latent as opposed to being active. Empowering the components ensures that they've been "turned on" and keyed to your specific goal.

Tools

Over time, certain symbols have become impregnated with certain associations, which, in turn, trigger the subconscious. The same precept holds true in spellcasting: Certain tools are used for their symbolic associations, thus reinforcing what you are doing. For example, if you are doing a spell revolving around transformation of some kind, you might select the *cauldron* as an important tool for your spell. On a practical level, the cauldron is the predecessor of the Crock-Pot or Dutch oven. It's a basic cooking implement into which you can toss meat, vegetables, and liquid, cover and simmer, and a couple of hours later you come back to it to discover a wonderful meal. Magically, the cauldron is associated with a similar function. There are several cauldrons of legend, which produce endless food, or revive the dead, or bring knowledge and illumination. In each case there is a shift from one state to another: from hungry to sated, from death to life, from ignorance to wisdom. The cauldron is a tool representing transformation of any kind.

A *cup* is a container, like a cauldron, but it is usually used in an act of sharing or commemoration. Often liquid is sipped from it to internalize some sort of transformation, or to internalize a desired shift in perception. A cup is more personal than a cauldron. In fairy tales, cups are used to celebrate, to share, and to honor; they often represent fulfillment or life. The Holy Grail of Arthurian myth is a cup, for example. Cups are associated with hospitality, love, communion and communication, mystery, and divination. A cup contains, which means it may be seen as confining something, or cradling it. Both the cauldron and the cup are associated with feminine energy and the womb of life.

The *wand* is associated with inspiration, and with directing your will. Several fairy tales involve a fairy godmother with a magic wand. A wand is like a pointer: it calls attention to your object, fixing it clearly in your mind. The wand also acts as a funnel, bringing the mass of energy and power you have collected down to a fine point, ensuring accuracy and efficient use of that power. Wands can be as simple as a chopstick, or as ornate as a wizard's staff. Like any other component or tool used in spellcasting, a wand is simply a prop; the true power lies in you, the practitioner, and how you gather energy from various places and weave it together. What you choose to use is up to you; you can gather a stick from the outdoors and decorate it as you like, or you can order a fancy pewter and crystal wand over the Internet. The key to acquiring a symbolic tool such as a wand is to experiment and keep notes, just as with any other component or tool, to ascertain if it's something you ought to use or not. The wand is associated with masculine and projective energy.

Another popular tool frequently mentioned in spellbooks is a *knife*, also referred to as an *athame*. In spellcasting, the knife is associated with severing yourself from a particular state; this action frees you to function within a new state. Whereas the wand is a more intellectual tool, the knife is associated with creativity and action. The knife too is associated with masculine projective energy. Many practitioners use a knife like a wand, directing energy and power down the blade through the tip toward their goal. Although the symbolism is slightly different, spellcasters use knives and wands interchangeably, as per their personal preferences.

Elements

Each of the four basic elements (earth, air, fire, and water) has certain energies associated with it. In the Middle Ages, they each constituted an aspect of the energy, which made up the body, as well. These were called the four humors. If these four humors were well balanced in your body and mind, then you were a healthy person. However, if you had an imbalance, it manifested in behavior, personality, or physical health issues. If you had an excess of earth energy, or phlegm, you were said to be phlegmatic. If you had an excess of fire energy, or choler, you were said to be choleric. If you had too much water energy, or melancholia, you were melancholic. If you had too much air energy, or blood, you were said to be sanguine. The system of humors gradually fell out of use as doctors further explored and understood the workings of the human body. These words live on in our modern vocabulary as adjectives for behavior or personality, but they're no longer used in medicine.

The four humors were also an important part of alchemy, the forerunner of modern chemistry. Like other sciences, it addressed both physical and spiritual aspects simultaneously, so that while on the physical plane alchemy was concerned with transforming lead into gold, it was similarly engaged on the spiritual level of transforming man's lowly soul into a transcendent and radiant light. The four elements have been a cornerstone of natural philosophy, metaphysics, and science of all kinds for a very, very long time. If you're interested in how the elements and other correspondences were classified in the Renaissance, and why, I highly recommend reading Agrippa's *Three Books of Occult Philosophy*, the complete text of which is now available and well annotated by Donald Tyson. This book is often referred to as the core text of Western occult study, and for good reason: it addresses the concept of magic in several forms, such as natural magic, mathematics, the elements, and various other subjects included in the study of "natural philosophy."

Agrippa based much of his work on the work of the classical philosophers, and if researching correspondences and associations appeals to you, the next place to turn is to Pliny's *Natural History,* an invaluable look at how Rome saw the world in the first century C.E. While today science addresses many of the areas addressed by Agrippa and Pliny, at that time explaining how the world worked was the job of philosophers (in a secular fashion) and clergy (in a religious setting). Natural philosophers believed that if the world was catalogued correctly, and that if you understood all the classifications, you could then manipulate or have control over the world around you. Sound familiar? It ought to: it's precisely what you seek to do with a spell.

By employing one or more of these elements in your spellcasting, you are in fact invoking the corresponding energies associated with the element. The correspondences associated with the elements come from various places, but mainly rest with the Western archetypes found within the collective unconscious, reinforced and perpetuated by natural philosophers and spellcasters throughout history.

Each element carries its own energies and associations. You can draw on the energy of one specific element to help power your spell, on all four for balance, or any number in between according to your needs. Another way to work with the energy of a specific element is to involve an elemental. An elemental is the spirit of the element. Some spellcasters find it easier to visualize the spirit of an element aiding their spellcasting, instead of the element itself providing energy.

Earth

The element of earth is associated with strength, stability, abundance, prosperity, and fertility. It is our source of life and shelter, and our physical form. Earth is often invoked in spells concerning the home, spells to improve business, spells concerning finances, and spells for stability of any kind.

The elemental, or spirit of the element, of earth is the gnome. If invoking earth itself is too abstract for you, then envision small dark humanoid creatures emerging from the ground to add their personal energy to your spell.

Air

The element of air is associated with movement, thought, communication, inspiration, and wisdom. Air allows us to speak, breathe, sing, and fly. Air is often invoked in spells for mental work, study, physical grace, and acquiring knowledge.

The elemental associated with air is the sylph. The Victorian depictions of fairies as long slender humanoid figures graced by dragonfly wings are very sylph-like. Envision them riding the breeze to where you are, raising energy to power your spell.

Fire

The element of fire is associated with energy, action, willpower, creation, and destruction. Fire is the heat of our blood and the warmth of the sun, as well as the mindless rage of the forest-consuming blaze. Fire is often used in spells to banish or remove something from our lives, to stimulate energy and action, and for creativity.

The elemental associated with fire is the salamander. Imagine little flames in the form of small reptiles, and you have an image of the salamander. Watch them dance in your hearth or in the flame of a candle.

Water

The element of water is associated with purification, emotion, psychic energy, dreams, and intuition. Water is the flow of the stream, the fall of rain, the shedding of a tear, and the cold bite of ice. Water is often used in spells calling for emotional balance, psychic work such as divination, spells calling on lunar energy, and spells to remove negativity.

The elemental associated with water is the nixie or the undine, a small humanoid figure with a fishtail, like a miniature merperson. They are easily seen in the breakers on a shore of a lake or ocean.

HERBS

Herbs, trees, and plants in general, are associated with the earth by virtue of the fact that they grow from it. However, each green thing has its own energies and corresponding attributes, which practitioners over the ages have discovered and reinforced. Many herbal correspondences exist by virtue of a system of classification created by the Renaissance natural philosopher Paracelsus (1493–1541), called the Doctrine of Signatures. This system proposed that the properties of plants could be ascertained by observing three things: the physical appearance of the plant; the environment in which it grew; and upon what sort of illnesses it had an effect. This system took these observations and assigned a planetary correspondence to the plant in question.

While later practitioners debated the validity of this system for medicinal use, the associations have persisted for spellcrafting. Planetary energy classifies basic energies according to the seven classical heavenly bodies (sun, moon, Mars, Mercury, Jupiter, Venus, Saturn—see the Planetary Associations section later in the chapter).

Before the separation of medicine and magic, practitioners prescribed herbal use to remedy a situation holistically, meaning they treated body and spirit simultaneously through a perceived linkage. As a result, many of the magical associations you can find listed for herbs were derived from the same source whence the medicinal information came. For example, if you drink a lavender infusion or rub lavender oil on your temples before bed, you'll sleep better. This is due to the influence lavender's botanical makeup has on your own body chemistry. Likewise, lavender is often used in spells for peace, relaxation, and tranquility. Herbs that warm the body, such as ginger and peppermint, are used both medicinally for fighting colds, and magically for strengthening courage and action.

Herbs are more than 90 percent water, and they serve as an essential link in the food chain. They feed omnivores and herbivores, and constitute a large portion of humanity's diet. Plant life can be found on most of the earth's surface, and under water as well. They demonstrate the visible cycle of life, from seed to sprout to full-grown plant, bearing flower then fruit, finally moving into a dormant state before beginning the cycle again.

The Top Ten Herbs in Spellcrafting

Herbs are a remarkably versatile component in spellcrafting, as seen in Chapter 8. The majority of herbs have more than one area of correspondence. The following herbs are staples in my spell supply cabinet due to their adaptability and availability.

LAVENDER

Lavender is an herb I turn to again and again. It's excellent for relaxation, sleep, love, and anything to do with children. Lavender is particularly good in house blessing and cleansing. It's a very gentle herb. I like to use it to help rebalance myself emotionally, spiritually, and physically. Lavender is associated with the planet Mercury, and the element of air.

VERVAIN

I add a pinch of vervain to pretty much everything. It has a terrific energy. Vervain is a versatile herb, which can be used for creativity, inspiration, purification, healing, divination, protection, prosperity, love, sleep, and tranquility. It is associated with the planet Venus, and the element of earth.

SAGE

Sage is excellent for purification of any kind. The traditional smudge stick is made from sage, or a base of sage with other cleansing herbs. Growing sage is said to lengthen the lifespan, and eating it is said to enhance wisdom. I find sage a very calming herb, and good for healing, prosperity, and business. Sage is associated with the planet Jupiter, and the element of air.

JASMINE

Jasmine is an herb associated with love, sweet dreams, and self-esteem. It makes a delicious tea. Jasmine is a delicate and exotic scent, which relaxes many people, and invigorates others. Jasmine is associated with the moon, and the element of water.

ROSE

Rose is a gentle purifier, and the scent of a freshly-picked rose is one of my favorites, although I find artificially scented rose products much too sweet and heavy. A spiritual scent, and a relaxing one, rose raises the spirits while relaxing the body. Rose is also used for healing. I save every rose given to me, and gently pull the petals off to dry them when the flower begins to droop. I use a pinch in any incense blend calling for feminine energy, and I always add them to house blessing and purification blends. Rose is associated with the planet Venus, and the element of water.

Sandalwood

Sandalwood is another purifier, and excellent for raising the spiritual vibration of an area. Sandalwood is an essential addition to any meditation or ritual blend I make. Sandalwood is associated with the moon, and the element of water. (Red sandalwood is associated with the planet Venus.)

Rosemary

Rosemary is good for intellectual pursuits, protection, removing negative energy, and enhancing memory. I use rosemary for positive thinking as well, and in any spell commemorating veterans or loved ones who have died. Rosemary is associated with the sun, and the element of fire.

Lemon

Purifying and clarifying, lemon is something I add to spells for joy and clear thinking. I use grated dried lemon peel, although in certain spells I like to use fresh lemon curls made from the zest, or fresh lemon juice. Lemons are associated with the moon, and with the element of water.

Cinnamon

Cinnamon is good for protection, activity, energy, money, healing, and love. I add cinnamon to anything that needs a good sudden injection of energy and action. Cinnamon is also used to raise spiritual vibration. Cinnamon is associated with the sun, and with the element of fire.

Bay

Bay leaves are excellent for wishes, for protection, to enhance wisdom, to remove negativity, and for money. Bay also is used to guard health, to celebrate victory, and for divination. Bay is associated with the sun, and with the element of fire.

Storing Herbs

How long should you keep herbs? That depends on what uses you have for them. If you use herbs medicinally, then a year is generally the use-by date. If you're using them magically, replacing them three years from the date of harvest or purchase is a good rule. Wondering what to do with them when you're cleaning out your herb cabinet? Add them to your compost pile, or bury them in the earth.

STONES

Stones are great to use in spellcrafting, because you can recycle them by cleansing and purifying them. Basically, this "washes" them clean of whatever energy with which you previously empowered them, as well as whatever energy they picked up during their work. Note that this does not remove their base energy. No matter what you do, you can never remove the basic energy encoded into the stone (or herb, or any component, for that matter). Once the stone has been cleansed, it's ready to go again: a blank slate for you to program or charge for a new purpose.

There are several ways to cleanse a stone:

Salt

In a small dish of salt, bury the stone you wish to cleanse and leave it for at least twenty-four hours. Depending on how deeply the stone requires cleansing or purification you might wish to leave it buried in the salt for up to a week. (Use the Sensing Energy exercise in Chapter 7 to get a good sense of how much purification the stone needs.) Be careful what kind of stone you're burying; stones with a high iron content react poorly to salt. If the stone is set in metal, do not use this method, as the salt will corrode the metal setting.

If all you have on hand is table salt, it will do. However, if you're serious about spellcraft, it's a good idea to invest in sea salt, a more natural form of salt. The less refined the salt is, the more natural energy it contains. Sea salt is only a bit more expensive than table salt, and easily found in most supermarkets now, as well as drugstores or health food stores. Kosher salt is good, too. Never use rock salt designed for outdoor use in winter, as it is toxic.

Earth

In a small dish of earth, bury the stone for three days. I often use a potted houseplant for this. Put a toothpick or some sort of marker in the surface of the earth above where you've buried your stone, though, or you might never find it again. In addition, beware of using a houseplant's earth if the stone contains a lot of negative energy; it will be absorbed by the earth (which is why you're using the earth to cleanse the stone), but it will in turn be absorbed from the earth into the houseplant, and the houseplant is likely to die.

Running Water

If you're fortunate enough to live near a stream, tie your stone in a piece of cheesecloth or old pantyhose, and with a piece of string fasten it to a branch or stone on the bank. Let the fabric-wrapped stone rest in the water for at least twenty-four hours. If you're in an urban environment, you can set the stone in a strainer or colander and put it in your sink. Turn the cold-water tap on and leave it there for a while. However, this method wastes a lot of water, so I don't use it. Instead, I pour bottled spring water in a dish, and set the stones in it. Water absorbs energy whether it's running or not; the movement simply adds more energy to the process and gets it done faster.

Water is an excellent purifier. If you add a pinch of salt to it, it becomes even more powerful. Again, however, if there's any metal attached to the stone, skip the salt and use pure water. Don't substitute earth for that pinch of salt in this technique, or you'll end up having to rinse off the stone under the tap anyway.

Sunlight and Moonlight

The easiest of the cleansing techniques involves setting your stone on a windowsill where the direct sunlight or moonlight will hit it. The number of days or nights you'll leave it will depend on how much negative energy has collected in the stone. Set the stone on a mirror to enhance the effect. Be careful not to handle the mirror so that it flashes the reflection of the light into the eyes, as it can damage eyesight. Make sure that the reflection doesn't focus on a flammable surface for an extended time, either.

The Top Ten Stones

These are the ten essential stones in my spell supply cabinet.

ROSE QUARTZ

The ultimate stone to enhance good vibrations! Rose quartz is a lovely stone that attracts and amplifies positive energy. It's used for love, self-esteem, and self-trust, and for comfort. It's a wonderful stone to use for children and friends.

AMETHYST

Amethyst is a form of purple quartz. It's excellent for protection, and for bringing the truth to light. It also enhances psychic abilities. The first stone my husband ever gave to me was a chunk of amethyst, and I used to keep it in the pocket of my coat. Now it sits on a shrine along with other stones.

AMBER

Amber is a stone that I love to use; it's often the stone I will use to represent myself in a stone trade with other spellcasters. Technically, it isn't a stone at all; it's petrified tree sap. Amber is associated with health, the sun, and creativity. I wear one to enhance my confidence, strengthen my health, and to honor the goddess with whom I do most of my spiritual work. (Note: Be very careful when purifying amber by the sunlight method. Remember, it's petrified tree sap, and it's capable of melting if the temperature reaches a high enough level.)

CITRINE

Citrine is a form of yellow quartz. It's good to defend sleepers from nightmares, to soothe digestion, and to promote creativity. I carry one in my cello case, and I add one to every creativity charm I make.

HEMATITE

This silver-toned stone looks like a dull mirror, and like a mirror, it's good at reflecting energy. It's primarily used to reflect negative energy from any source. Hematite is also used to help ground energy, so if you're spacy, hold or wear a hematite.

SODALITE

This blue and white veined stone is used to enhance wisdom, and to balance emotion. It's good for communicators of any kind, such as singers, actors, speakers, writers, and so forth.

CLEAR QUARTZ

This multipurpose stone functions well as a battery. A lot of New Age practitioners carry this stone or wear quartz jewelry, because it provides an alternate energy source. Quartz cheerfully allows you to use its energy, and there's plenty of it to borrow. Clear quartz is also good for scrying, for attuning with lunar energy, and enhancing any sort of spell. If you charge it to absorb negativity, it can do that too. Clear quartz is one of the most versatile stones available today.

TIGER'S EYE

A shiny, satiny stone in shades of gold and brown, tiger's eye is used for luck and fortune, as well as confidence and courage. It can also be found in shades of brownish red, which are excellent to strengthen the courage aspect. If it is found in shades of blue, it's termed a falcon's eye or hawk's eye.

OBSIDIAN

This is actually volcano glass. A shiny black stone, it's often found in shards. Obsidian is my stone of choice to use against nasties of any kind. Black obsidian in the shape of an arrowhead protects both by virtue of the stone's energy, and the act of defense associated with the weapon.

MALACHITE

A beautifully banded green stone, malachite is used for fertility, mothers, and the earth. I use it for healing, and for grounding. I love to meditate with a chunk of malachite in my hands; it helps me achieve a serene state in next to no time.

CORRESPONDENCES

Make a list of five foods, flowers, trees, and colors you like, and then make a list of five you dislike. Look up the correspondences for each of them (either in the appendices of this book, or in other books). What sort of patterns can you discern in your results? What does this say about you as a person? If there is a marked imbalance, can you think of a way to help correct the balance by introducing new correspondences in your life?

Numbers

Those glossy spellbooks often tell you to perform an action a certain number of times, but rarely tell you why. Western occult practice has developed its own numerological correspondences, and what follows is, once again, a general list.

0. Zero is associated with the potential for anything.
1. The number one is associated with independence, confidence, initiation, and the beginning of new projects and cycles.
2. The number two is associated with balance and harmony, a choice, partnership, and working together.
3. The number three is associated with creation and creativity, expansion, offspring (the logical next step after partnership: two increases to three), development, and adaptability.
4. The number four is associated with stable foundations, manifestation, order, and commitment.
5. The number five is associated with activity, change, challenge, and risks.
6. The number six is associated with calm, peace, love, and family.
7. The number seven is associated with spirituality, introspection, and study.
8. The number eight is associated with work, order, leadership, and achievement.
9. The number nine is associated with the final stage of a cycle, completion, revelation, wisdom, and forgiveness.

10. Although the number ten can be reduced to the number one (see below), it is a number that includes both one and zero. It is the transition between the end of one cycle and the beginning of another.

All other numbers can be reduced to single digits by adding up the individual numbers within them. For example, 694392 can be reduced as follows:

6 + 9 + 4 + 3 + 9 + 2 = 33, which is further reduced as 3 + 3 = 6

The Tarot, one of the most popular forms of divination, uses numerological significance combined with the symbolism of the four basic tools listed above to organize the fifty-six cards of the Minor Arcana. The first twenty-two cards, or the Major Arcana, are numbered zero through twenty-one.

Using numbers in spellwork doesn't mean that you have to involve mathematics or follow complicated formulae (although if you're fascinated by the magic of numbers, then by all means, go ahead). You're already using number magic by choosing a certain number of components or repeating a spoken charm several times. Many spells default to using three components or saying something three times, as three suggests increase and growth. I tend to use multiples of three or five, as five is also associated with change. If you wish to do a spell for stability in a situation, for example, you might wish to speak an invocation or repeat the symbolic action four times, as four is the number associated with stability. Another way to use number energy is to repeat a spell a specific number of times; in the example of performing a spell for stability, you might decide to perform the spell for four days in a row.

Planetary Associations

These just might be the granddaddy of all correspondence systems. If you read through other books of correspondences, you'll discover that almost everything is assigned to a planet. Planetary influence is perhaps the most common form of classification. These correspondences are derived from Greco-Roman classical mythology; classical philosophers used planetary associations to categorize the world around them.

You'll notice that the ancients included the sun and the moon as planets. Although the luminaries don't qualify as planets in modern parlance, except in astrology, they have great influence over our lives and behaviors. If you're wondering where the planets Uranus, Neptune, and Pluto are, they weren't visible to the naked eye. Thus, they weren't officially proven to exist until 1846, 1781, and 1930, respectively.

Sun

The sun is associated with active energy, health and healing, men, power, leadership, authority, success, and sports.

Moon

The moon is associated with receptive energy, women, travel, the sea, hunting, cycles, reproduction, dreams, psychic work, and intuition.

Mercury

The planet Mercury is associated with learning, intellectual pursuits, communication, gambling, medicine, commerce, deception, theft, and androgyny.

Venus

The planet Venus is associated with music, dance, all arts, social occasions, gourmands, attraction, love, emotion, and female sexuality.

Mars

The planet Mars is associated with aggression, destruction, conquest, violence, animals, and male sexuality.

Jupiter

The planet Jupiter is associated with good fortune, growth, rites of passage, expansion, career, and bureaucracy.

Saturn

The planet Saturn is associated with the past and time in general, aging, death, abstract thought, higher study, and agriculture.

Days of the Week

The daily correspondences are derived directly from the planetary associations. Each day has a patron planet, which defines the energies associated with it. These days are also discussed in Chapter 5.

Sunday: As the name suggests, Sunday is ruled by the sun. Energies associated with this day are health, family, and prosperity. Colors associated with Sunday include yellow and gold.

Monday: Monday is ruled by the Moon. Energies associated with this day include psychic work, fertility, and mothers and children. Colors associated with Monday are silver and blue-greens.

Tuesday: Tuesday is ruled by Mars. Energies associated with this day are action, movement, and men. Colors associated with Tuesday are reds.

Wednesday: Wednesday is ruled by Mercury. Energies associated with this day include commerce and communication. Colors associated with this day include yellow.

Thursday: Thursday is ruled by Jupiter. Energies associated with this day are career, business, and prosperity. Colors associated with this day include greens and browns.

Friday: Friday is ruled by Venus. Energies associated with this day are love, romance, money, and women. Colors associated with this day are pinks, reds, and greens.

Saturday: Saturday is ruled by Saturn. Energies associated with this day include age, death, philosophy, wisdom, and higher education. Colors associated with this day include blacks and reds.

Angels and Deities

Many people invoke the energy of a deity or an angel which corresponds to their purpose. While deities and angels do have spheres of responsibility and corresponding energy, a spellcaster doesn't plug them into a spell the way a color, stone, or herb is used. These are entities, not objects, and the process of including their energy is different. I mention them here, because it's often in the process of sorting through correspondences that a spellcaster ponders whether or not to invoke deity or angelic energy, and which to choose. Chapter 7 addresses the use of angelic and Divine energy in spellcraft.

Angels

Angels are spiritual beings, existing in several cultures and religions before the formation of Judeo-Christian religions. Anyone may call upon them. These are the four archangels that you are most likely to be familiar with.

RAPHAEL

Associated with the direction of East, and the element of Air, Raphael is usually portrayed as carrying a caduceus, dressed in yellow and purple, or greens and blues. Raphael is a healer, both of the earth and of mankind. He is also associated with creativity and harmony.

MICHAEL

Associated with the South, and the element of Fire, Michael is usually portrayed in armor holding a sword or scepter. He is a warrior, associated with justice, loyalty, and defense.

GABRIEL

Associated with the direction of West, and the element of Water, Gabriel is usually portrayed in shades of blue, and is sometimes portrayed as female. Gabriel is associated with mercy, hope, and birth, and serves as God's messenger.

URIEL

Associated with the direction of North, and the element of Earth, Uriel (sometimes spelled Auriel) is portrayed in shades of brown and green, sometimes carrying a scroll. Uriel is associated with intuition, and mystery. Sometimes Uriel is called the Angel of Death, which is not meant to be a terrifying appellation; rather, it is a solace, for to be gathered into the arms of this angelic being after life is a comfort.

According to Agrippa, the angels associated with the elements are:
- *Air:* Cherub
- *Water:* Tharsis
- *Earth:* Ariel
- *Fire:* Seraph

The angels associated with the planets are:
- *Sun:* Michael
- *Moon:* Gabriel
- *Mercury:* Raphael
- *Venus:* Uriel
- *Mars:* Camael
- *Jupiter:* Sachiel
- *Saturn:* Cassiel

Deities

Many different aspects of the Divine are called into spellcasting by various practitioners. As I said in Chapter 1, the best way to handle this is to work with the deity you already worship. Deities may be invoked to bless your work, or to add their specific energy to your spell. Here is a selection of common deities often invoked in spellcasting. You will notice that they are mostly goddesses. This may stem from the fact that spellcasting was often referred to as "low magic" and practiced mainly by women of rural areas, as opposed to the "high magic" of clerics, philosophers, and educated men.

Isis

Isis is the Egyptian great goddess who, over time, has become associated with many forms of energies. She began as a deity associated with magic and motherhood, and evolved to lunar and solar energy, the secrets of life, wisdom, hidden secrets and mysteries, women and children, and fertility.

Aphrodite

She is the Greek goddess of love and attraction. In the Roman pantheon, her equivalent is Venus. Aphrodite is often invoked in matters of beauty and romance.

Apollo

The Greek god of light and inspiration, Apollo is associated with prophecy (the oracle at Delphi functioned under his patronage), creativity, including music and drama, success, knowledge, logic, and intellectual pursuits.

Hecate

Originally a maiden goddess associated with light, Hecate became absorbed into the Greco-Roman culture as an older goddess associated with the night, magic, revenge and justice, and the spirits of the dead.

Brighid

A pan-Celtic hearth goddess, Brighid is associated with the creative fire of artists, smiths, and healers. Often invoked for inspiration, Brighid is also the guardian of women, animals, and the life-sustaining flame of the home.

Cernunnos

Cernunnos is the Celtic god of the woodlands, usually visualized as a man with stag's antlers. He is both the hunter and the prey. Cernunnos is often called on for matters concerning forests and wild animals, as well as strength and success.

Lugh

Also known as Llew, this Celtic god is invoked for success and skill, both in martial and other matters. He is often associated with the sun, although none of his myths directly relate to solar energy. It is entirely likely the association came about due to the Roman custom of equating local Celtic gods with their own deity figures.

Colors

Everyone who has opened a brand new box of crayons knows the potential energy that lies within color. Interior decorators know that color has a major impact on our state of mind, and our physical state. Spellcrafters are further aware that color possesses energy, and like any other energy it can be used in a spell.

The average spellbook will tell you that you have to use red things for love spells, green things for money spells, and so forth. Charts abound with correspondences for sea blue, chartreuse, and cyan. These charts are a general guideline for a practitioner. Psychological tests have revealed that in general, the average person will react differently to various colors. Red energizes people. Green soothes them, which is why hospitals use shades of green in their decor. Orange hurries people up, which is why so many fast-food restaurants used it in the seventies and eighties.

A general guideline is all well and good, but the more personal your spell the better and, therefore, it makes sense for any practitioner to put together his or her own list of color correspondences. I used pink in two spells relating to friendship and self-love, just like the books told me to, until I realized that the spells fizzled due to the fact that I don't like most shades of pink. Since I've not yet found supplies in the one or two shades of pink I like, pink is forbidden in my spellcraft.

Exercise: Create Your Own Color Correspondences

Create your own color chart to accurately reflect the power which color holds for you. On your next trip to the hardware store, grab a handful of paint chip cards. Make sure you have at least the basic colors such as blue, green, red, yellow, orange, purple, brown, pink, white, and black. Bring them home and cut them up into separate chips. Glue the chip to the blank side of an index card. Meditate on the color for a while. Gaze at it and write down all the feelings it evokes and the associations the color has for you on a blank piece of paper. Don't do the whole pile of chips at once; do one or two per day. When you're finished, copy the feelings and meanings each color has on the lined side of the appropriate index card. You now have a set of reference cards for your own personal color correspondences. Keep them in a recipe box decorated to your taste, or punch a hole in a corner of each card and string them onto a ring or tie them together with a cord.

Appendix 2 has a table of general color correspondences for you to consult, but as always, they're not set in stone. Color evokes a very personal response from everyone, so take the time to create your own table of color correspondences to help power your spells correctly.

Final Words on Correspondences

Hopefully you now have a better understanding of what correspondences are and where they have come from. With this knowledge, you can begin to draw various ingredients and components into your spellcrafting and understand why they are associated with your goal. Even better, with this knowledge you now understand that a correspondence isn't engraved in stone; if you discover that something doesn't work for you, for whatever reason, you can return to your lists of correspondences and select an alternative. (For more information regarding replacements and substitutions, see Chapter 11.) There isn't one item that demonstrates the corresponding energy better than the rest; the aggregate of correspondences that exists for every object in spellcasting has been developed over time, by extensive experimentation and practice. What works best for you will depend on your own experiments and on practice. You have the benefit of being able to consult the existing list of correspondences, however, and narrowing down your own top ten lists. I recommend developing lists like this; it will ensure that you have versatile components on hand, and it will cut down on the clutter you will acquire as you expand your spellcrafting abilities. Why bother buying a new herb if you have one that answers the purpose already?

Be advised, however, that tastes change, and what doesn't work for you now won't be a writeoff forever. Keep an open mind, and, every so often, try correspondences that haven't worked for you in the past. As your personal energy evolves, so too does your interaction with your components. Likewise, some correspondences that used to work for you may slowly phase out of your spellcrafting. Your personal system of correspondences is not written in stone. As a spellcrafter, you must remain flexible and adaptable, willing to give things a second chance as well as venturing out into new territory.

Of course, that's part of the fun of spellcasting: experimenting with new components and ingredients. It can get expensive quickly, though, so practice restraint, and, as always, keep good notes!

7

raising energy

How does a spellcaster "raise energy" to make the spell go? This tricky step is examined in detail, and tips and techniques of raising energy are explored. These techniques can also be extended to other areas of your life requiring positive energy.

꒜

Part of the energy required for a spell comes from the ingredients, or components, and their correspondences. If that were all, though, spell-casting would be a passive act: A plus B equals C, every time. And as you know by now, this isn't the case at all.

So what's the variable? What's the magic that combines the energy of the ingredients, catalyzes them, and activates them, thereby achieving your goal?

That magic is called energy, and it's the hardest thing to define for any teacher trying to communicate the concept. In high school, we learn the difference between potential energy and kinetic energy: potential energy describes the energy a body possesses at rest, kinetic energy describes the energy the body possesses while in motion. A tablespoon of mint leaves possesses potential energy until you activate it and use it in a spell, at which point its energy becomes kinetic—just not in the way it would become kinetic energy if you threw it at someone.

The Language of Sensing Energy

One of the major obstacles with teaching people about energy is the simple fact that everyone senses or experiences energy in a different way. One person might feel a warm tingle, another a cool tingle; one person might feel like the substance is pulling them toward it, others feel as if it's pushing them away. Some people smell odors. Yet others experience emotion.

My husband often explains energy work by pointing out that we have a literal field of electricity around us, which is a form of energy. In order to sense the energy of something else, imagine your personal energy field contacting the energy field of the substance or object, and "feel" it with your energy instead of your physical hand. When I raise energy for a spell, I can feel it rise within me like a rush from my solar plexus up through my throat. My throat chakra overflows, and I feel as if I'm in two places at once.

When you raise energy for a spell, you yourself act as a conduit. You also serve as the binding energy, which melds the energies of the components you have chosen to use.

"But *how*?" frustrated students ask me. "*How* do I sense energy?"

It all comes down to this: you just *know*. This is why the word "sense" is used so often when energy is being discussed. Any of the established five senses can be used to detect energy, and any number of unestablished senses. You already know that spellcrafting isn't a quantifiable practice. This shifty energy issue is part and parcel of it all.

In the chapter on correspondences, I spoke at length about the energy associated with objects and substances such as herbs, colors, stones, elements, and so forth. I also recommended that you keep detailed notes about your practice so that you could refine your personal list of correspondences. To help you do that, here are a couple of exercises to fine-tune your energy-sensing skills.

Exercise: Sensing Energy

In a quiet place, arrange yourself comfortably with three different stones, a pen, and your record book or journal. These do not have to be semi-precious or expensive stones from a metaphysical shop; you can use stones from the garden or from a river, if you like. Make sure they're physically clean as well as cleansed with salt or earth, as described in Chapter 6.

Pick up the first stone in your hands, and close your eyes. How does the stone feel to you? Is it heavy, or light? Is it warm, or cold? Where do you think it came from before you found it? What do you think it would like to be used for? Do you think of a certain color or emotion when you hold it? Does it remind you of something else you've touched or handled in the past? In your journal, describe the energy in as many different ways as possible. Allow yourself plenty of time with each stone; don't rush the exercise. Don't force it, either. Remain relaxed, and you'll discover that sensing energy is easier than you expect it to be. I remind students frequently to relax during energy work; the natural tendency is to tense up the body when exerting your will, and reaching out your senses to acquire new information seems to trigger all sorts of "pushing" behavior. Relax, and allow the energy of the object or substance to flow to you.

Sensing energy isn't about getting answers correct; it's about interpreting new information in a fashion that is uniquely yours. When you learn to sense energy, you are essentially creating a new language by which you will communicate with the world around you. This language is different for every person. What you get from this stone will likely not be the exact same information I would pick up from it. However, a remarkable amount of our observations would be similar interpretations of the stone. This further illustrates the common system of correspondences that exists. The unique observations would represent how our personal energy reacts with the energy of the stone. Perhaps your personal energy would mesh beautifully with rhodochrosite, and you'd sense a wonderful attractive energy within it. I, on the other hand, get next to nothing from rhodochrosite (must be the pink color!). This is an example of how two individuals could have different reactions to the same object, and how we would choose to use the object as a component in a spell or not.

This is a terrific exercise to do whenever you acquire a new stone or gather a new herb. Before you look it up in a book, give yourself the opportunity to sense the energy and note down your personal observations. You might be surprised at how close to the general correspondences your observations are. And if they're completely different, give yourself the benefit of the doubt: who knows how your energy works best, you or an historical list of associations? Remember, although a spell's energy comes partially from the correspondences, a lot comes from you, too. If you can't get along with the energy of your components, why use them?

Exercise: Kim's Game, Energy-Style

Kim's Game is a memory-sharpening exercise often used by groups such as Scouts and Guides, inspired by Rudyard Kipling's protagonist in the book *Kim*. In the regular Kim's Game, a small collection of random objects are placed in front of you, and you're allowed a specific amount of time to look at them. Then, the objects are covered by a cloth, and you must recite from memory what the objects were. To vary the degree of difficulty, sometimes you are challenged to recite the order of the objects, and as many details about each of them as you can remember. Kim's Game teaches you to observe.

In this version of Kim's Game, however, you're going to use your energy-sensing skills instead of your eyes. You'll need a partner for this exercise.

1. Have your partner set out half a dozen objects in front of you.
2. One by one, pick them up and sense the energy of each of them. This doesn't mean physically feeling them all over; instead, imagine your senses extending beyond your physical fingers to pick up information regarding the energy contained within the object. Allow these "energy fingers" to reach out and pick up as much information about the object as they can.
3. Close your eyes. Your partner will change the order or placement of the objects.
4. With your eyes still closed, have your partner guide your hand to hover over one of the objects. Without physically touching it, extend your "energy fingers" to sense the energy of the object, and identify it aloud to your partner. Don't open your eyes! Let your partner write your description of the energy down, and what object you think it is.

5. Allow your partner to guide your hand to hover over another object, and repeat the energy-sensing and identification.
6. When you have sensed all the objects, and your partner has written your final identification down, open your eyes and check your score. How many of the objects did you correctly identify by sensing their energy alone?
7. Switch places and allow your partner to have a turn.

Make this exercise even more of a challenge by covering the objects with a cloth before you do the first sensing, so that you cannot use your sense of sight or touch to help you acquire your energy reading. Your partner will have to number the objects before she covers them so that she can keep track of them when they're moved around in the middle of the exercise.

Techniques of Raising Energy

There are a variety of methods used to raise energy and to build or collect power in order to fuel your spell. Some will be more appropriate to your goal than others.

Meditation and Concentration

This is the purest form of energy you can use, as it comes completely from you. It involves clear visualization, strong intent, lots of focus, and self-discipline, not to mention patience.

Creative visualization is one of the most valuable tools a spellcaster has in his or her toolkit. Essentially, creative visualization is the use of a strong imagination to create a new reality or to change the outcome of a situation. We usually use our imaginations to daydream, or to escape reality. By visualizing yourself in the new reality, which shows you have succeeded in your spellwork, you are increasing the chances of that reality coming to pass, because you are lending energy and belief to it. Remember, thoughts are a form of energy, just as matter is a form of energy.

Visualization is the key that accompanies every action you perform as you craft and cast a spell. When you perform an action with intent, it means that you perform the action with the awareness of it adding to the manifestation of the outcome you have visualized.

Exercise: Creative Visualization

Sit quietly in an area where you will not be distracted. Clear your mind and take three deep breaths, releasing stress and tension with each exhalation.

Close your eyes and build a mental image of your goal. It may be a new car, or a test handed back with a perfect score, or a harmonious relationship. Keep this image in your mind as long as possible. You may wish to create a little movie out of it from your point of view: taking the keys, getting into the new car, feeling the seats, smelling the new car smell, the sound of the new engine as you put it in gear and drive out of the dealer's lot.

It's important not to get hung up on *how* you visualize. Several of my students become agitated or upset because they don't "see" things when they use their imaginations; instead, they feel things, or they "just know it's there." Use whatever method works for you.

~~~~~~

For more information on creative visualization, read Shakti Gawain's *Creative Visualization*, or Denning and Phillips's *Practical Guide to Creative Visualization*. Chapter 13 also addresses creative visualization.

Chants and Invocations

In the past, practitioners often considered this an all-encompassing category covering any use of the voice. However, modern Wiccan author Silver RavenWolf splits this into two separate categories: Chants and Sacred Breath, and Aspecting and Invocations. This division makes more sense, as you'll see.

CHANTS AND SACRED BREATH

The concept of words of power is hardly new. Magic words such as "abracadabra" or phrases such as "open sesame" are scattered throughout the vocabulary of our popular culture. In the Book of Genesis, God's words bring forth the world, and God's breath is what gives life to the body of dust, creating the first human. A chant is a spoken rhyme or verse channeling your intent. The word *incantation* is sometimes used to describe spoken magic such as this, although it implies a longer vocalization. A chant is often repeated several times until the practitioner feels that enough energy has been raised. Chants are often used in group spellcasting to raise energy, as a cooperative practice.

A chant is similar to an affirmation (a positive statement meant to reinforce a new reality—see Chapter 8), except it's repeated over and over, the volume and intensity rising to build the energy. A rhyme seems to help the chant build, although it might not be prize-winning poetry. When you create a chant, make sure it flows; an awkward chant will make the energy difficult to flow smoothly. Here is a simple chant for prosperity:

Gold and silver from all the land,
Flows to me, into my hands.

Chant this over and over, while visualizing depositing large amounts of money into your bank account.

It's important not to visualize the origin of the money, or of any of your desires. When you do that, you're restricting the energy of your spell and it no longer has the freedom to draw on any source to manifest your desire.

Sacred breath is a concept that exists in several cultures. I've already used the example of God breathing life into the first human. Many old charms and spells call for the practitioner to breathe upon an object, infusing it with energy. Think of this act as exhaling your will and your energy, directing it toward your goal. When you inhale, visualize drawing in the energy of your components and your environment; when you exhale, direct that power toward your goal.

ASPECTING AND INVOCATIONS

In the previous chapter, I mentioned correspondences for deity and angelic energy, but I pointed out that neither angels nor the Divine exist to simply be tossed into the mix to augment the energies you weave together into your spell. You don't tell God or the angels what to do; you ask them for help. Aspecting and invocations are both forms of involving Divine or angelic energy.

An *invocation* is a form of using words to invite a deity or angel into your space. *Aspecting* is invoking the deity's energy into your own body instead of into the space around you. In essence, it's a mild form of voluntary possession. It can be remarkably successful if your spell involves an inner transformation of you, the spellcaster; by aspecting a deity closely allied with the personality traits your spell is intended to enhance, you can literally change from the inside out. I cannot stress enough the necessity of thorough research before you invite a deity to share his or her energy with you through aspecting: if you simply run your finger down a list of correspondences and decide to aspect Kali, the Hindu goddess of death, destruction, and strength, without doing more reading, you're going to experience a nasty shock when Kali's energy begins to flow through your life and you begin to walk all over people, heedless of their pain or suffering, or, worse, provoking it and enjoying it.

Previously I've used the analogy of a spell being like knocking on a deity's door: if they peek through the spyhole and don't know you, they have absolutely no reason to open that door and gift you with their energy. If, however, you get to know them over a period of time, they'll be much more open to the idea of helping you out now and again. One of my friends planned a "dinner party" for the pair of deities he was planning on working with. It is a marvelous idea: in meditation, you have the opportunity to introduce yourself to the deity, tell him/her about yourself, and ask about his/her likes and dislikes. In the physical world, a meal or special beverage can be created to honor the deity.

Once you have a personal relationship of some sort with a deity, you may invoke them in a spell. To invoke is not to command: a deity is not a figure to be ordered around. A deity may be invoked by words such as the following:

Bright Apollo,
Lord of light and song,
Descend upon this place
And lend to me your aid!

Invoking, by the way, is not commanding something to appear. That's evoking. A ritual magician *evokes* a spirit from one place into a confining circle of protection. That sort of act isn't spellcraft; it's ceremonial magic, which is a different subject altogether. Spellcraft does not deal with spirits or demons, as you've probably figured out by now.

Historically, such practices were enacted by figures such as John Dee, Albertus Magnus, and other magicians. Invoking may also be defined as inviting something; evoking is to call something out. You can *invoke* a deity into your spellcrafting space; you *evoke* your own courage out from where it's hiding in a stressful situation.

If you wish your actions to be influenced by divine energy itself, you may choose to aspect the deity instead. When aspecting, your own mind, spirit, and personality stay exactly where they are. The energy of the deity acts as a coat of varnish over your own energy, so that you remain yourself but see and interact with the world through the divine energy. Basically, you will display *aspects* of that deity.

For example, if you were about to begin nursing a sick member of your family, you might aspect Brighid, the pan-Celtic goddess of healing. Here's a sample invocation by which you could appeal to the goddess Brighid in order to aspect her.

Bright Brighid of the healing waters
Descend upon me this day
To lend your energy to my task
Of healing my loved one.
Blessed Brighid of the cleansing flame,
Let your energy fill my body,
My hand are your hands;
My words are your words.
Mother, daughter, sister Brighid,
Come to me now!

Imagine what it would be like to *be* the goddess Brighid, and allow that feeling to permeate your body. Then go about your task.

The energy you embody while aspecting will slowly fade away over time. However, if you choose to aspect a deity for a specific task, once the task is over, I recommend releasing that energy with thanks. In fact, I don't recommend hanging on to the deity's energy any longer than you have to; it can have odd side effects, particularly if you don't do it often, or if you choose to aspect a deity you don't know very well, as in the Kali example above. Declaring a time limit is a good idea, such as "descend to me for seven days."

Once you're done, release the invoked deity with respect and thanks. Acknowledge their help and affirm that you are once again wholly yourself.

Sacred daughter of the flame,
I thank you for your generosity and your company.
Return to your realm, with my heartfelt gratitude.
Brighid, I release your energy, and reclaim my self.
Go in peace.

Ground as you would after any spell. The shift in energy might catch you by surprise. Sitting down and eating something after aspecting is always an excellent idea.

What makes aspecting different from drawing down the moon, for example, is that you don't release it at the end of the spell. The link is kept open, and you walk around with this deity or entity's energy until your specified time period has passed. It's like an extended spell.

To improve your ability to aspect, I recommend taking drama workshops. Live theater was among my best training in energy work. Not because an actor "pretends" when on stage, or because a spellcrafter "pretends" to do magic, but because each knows how to handle energy given to them by fellow actors (or components), how to shape it in such a way that it becomes something greater than it was, and then deliver it to an audience (or a goal). Drama has also helped train me for aspecting. In one way, aspecting is like taking on a character for a specified time. Many actors will tell you that they "become" the character they are portraying while in performance. Aspecting is similar in that the spellcaster asks a deity to lend its point of view for a period of time.

Incense

The use of incense affects you by changing the energy of your area or of your physical or mental state. Burning incense is one of the most common methods of raising energy in spellwork: as the incense burns, it releases the energies inherent in the herbs and/or oils used to make it. Incense sticks release energy and scent slowly over a period of time. Loose incense blends burned on charcoal release energy in a faster, more immediate fashion very suitable to spellcasting. Additionally, incense sticks are usually created to have pleasant scents, while herbal and resin blends are created for certain goals, regardless of the aesthetics. See Chapter 8 for information on how to create and use incense as a spell all by itself.

Potions and Oils

It's not always convenient to use an herb in its natural fresh or dried form. Turning it into some sort of liquid form is an option that expands your choices. The most popular potion is the kind you drink. It might surprise you to learn that the herbal tea you make is actually a potion. Potions don't have to be potable to be used, however. Oils, whether applied to your skin, used to anoint objects, or warmed in an aromatherapy burner, count as potions too. Theoretically, anything that involves liquid is classified as a potion. Potions can also be bottled and used as a talisman. You can carry them, or leave them somewhere to work their magic on an area.

Please, please, please have the sense to look up the medical functions of any herb you decide that you want to use in conjunction with your body, whether it be as a tea to drink, an oil to apply, or whatever. Spells are designed to improve your life, not end it. If you have sensitivities or allergies, take them into account when you use herbs to help raise energy.

Infusions are often used to help raise energy in some way. An infusion is similar to the basic tea-making preparation: with visualization, pour boiling water over a teaspoon of empowered herb and allow it to steep for five minutes. Once you have strained it, you may use it for a variety of purposes: as an addition to wash water, as an anointing fluid for tools, as an addition to bath water, and so forth. A decoction is a similar process, for bark or root matter, where the herb is boiled in the water for a specified period of time.

Herbs can also be soaked in alcohol of at least 90-proof, or cider vinegar to produce another form of potion. Fill a clean jam jar with fresh empowered herb matter, and pour the alcohol or vinegar over it until it reaches the neck of the jar. (If you choose to use dried herbs, fill only half the jar.) Cap it tightly and allow it to sit for two to three weeks, shaking daily. If the level of the liquid decreases, add more liquid. Strain the contents through cheesecloth or a stocking, wringing the herbal matter out well. If you use alcohol, the result is called a tincture; if you use vinegar, it is either a tincture or an herbal vinegar.

Like infusions, you can add drops of these to a bucket of water to wash the floor, to your bath, or to a glass of water to be imbibed.

For more information regarding herbs, incenses, and potions in spellcrafting, see Chapters 6, 8, and 11.

Home-made herbal oils can be made by steeping herbs in warmed oil over low heat, or by the process of *enfleurage*: steeping them in a glass jar of oil left in a sunny window over a period of time. Don't worry if they're not as strong as essential oils; they carry the energy of the original herb, which is all that matters. And because you've made them yourself, they carry a bit of extra power for your personal spells. There are plenty of good oil books on the market; check out Scott Cunningham's *The Complete Book of Incense, Oils and Brews* and *Magical Herbalism* for recipes and tips.

Dancing

At the beginning of this chapter, I gave the definition of potential and kinetic energy. These two energies are associated with physical objects and bodies. Physical motion produces energy on a physical and astral level. Rhythm of any sort can put you in a different state of mind, which is essential for spellwork. Using a drumming recording can help, or you can purchase a small drum and direct your own rhythm to raise and release energy during spellwork.

Drumming is a deceptively easy way to control rhythm and energy, and is remarkably effective. My husband and magical partner uses a *bodhran*, an Irish drum which is played with a special drumstick called a tipper. He can control the pace and energy of a ritual or spell simply by modifying the beat he uses, the volume, and the speed. Two of my original coven mates played *djembes*, taller drums played with the hands, which require slightly less coordination than a bodhran and can be found in several sizes. I used a tambourine for a time, which gave me the option of hitting the skin or using the rim with the cymbals. Now I just clap. Like other tools, drums and tambourines are great, but you might not have them available when you want or need them. You always have a pair of hands with you. Every drum has a different energy signature, which appeals to various people in different ways.

End your drumming with a good bang when you release your spell. When you begin with a certain beat, you might find yourself evolving into a different beat as you move through different headspace. That's fine. It demonstrates that the energy is changing as you build it up.

Experiment with rattles as well. Nothing gets the blood moving like a good maraca or gourd rattle wrapped in a net of shells or wooden beads. Nothing dispels negative energy faster, either! If you have nothing else, put dried beans or lentils in a glass jar and cap it.

Offerings

Most cultures have engaged in some form of sacrifice to their deities for a variety of purposes, usually an animal sacrifice. The blood from the sacrifice represented life energy, among other things. In fantasy novels, villainous sorcerers often use the deaths of innocents to power their magic, and the reason for that is partially based on the fact that shedding blood and causing death releases energy. It's not very pleasant energy, however, and if you're tempted to go out and sacrifice a gerbil or something to power a spell, think again. The means affect the end, and if you employ pain or suffering to attain your need or desire, pain and suffering will come back to you courtesy of that ever-present web of energy which connects you and everything else in the world.

An offering is a much more positive version of a living sacrifice. Traditionally, offerings have consisted of fresh flowers, food, beautiful objects, crafts, and other such things. One of my friends now leaves a regular offering of a medium coffee with two creams and two sugars for her house spirits. She says it keeps them happy, and things don't vanish or become misplaced as often as they used to. I pour an offering of cinnamon schnapps for the Norse goddess Freyja when I work with her; she seems to enjoy it quite a bit. When I make scones, I leave some on my altar for the Celtic goddess Brighid, the goddess I serve. In the past I have also poured milk and honey at the base of a tree in thanks for strength, buried a stone in a flowerbed, and cast herbs into the St. Lawrence Seaway, which flows past my city. An offering is a free-will gift to whatever power you wish to draw upon for your spell or work. It is not a bribe, or a trade.

The offering doesn't physically vanish, of course. Some cultures believe that the deity or entity partakes of the spiritual essence of the food, leaving behind only the physical dross. That physical dross, of course, is left right where you placed the offering. What do you do with it afterward? Different practitioners have different solutions. Some leave the offering for a specified period of time—for example, twenty-four hours, or three days—then dispose of it. The offering may be left outdoors, where the elements reduce it to its basic components, or it is eaten by animals; it may be burned; it may be buried; or it may be tossed into a moving body of water. Just placing it in the trash is perceived as disrespectful. Think carefully about how you will dispose of the remains of the offering; consider your environment, and consider also the purpose of your spell. If the spell called upon the element of earth in some way, then you might chose to bury the offering. If it called upon the element of water, you might choose to dispose of it in running water.

If your offering was a piece of art, writing, or music, obviously the animals won't eat it. You might choose to preserve it, as a symbol of what you created in honor of the deity or spiritual entity in question; or, you may choose to destroy it, as a demonstration of how completely the offering is devoted to that entity.

Sex Magic

Sex on its own raises a lot of energy. When used with intent, it's pretty powerful stuff. There are so many issues bound up with sex, however, that I don't advise using it for powering spellcraft. First of all, there exists a major ethical issue: it's cheating to have sex with an unsuspecting partner and use the resulting energy to power your spell. Your partner should have full knowledge of your intent and give his or her full consent. Second, it's hands down the most difficult method by which energy is raised. Think about it: you have to focus on your goal the entire time, focus on pleasuring your body (and that of your partner, if you have one), control the rate at which you excite and raise the energy, and control the exact moment of release (again, if you have a partner, simultaneous release). Save sex for fertility spells; that's what it's best suited for.

Choosing a Technique to Raise Energy

Your spell might be ideally suited for one or two of these techniques, but not others. Other times you might be at a loss as to which technique to choose. In a situation like this, take a look at the spell itself. Does it have specific cultural origins? If so, is one of these techniques close to how the original practitioners within that culture might have raised energy?

Your goal might also help determine which technique to employ to help power your spell. If you intend to cast a spell to put an end to physical harassment in your life, choosing sex as a means of raising energy might not be the best technique. If you're creating a talisman to protect your garden, perhaps creating a potion to sprinkle over the earth or blending an herbal incense to burn would be appropriate.

There's nothing wrong with using more than one technique to raise energy. In fact, many spellcasters will burn incense, chant, and drum to raise the energy necessary to power a spell. However, just like correspondences or tools, you don't have to use *all* the techniques in order to raise a maximum of energy. Less is usually more in spellcraft. It takes a lot of focus and energy to handle the various elements you're pulling together and combining to create a method of achieving your goal. Using every single technique is more likely to distract you than help you focus on your goal as you raise energy.

You may have noticed in the spellbooks you've read that there tend to be two kinds of spells: the ones that keep it simple, using the assumption that a simpler concept frees you up to focus all your intent on a simple sequence; and those that make it complicated, using the assumption that the more steps and ingredients you have to keep track of, the more you'll have to concentrate on. Each genre appeals to different types of people. Try both, and determine which kind of spell works better for you. You might discover that there are times and situations requiring a simple spell, and others calling for complicated spells. One is not necessarily more powerful than the other. As always, you are the final factor in determining how much energy is channeled into your spell to create change.

Grounding the Power

The opposite of raising power is, of course, grounding it. You can't keep the energy level running at high twenty-four hours a day, seven days a week; you'll burn out. You also won't be able to function normally; your perceptions will be wonky. After you've raised energy and used it for your goal, you need to ground in order to rebalance your system. Grounding equalizes your personal energy level, just in case extra energy from the spell is hanging around. Refer back to Chapter 3 for more information on grounding.

What's a Circle and Do You Need One?

This is one of the top five questions that I am asked regarding spell-casting, no matter where I am, and no matter what the subject of the workshop or class might be. Many spellbooks tell you to create a "magic circle" or a "circle of protection," and each one gives you a different method by which it must be done. Others ignore the concept completely. What's a spellcaster to do when faced with all this conflicting information? What if you've done spells in the past without a circle, and they've worked perfectly well?

The short answer is that no, you don't absolutely need a circle in order to cast a spell. The long answer, however, is more complex.

A circle isn't just a physical marker; it's a barrier of energy, created by your will and intent. Let's say that you've decided to boil some water on the stove. In order to do that, you need some sort of container to hold the water, such as a pot. If you want the water to boil faster, you put a lid on it. A circle is like a pot: it serves as a container for the energy you're stirring up into the spell. It keeps it all in one place until you're ready to pour it out, or send it toward your goal.

The pot, or circle, also acts as protection. If you poured water directly on the stove, it would not only end up as a big mess, when you tried to collect it up again it would have bits of dust and other unidentifiable kitchen stuff in it. A circle keeps the energy sympathetic to your goal inside, and all other energies that might dilute, taint, or distract it on the outside.

The circle also serves a psychological function for you, the spellcaster. By taking the time to create a circle physically and with energy, you are reinforcing the idea in your mind that your working area has been set apart as unique and special. Inside the circle, the spell connects the current reality and your desired reality. In this instance, the circle helps you focus on your goal, and brings you closer to it.

When should you cast a circle? Ask yourself the following questions:

- Am I in a familiar place?
- Am I likely to remain undistracted?

- Is my spell complicated?
- Is my spell going to take a long time?

If you answer yes to two or more of these questions, it's probably a good idea to create a circle before you cast your spell.

You won't always have the time or opportunity to create a circle before you cast, though. Spontaneous spells cease to be spontaneous as soon as you pause to cast a circle. However, in situations such as this, or when you don't feel that you need a full-blown circle, try this short charm:

World above, world below,
Energy come, energy flow,
Bright Divine light circles round me,
Mountains and sky, flame and sea.

This charm brings to mind the Hermetic "as above, so below" principle which allows symbolic action to create change on a larger scale, as well as calling on the guiding force of the universe and the four elements for protection. It's not a circle with a lot of bells and whistles, but if you speak it with intent while visualizing, it serves a similar purpose.

Casting a Circle

There are as many different ways of casting circles as there are spell-casters to cast them. No way is more correct than any other. Let's take a look at a basic circle casting, which can be used as a template.

To help your visualization, you can lay a long cord or rope on the floor around you, or sprinkle flour or salt on the ground to mark the circle's circumference. Some people like to use a tool such as a wand or a knife to help them create a circle because each acts as a method of focusing the energy. The energy is visualized as flowing from the spellcaster through the tool and out of the end, rather like piping frosting through a pastry bag fitted with a fine point tip to write on a cake.

Stand before your prepared workspace, or in the center of where you intend your circle to be. Close your eyes and relax. Take three deep breaths to settle yourself, exhaling any stress or tension. Feel the energy lying within you; then reach down to feel the energy of the earth, as in the grounding exercise. Draw the earth energy up into your body and down your arm to your hand. If you are using a tool to help you draw the circle, visualize the energy flowing through it and out the tip; otherwise, hold your hand out at approximately waist level, with the palm down. Point your fingers toward the edge of the forming circle. If you have some sort of physical guide such as the cord or salt, point at it.

See and feel the energy flowing out from your fingertips in a stream of light. Slowly turn around in place clockwise, or if the circle is large, walk around the inside edge, allowing the light to trail from your fingertips or the tip of your tool. When you reach the point you started at, make sure the ends of the light join. Visualize the band of light stretching up and down to form a dome over your head, and a bowl under your feet and the ground, creating a sphere of energy and light around you. Some people like to raise their hands to indicate the light stretching upwards to join over their heads. If you have used salt or a cord, the edges of your visualized energy circle should touch the physical marking of the boundary.

When the circle seems complete and solid around, above, and beneath you, take another deep breath and stop drawing the energy up from the ground. Congratulations; you've cast a circle.

An energy barrier such as a circle is meant to protect what's inside it. It exists so long as you respect it and leave it in place. If you forget about it and walk through it, it's gone; you've popped it like a soap bubble. Manipulating energy requires a lot of visualization and belief in what you're doing. As long as you trust yourself, you're succeeding. If you doubt yourself, or stop concentrating, or even worse, forget what you're doing, you'll lose it.

Taking Down a Circle

While walking through the circle will destroy it, the energy will remain hanging around, leaving things unbalanced. It's much better to perform a set of actions, such as the ones you did to raise the circle, in reverse. It's more respectful, and it enforces the belief in your subconscious that you can indeed handle energy.

Stand in the center of your circle and extend your hand toward where you began. Slowly turn in place *counterclockwise*, or walk around the perimeter of the circle counterclockwise, drawing the energy back into your hand or tool of choice. Remember to shunt the excess energy down into the ground. When you reach the beginning again, do something physical like stamping your foot or clapping your hands sharply to stop the flow of energy.

If you need to ground in order to re-establish your personal energy balance, do so.

Elements and Circles

Lots of spellbooks direct you to invite or summon each element into your circle. This is done for a variety of reasons, such as ensuring a balance of elemental energy, for protection, and so forth. In spellwork this isn't absolutely necessary, unless you intend to work with the elements as part of your correspondence system or in raising energy.

If you do choose to call elements into your circle, a simple invitation such as the following works nicely:

Element of [element name],
I invite you into my circle to help me achieve [name your goal].
Welcome!

What you invite, you have to say good-bye to at the end of the spell; it's good manners.

Element of [element name],
Thank you for helping me achieve [goal].
I bid you farewell.

SPELLCRAFT AND THE DIVINE

Spellbooks often list invocations to dozens of ancient deities such as Aphrodite, Hecate, and Diana. In Chapter 6 we looked at some common deities and their associated energies. Why are these called upon in spellcasting?

Faith is a very strong source of power for changing reality. This is how certain healers can lay hands on someone who is ill, and heal them in the name of God. Both the healer and the invalid have faith that the Divine will cure them.

By involving God (in one of the Divine's many forms) in your spellcasting, you can draw on the love and faith you bear in the Divine. If you have deep, unshakeable faith, and your goals are ethically righteous, the results can be truly astounding. However, invoking a deity simply because they are associated with your goal is not only pointless, it's rude. Do you know who Aphrodite is? No? Then why would you invoke her power in your spell?

Deity is a cultural expression of the Divine aspect of the universe. You can call it God, the universal consciousness, the Creator, Goddess, or Spirit; it all comes down to the same basic conception of something greater than we are, whose love and power flows throughout the cosmos. Wars have been fought over whose cultural expression of the Divine is the "real one." If the Divine could be limited by what we envision, then the Divine wouldn't be the Divine.

If you have an established personal relationship with the Divine in some form, then by all means, call on that deity's aid in your spellcasting. If not, then you're going to have to work at creating a relationship before you invite them over.

Working with a deity isn't like looking up an herbal correspondence for a spell. Flipping through a series of tables and saying, "Okay, I'll use a blue candle, some amber, thyme, and Isis for a healing spell" misses the point entirely. A deity doesn't exist solely to pass out power to spells; a deity exists to guide a certain aspect of a culture, who in turn offers the deity honor and respect through specific forms of worship. If you consider Hecate a fictional character from classical mythology, then asking for her help in a spell would seem pretty pointless.

If, however, you have chosen to research and study the deity, and you encounter the deity in meditation, then you've at least introduced yourself. Deities from ancient or foreign cultures were once widely worshiped and honored by citizens and votaries. These deities are not fictional; they are simply an alternate expression of the Divine. When you encounter a deity invoked in a spell with whom you are not familiar, you have to understand that at one time this deity was everything to his or her culture, very possibly for millennia. These ancient deities aren't minor spirits you can just summon and insert into your spell. They're powerful echoes of history and emotion, and they still resound today in various lands and in the hearts of many modern men and women.

8

methods of magic

This chapter takes a look at a variety of spellcasting principles, such as sympathetic magic and imitative magic, as well as techniques such as candle spells, knot spells, color magic, and so forth, that can be used alone or in combination for positive change.

❧

In *The Golden Bough,* a late nineteenth-century study of magic and religion in various cultures, social anthropologist James Frazer notes that there appear to be two very basic laws by which a practitioner operates while spellcasting:

> If we analyze the principles of thought on which magic is based, they will probably be found to resolve themselves into two: first, that like produces like, or that an effect resembles its cause; and, second, that things which have once been in contact with each other continue to act on each other at a distance after the physical contact has been severed. The former principle may be called the Law of Similarity, the latter the Law of Contact or Contagion. From the first of these

principles, namely the Law of Similarity, the magician infers that he can produce any effect he desires merely by imitating it: from the second he infers that whatever he does to a material object will affect equally the person with whom the object was once in contact, whether it formed part of his body or not. Charms based on the Law of Similarity may be called Homoeopathic or Imitative Magic. Charms based on the Law of Contact or Contagion may be called Contagious Magic. (Frazer, 1951, pp. 12–13)

Both the Law of Similarity and the Law of Contagion function on the principle of sympathetic movement: like produces (or attracts) like, and will continue to do so even at a distance.

Let's look at these two laws in more detail.

The Law of Similarity

The Law of Similarity states that "this is that." In other words, an object that is unrelated to the subject of the spell is visualized, seen, and treated as being that subject. This means that whatever happens to the magical object, happens to the subject.

This is one of the most familiar methods to practitioners of spellcraft. With this type of representational spell, you establish a relationship between two objects, drawing a connection between the objects used in the spell or charm and the focus of the spell or charm. For example, creating a doll (also known as a *poppet*) to represent the person you intend to heal is an illustration of imitative magic, as the doll will serve as a focus for your spell, a physical representation of your goal. Imitative spells for conceiving and bringing a child to healthy term might include mimicking the physical signs of pregnancy, birth, and tending to an infant.

The Law of Contagion

The Law of Contagion states that "this was that, and still is." Using a lock of someone's hair to help connect a spell to her is an example of contagious magic, as is using a piece of clothing worn by the target. Whatever happens to the object will also happen to the person, even though they are no longer in physical contact.

Just as a cold is contagious, so too can a spell be passed on by touch. Contagious magic is also known as transference magic, and it describes a process whereby "this *enters* that." Transference magic in a spell moves energy out of one place or person and into something else, with the intent that the transfer will affect the recipient. In a spell that operates on the principle of contagious magic, an object or place is empowered and left somewhere to affect individuals who come into contact with it. Depending on the intent of the spellcaster, the power doesn't necessarily pass completely upon contact; it can remain in the item to "infect" anyone who passes or touches it.

The use of the words contagious and infect shouldn't indicate to you that this is a negative method of magical motion; they describe the action, nothing more.

Now that you understand these two basic magical principles, let's look at the various ways to employ them.

MAGICAL METHODS

Spells take several different shapes and forms, depending on the desire of the spellcaster. Some practitioners specialize in a few methods; others use whatever is at their disposal, according to how they feel at the time. Others work in phases: they will use herbs for a while, then slowly move on to image magic, candle magic, and then on to herb magic again. Practitioners will often use several methods in the same spell.

No one method is stronger than any other. A spell is merely a form or structure for your intent. And no, you don't have to use all of them. Once again, more is just that: more. More complicated, more planning, more supplies, more mess. A simple spell is not necessarily easy, or weak.

Words of Power

The concept of "magic words" has permeated our culture. The idea of a word so powerful that a single utterance can change reality is curiously attractive to us. Words are the world's major method of communication, and they have great impact on our psyches and surroundings. As children, we chant that "sticks and stones may break my bones, but names will never hurt me," but that isn't true: names do hurt us, terribly. Words can wound deeply, but they can also soothe and heal. Saying something aloud confirms it, and brings it from the emotional realm into the physical realm by way of the moving air striking the eardrum. We don't just hear words; we feel them. Words are physical manifestations of thought or will. As such, they are extremely powerful.

The issue of foreign languages being used in spellcraft arises every once in a while. Some practitioners believe that if you can't speak the language, you have no right to use it magically. From a respectful point of view, this fact has a flip side: if you don't speak the language, chances are good you're going to really concentrate on what you're saying in order to get it right. Therefore, the focus is greater. This works equally well for written magic. Using foreign alphabets or codes forces you to concentrate on what you're doing. If this sort of thing causes you to focus on the form rather than the content, then using foreign alphabets might not be for you. In that case, stick to your mother tongue.

Affirmations

Affirmations are a remarkably powerful form of word magic. By drafting a positive statement and repeating it several times at various intervals, we can train our minds to accept a new reality. In essence, it's changing yourself or your environment from the inside out.

Affirmations are particularly suited to altering an attitude toward something. For example, if you're terrible at budgeting and suffer from a lack of money at the end of the month, you might create an affirmation along the lines of, "I am a successful financial manager." The very word "affirmation" reflects the positive nature of this technique. You affirm, or support, the new reality that you desire to manifest. It's a type of positive programming. Just as repeating a negative observation such as, "you'll never make anything of yourself" to a child can have a deep and lasting psychological impact, so too can positive affirmations change your life.

While the basic idea of the thing might seem rather simplistic, the truth is that we absorb a great deal of information on a subconscious level every day that shapes and molds our outlook on life. Advertising works on this level, for example: by exposing the name and presence of a product over and over in different places through a variety of media, it eventually becomes familiar to us, and a viable option for consumption. By repeating a statement over and over, you can in effect "advertise" a new reality to your subconscious.

Affirmations are excellent for working on prosperity issues, self-esteem and confidence issues, expanding awareness and tolerance, and enhancing your intuition.

Affirmations are very personal things, and what works for one person might not work for another. Additionally, affirmations work best on the self and your immediate environment. Writing and repeating affirmations to change someone else's life is a waste of time, as well as being unethical.

Affirmations can be used as support for any spell, but they work well on their own. You can create sacred space to repeat an affirmation, or repeat it every time you look at your watch, each time you open a door, when you hang up the phone, or when you sit down to eat. If you can't create sacred space, then take a moment to close your eyes, take a deep breath, and exhale slowly while relaxing your body. Repeat the affirmation aloud so that you hear it with your own ears, or silently if you're uncomfortable with being overheard. You may choose to repeat it any number of times, or only once each time. State the affirmation with confidence.

An affirmation should always be phrased in the present tense, and should always be stated in positive terms. "I am a creative person" signifies to your subconscious mind that you are a creative person right now and you have only to realize it, whereas "I will be a great artist" sends the message that your artistic success will always lie sometime in the future, never now. "I'm not scared" doesn't work as well as "I am courageous," mainly because our minds grab onto the key concept of fear rather than the negative which accompanies it.

Affirmations can be written down, as well. Writing something over and over entrenches it in your mind. There's a reason why lines were often given out as punishment in school: ever-hopeful administrators sought to reinforce the resolution to be good in the minds of young offenders. Pity they always used negative phrasing, such as "I will not pull Teresa's braids"; perhaps if the lines had been phrased positively, the practice might have had some sort of psychological benefit.

Charms

This form of word magic exists in every culture. A charm is often defined as some sort of spoken spell. The word may be etymologically connected to "incant," meaning to repeat, "enchant," meaning to ensorcel through song, and "chant," meaning to sing. Charms are rhythmic, vary in length (although are often short to enable easy memorization), and often rhyme in their original language.

Charms are used in several cultures. For example, the Scottish charms collected in Alexander Carmichael's *Carmina Gadelica* are spoken at various times for various purposes, among them healing and blessing.

COMMON HEALING CHARM

This charm is found in different forms from different European cultures, but the premise is the same in each:

> *Calum Cille rose early*
> *He found his horse's bones*
> *Leg crosswise;*
> *He set bone to bone,*
> *Flesh to flesh,*
> *Sinews to sinews,*
> *Hide to hide,*
> *Marrow to marrow,*
> *Christ, as you healed that,*
> *May you heal this.*

In charms like this, the words link together into a whole, step by step, just as the healing is intended to link the wounded parts of the body together again.

You can use a traditional folk charm such as this, or you can write your own to suit the situation. Even repeating the same words over and over while visualizing has a cumulative effect upon energy. Repetitive sound creates an altered state, and the use of mantras is a common technique in meditation to give the conscious mind something to focus on. Chanting a rhyme or charm over and over serves a similar purpose in spellwork.

Candle Magic

Candle spells use the power of fire and light to accomplish your purpose. Candle spells are very common, both alone and as an element of more complex spells, most likely due to the fact that there is a very obvious feeling of energy being used and moved when you light one. Candle magic is a simple example of basic sympathetic magic. The candle (and its color, if you incorporate it into your visualization and correspondences) represents your goal, or your obstacle.

Candle magic can be quite elaborate, with candles representing you, the goal, and the obstacles, all set up in a pattern on your workspace, or it can be as simple as charging a candle with your purpose and burning it to release your desire into the universe.

Candles are easy to obtain, and they are remarkably adaptable to the spellcaster's visualization. As the candle melts away, you can see it as your obstacle being removed, or as the energy contained within the candle being transformed and released by the flame to do its work where it is needed.

The easiest way to use a candle in a spell is to obtain a new candle that has never been used for any other purpose, hold it and empower it with your personal desire or need, and then light it. To add a bit more supportive energy, you may choose a candle color according to your purpose.

To add even more energy, and to further attune the candle to your goal, you may carve symbols or words into the candle. The tool often used for this is called a burin, which is basically a little stick with a pointed metal end. My husband made one for me by sanding a six-inch long wooden dowel smooth, rounding the edges, hammering a finishing nail halfway into one end, and then cutting the flat head of the nail off with wire cutters and taking off any rough bits of metal with a file. You can use an awl from your toolbox, a fine knitting needle, a tapestry needle, a long nail, a dead ballpoint pen, or a stylus. Many authors claim that a traditional method is to "carve your candle with your magical knife," but maneuvering a knife to carve little words or symbols is rather a challenge. (Authors also claim that a magical knife ought never to be used to cut anything in the physical realm, which is slightly confusing because a candle is something physical.) In my opinion, focusing on handling the knife in order to make the correct symbols with the tip keeps you, thoroughly frustrated, in the here and now, as opposed to being focused on the goal you're inscribing into the wax. There's nothing like fumbling with tools to take you out of the correct frame of mind.

I like to carve my entire spell out onto my candle, using my burin as a pen and carving cursive letters into the wax just as if I'm writing. I turn the candle slowly as I go, so my spell ends up spiraling up or down the candle. If I'm drawing something toward me, I begin writing at the top and spiral down the candle. If I'm banishing something or sending something away, I begin at the bottom and spiral up the candle. This act instills a lot of energy into the candle, since I'm concentrating on my goal throughout the act.

If you use rolled beeswax candles, carving will be difficult; in that case, write down what you want on a slip of paper and tuck it under your candleholder.

Another method of adding energy to your candle magic is to anoint the candles with oil. The easiest way to do this is to take a dab of olive oil on your index finger and rub it onto the candle. Traditionally, if you are drawing something toward you, you rub from the top down or from each end toward the middle of the candle. If you are pushing something away, rub from the bottom to the top or from the middle to each end.

For candle magic, you should use the best quality candle you can find. Beeswax is ideal, because it burns cleanly, with little soot, and it releases positive ions as it burns. It also smells slightly sweet. With candles, you often get what you pay for, although in my experience very expensive candles aren't worth it. Mid-priced, middle-of-the-line candles are often the best kind to use. Experiment with burning any new brand of candle before using one in a spell; that way you won't ruin a spell. Freezing candles for a few days seems to make them burn better.

Begin with a wick trimmed to about a quarter-inch, and once you've lit the candle, keep the wick trimmed to that height as it burns, especially if you're using a lower-quality candle. You might not want to mess with a spell candle, but, trust me, it's for the best. Think of it as maintaining the flow of energy through your spell. If your wick is too high, it will smoke and flicker wildly, resulting in uneven burning. Keep an eye on it. If you must trim it, you can use a sharp pair of scissors, but make sure not to put out the candle if you cut the upper portion of the wick off. If the bit you cut off carries the flame with it, carefully touch it to the remaining wick to transfer the flame. Be careful not to cut the wick too low; the liquid wax will drown the flame and you'll have to pour out some of the liquid wax in order to light it again. Whether or not this actually affects the spell depends on the practitioner; if you think of the candle going out as a bad omen, or as slowing down the spell, that's precisely what will happen. If you think of it as maintenance to ensure success, or as simply a small hiccup in the process of your spell's ultimate manifestation, that's how it will happen. Keep a record of what you have to do to your candle and compare it to the outcome to figure out if messing around with the candle as it burns influences the goal.

Always use a candleholder appropriate for your chosen candle. Nothing blows a carefully structured spell apart faster than a candle that tips over, flares up, or dissolves into a gooey lake of wax faster than you can run to clean it up. You might reserve a candleholder or two just for spellwork. For example, I have an ankh-shaped holder, which I use for health and healing spells, and an acorn and oak leaf holder, which I use for spells involving abundance, security, and growth.

If you have pets, choose your workspace for candle spells carefully. I have one cat who is oblivious to flame and who has walked into candles three times, and I have another cat who likes to jump up on my altar to drink the holy water I keep in an earthenware chalice; apparently it tastes better than the water from the dish next to her food. I use jar candles a lot now to protect the flame and my cats. Use glass candleholders with caution; when the candle burns right down to liquid wax and a wick floating in it, the heat can often shatter the holder. Fancy holders can look spectacular, but if they're very detailed wax gets into the design and is almost impossible to get out. Clean your holders frequently, after each spell if you want to keep them as neutral as possible. Popping them in the freezer for an hour often makes it easier to remove the wax. If that doesn't help, soak the candleholder in very hot water and be prepared to pick out the softened wax with the point of a paring knife.

There are many different kinds of candles you can use in spellwork. Most practitioners automatically use taper candles when they do a candle spell, but there are many other kinds of candles available. Think of birthday candles as miniature tapers, and use them when you don't have the time to watch a twelve-inch taper burn all the way down. Votive candles and tea lights are also excellent alternatives to tapers, and you can carve and anoint them easily (just tip the tea light out of the metal container, then back in to burn it). The size of the candle does not reflect how much power it provides to your spell.

Novena candles, at about ten inches high, are great for long-term spellwork, and because they're encased in glass they don't drip. Best of all, you can reuse or recycle the jar once the candle is gone. In my experience, novena candles tend to be made with poor quality wax and wicks, so experiment with different brands until you find one that burns evenly and well. If the candle is not removable, anoint or carve the upper surface of the candle.

Some candles come suffused with scent. I like to burn scented candles for ambiance or to relax after a day of work rather than in my spellwork. I prefer a neutral candle that I can use as a starting point, rather than being tied to what the manufacturer has provided. White candles are often scented with vanilla, which is lovely for romance or comfort but not for justice or removing obstacles, for example. White is a universally applicable color in spellcraft; the scent of vanilla is not. Remember, scent possesses energy, and if the scent doesn't correspond with your goal, it isn't supporting your work. If it isn't supporting, it's useless, or worse, an obstacle.

Basic dos-and-don'ts of candle magic include never reusing a partially burned candle for another purpose, and not blowing the candle out when you stop burning it. Some practitioners say this is because you "blow the wish out of the candle"; others say it's disrespectful to the element of fire to use the element of air to destroy it. In either case, you run the risk of spattering wax. Use a candle snuffer, or pinch the flame out with your fingers. Do it quickly and decisively, in order to not burn yourself. This way, the energy remains in the candle and the wick, ready to be relit.

If you are interested in candle magic, refer to Raymond Buckland's classic works *Practical Candleburning Rituals* and *Advanced Candle Magic: More Spells and Rituals for Every Purpose.*

Cord Spells

Sometimes you have to do a spell in advance. Where can you store the action of the spell? In a cord! Traditionally sailors carried knotted cords given to them by witches. When they were becalmed, the sailors would untie a knot to release the wind magic placed in the knot by the spellcaster.

When selecting the material for a cord spell, try to use something as natural as possible, such as cotton, silk, wool, or linen. The material you use doesn't have to be a cord at all, of course; you can do knot spells with yarn, embroidery floss, tapestry wool, and strips of material. Knot and cord spells aren't just tying a knot; all sorts of weaving can be classified as cord magic. If you knit, crochet, needlepoint, or weave, you're performing some sort of cord and knot magic. After all, we commonly refer to someone "weaving a spell." If you have long hair, braiding it can be a spell. When women were accused of witchcraft by the Inquisition, their hair was cut off in order to prevent them from braiding spells in their hair. The motion of weaving something in and out, creating a new item out of various separate strands, is very powerful.

When you specifically choose to use a knot spell for a particular situation, remember that you might have to undo it at some point. The symbolism lies in the act of tying the knot, not in how tightly you pull it.

There are a variety of creative ways to employ cord and knot magic. While knot magic is good for containing energy, either temporarily or to capture it permanently, these other kinds of cord magic are good for abundance and manifestation spells.

Embroidery and Cross-Stitch

Once considered a lady-like talent, which kept hands busy and decorated clothes, embroidery is a remarkably powerful spell technique. Incorporate color correspondences, and image correspondences. For example, flowers and vines usually represent life; fruit or vegetables represent abundance and plenty. Clothes can be embroidered with protective symbols, or symbols which draw positive energy to the wearer.

Tapestry

Tapestry and needlepoint are heavier versions of embroidery and cross-stitch. There are printed images available on heavy woven tapestry canvas to use if you don't trust your own imagination or layout skills. Plain canvas is also available upon which you may plot your own images, or follow a paper pattern by counting squares.

Looms

Weaving is a wonderfully relaxing and creative form of spellwork. In elementary school children often make placemats by weaving strips of paper together. The process of weaving takes separate cords and creates a larger unit from them. My grandfather was a weaver, and one of the rooms in his house was filled almost wall to wall with a huge wooden loom, with skeins of wool in various weights hanging from the ceiling around it. I still cherish one of the pillow covers he wove. Investing in a loom would put most of us severely out of pocket, but if you check your local toy store, you can often find children's weaving kits, which are made on a smaller scale. Weaving is ideal for spells bringing people closer together, or for spells of celebration.

Knot and cord spells can be complex and time-consuming, true labors of love, or they can be as simple as making a braid or tying a single knot, as in these two cord spells.

Witches' Ladder

This spell is excellent for protection, abundance, and happiness. To further enhance the spell, choose colors and charms that correspond with your goal.

Timing: Midday; summer; hour of the sun; hour of Mars; Sunday; Tuesday; moon's second quarter; moon in sign of Leo; or your personal power time

Supplies:
3 lengths of cord, yarn, string, wool, or embroidery thread: each
    measuring 3 feet
Beads, feathers, small pendant charms associated with your goal
Needle and thread (optional)

Steps:
1. Empower the supplies for protection.
2. Tie the three lengths of cord together at one end.
3. Visualizing your goal, slowly begin to braid the three cords together.
4. When you feel it is right, pause in the braiding to slip a bead over one of the cords, or slide a small charm over one of the threads. If your cords are too wide for the beads and charms, finish braiding the entire lengths of cord and tie them off. Using the needle and thread, sew the beads and charms at various intervals to the braided cords. Weave the feathers into the braid, or sew them on. As always, perform each action with intent, and visualize your goal while you're doing it.
5. Hang the witch's ladder in the area you wish protected. You may loop it and tie the ends together to make a circle, or tuck it in a small space.

Knot Negativity

I cast this spell with the end of a shoelace if I'm wearing lace-up boots or running shoes, or with the ties on my shirts and skirts. The best thing about this spell is you only need a couple of inches of whatever you're using. In a pinch, you can use a shirttail, a sleeve, a scarf, a purse strap, or a sock. (Yes, you'll have one bare foot inside a shoe, but if it's all you've got, use it.)

Timing: Whenever necessary

Supplies:
One cord, any length

Steps:
1. When you feel negative energy rising inside you such as anger or fear, or coming at you from an outside source, visualize the negative energy coalescing in front of you. Hold the length of cord taut between your fingers and say,

   I command you to halt; I bind you where you are.
   You can no longer harm me.

2. Tie the cord into a simple slipknot, visualizing the cord being tied around the negative energy. Take a deep breath, then exhale and let the tension leave your body. Allow the cord to dangle again.
3. At the end of your day when you are in a safe place, untie the cord and allow the energy to dissipate.

There are plenty of other ways you can use cord magic to weave a spell. Try corking, playing cat's cradle, making a dream web or dream catcher.

Color Magic

You can draw energy from color to power your spell. Use those reference cards you made from paint chips when you explored color energy. When you need to energize a healing spell, for example, pull out the card containing the color you associate with healing glued to it. In my case, that color is either pale blue or green. Hold the card in front of you and imagine the color rising from the paint chip into the air, building up into a whirl of energy. When you feel it is ready, send it off toward your goal.

Other ways in which you can use color are in food, your wardrobe, and your environment. We unconsciously surround ourselves with color all the time; now, use it consciously. Is a room in your house ho-hum, or downright unwelcoming? Try adding the colors you associate with comfort and relaxation, and see what happens. Use accents like throw pillows, colored candles, blankets, new art, or area rugs, and see how the energy of the room changes. Remember to keep notes!

Symbol and Image Magic

Symbol and image magic function according to the imitative magic principle outlined by Sir James Frazer. By creating an image of what you seek to affect with your spell, you possess a direct means by which you can influence that object.

Symbols may be carried, buried, kept safe, or burned to release power; they may be on paper, wood, metal, wax, tattooed, or drawn on the body. The options are endless.

A common aspect of symbol magic involves the concept that scribing a particular symbol onto or into something will infuse the object with that symbol's corresponding power. The practice of signing someone with a cross to bless them is an example of this magic: the power of the symbol is such that by drawing it on an individual's forehead, the corresponding energy of the symbol is transferred to the individual.

Modern image magic now uses photographs of people you wish to protect. A common practice is to slip a photo under a candleholder and burn a candle corresponding to your desire for the person. For example, if a family member was attempting to immigrate to be with the rest of his or her family, a practitioner might put the photograph of the immigrant under a yellow candle to represent good communication throughout the immigration process, or an orange candle to speed up the process.

The use of dolls or poppets in magic is cross-cultural. The best-known example of this is the stereotypical voodoo doll. It might surprise you to learn that this is not necessarily a negative process since poppets are often used for healing or protection.

More modern uses of image magic include drawing energy from postcards with images that you feel are powerful, or from places you have visited which touched you in some way, evoking a strong emotional response.

Each planet has a symbol, and a series of planetary seals as well. Planetary seals are drawings of certain objects, numbers, Hebrew letters, and words that have been assembled to vibrate with a particular expression of energy associated with an aspect of the planet in question. Practitioners often enscribe these on wax disks or soft metal to create amulets and talismans (see below). These and other symbols of power can be found in books such as *The New Revised Sixth and Seventh Books of Moses* and *The Mystery of the Long Lost 8th, 9th, and 10th Books of Moses.*

The use of hex signs by the Pennsylvania Dutch is an example of a cultural use of symbols as spells. Through the careful combination of traditional symbols and colors, a hexmeister can create an example of image magic that can be any size, and displayed indoors or outdoors.

Many practitioners develop their own personal symbol with which they sign magical work, or use to represent themselves in spellcraft. Symbol dictionaries are an excellent source of images used in various cultures for a multitude of purposes.

Green Magic

Green magic encompasses spellcraft that uses herbs, flowers, trees, and plants as the focus for the power. Spellcraft of this type is one of the most common practices, likely due to the living energy contained within the components. It's easy to hold a plant and feel the life inside it. Things that come from nature possess great power.

Growing, harvesting, and drying your own herbs for spellcrafting is a rewarding experience. There's something magical about using your own mint and sage in a spell for concentration. One of the best ways to start working with green magic is to plant a small garden. Understanding how seeds germinate, establish roots, and draw on the energy of the sun and rain and earth to grow is an ideal way to learn how green magic functions. Even if you don't have access to a bit of land, you can plant a window box of herbs for your kitchen and have fresh herbs year-round.

Spells using plants and trees offer the spellcrafter a wide range of possibilities. Woodcarving a pattern or scene as a spell to bring something into fruition is a wonderfully creative way to use tree energy. Building a birdhouse or a piece of furniture from woods chosen for their associations can also be the steps of a spell.

Potions

Potions is a charming word for teas and blends involving liquids of some sort. A potion designed to be ingested must be well researched for safety and recommended dosages. I trust John Lust's *The Herb Book* for information such as this.

Rather than making an infusion and pouring it into your bath, you can blend your own bath salts with dried herbs to create a unique spell experience.

Purifying Bath Salts

Salt is a purifying substance, as is water. Combined with herbs carrying purifying energy, the bath can be a sacred place for washing away negative energy, thoughts, and refocusing on your heart and soul.

Timing: sunset; midnight; moon's third quarter; Sunday; Monday; moon in sign of Cancer; moon in sign of Pisces; hour of the sun; hour of the moon; or your personal power time

Supplies:
½ cup sea salt
1 cup Epsom salt
2 teaspoons dried rose petals
1 teaspoon dried lavender flowers

Steps:
1. Empower the ingredients. Grind the dried flowers finely while you visualize your goal.
2. In a covered jar, shake the two salts together. Open the jar and add the herbal powder. Close the jar and shake to blend thoroughly.
3. To use the salts, add two tablespoons to a bath under warm running water. When the bath is full, immerse yourself, visualizing the negative energy clinging to you dissolving away in the water. Feel the purifying salt, rose, and lavender soaking into your body, cleansing your aura. Stay in the water as long as you like, meditating on the white light of purity.
4. When you step out of the bath, dry yourself gently with a clean towel.

Florida Water à la Montreal

Waters and washes are potions that are used to wash things. The famous Florida Water is a wash. So is a cup of basic mugwort tea brewed to wipe over your new crystal ball. Florida Water is used for cleansing negative energy from pretty much anything. It can be used as an offering to angels, ancestors, spirits, or deities, and to anoint candles for protection or good fortune. There are lots of recipes; try different ones until you find one that you like. I experimented, and this is my recipe. You'll need a few clean, empty wine bottles with corks to store it. Alternatively, you can use a large plastic jug, like the ones juice or bottled water are sold in. Normally I don't like keeping magical potions in plastic containers, but glass jugs with lids are hard to find. You'll also need a jar with a lid, and a bucket in which to mix it.

Timing: I recommend mixing your wash around the full moon, but if you wish to empower it with a certain lunar energy (such as banishing power), choose the corresponding lunar phase. I also usually do each step around noon, when the sun is high. You can also make it during your personal power time.

Supplies:

1 tablespoon lavender flowers	1 fresh lime
1 tablespoon vervain	4 liters distilled water (one gallon)
9 cloves	2 liters 90-proof alcohol, or higher
1 fresh lemon	(two quarts)

Steps:

1. Empower the supplies for cleansing.
2. Slice the lemon and the lime in half. Squeeze the juice into a large jar. Chop up the rind and what remains of the fruit into small pieces and put them in the jar as well.
3. Add the lavender, vervain, and the cloves to the jar. Fill it up with the 90-proof alcohol. Cap the jar and leave it for at least one moon cycle. Shake daily, visualizing the Florida Water growing in power and energy each time.
4. In a bucket, pour the water and the remaining alcohol. Strain the herbal mixture into the bucket, wringing it well to get the last bits of liquid out of the herbal matter.
5. Stir the Florida Water gently, visualizing it glowing with positive energy. Decant it into the bottles or jug, and cork them.

METHODS OF MAGIC

You can use this potion for almost anything you can think of. Mop your front doorstep with it. Scrub your kitchen floor. Wipe down the walls and doors. Pour some on a bit of clean white cloth and gently wipe your spellcrafting tools. If you're desperate to break a cycle of bad luck, dip your finger into the mixture and touch the center of your forehead, your heart, your palms, and the soles of your feet, visualizing the water repelling the murky bad luck and energy hanging around you.

Substitute the herbs and fruit with drops of oil in the following amounts: six drops of lavender, three drops of clove, four drops of lemon, four drops of lime, and two drops of vervain. Many Florida Water recipes call for bergamot; if you cannot find or make vervain oil, use bergamot instead. If you have floral waters on hand, you can substitute them for the oils or herbs (orange water can replace the lemon).

You can also personalize your washes with an ingredient that's uniquely yours. Some practitioners add a splash of their personal perfume. I sometimes add a splash of my father's homemade pinot noir to my Florida Water. It's just one more ingredient that corresponds to my comfort and protection. In spellcraft, use what you've got, and use what works for you.

Potpourri

Combining dried flowers and herbs for potpourri is an age-old practice. This potpourri functions as a slow-release spell.

Peace Potpourri

Potpourri is an excellent form of spell for peace; it is quiet and always present, just as we often wish peace to be.

Timing: Monday; Friday; moon in the second quarter; midday; hour of the moon; hour of Venus; or your personal power time

Supplies:
Choose between three and nine herbs and flowers with the corresponding
    magical properties of peace (see Chapter 6 and Appendices).
    Suggestions: lavender, rose, myrtle, chamomile, jasmine, violet
1 teaspoon orris root powder
Bowl, dish, or jar
3 drops of essential oil (optional)

Steps:

1. Empower each of the herbs and flowers for peace and tranquility.
2. Place them in the bowl and mix the herbs gently with your fingers, visualizing your goal.
3. To fix the scent and help preserve the potpourri, stir in a teaspoon of orris root powder. You may add a few drops of oil to enhance the scent, but do so carefully and blend well. If your potpourri is too damp, it will grow mold and mildew, and that's not the kind of green energy you're looking for at all!
4. Place the potpourri in a pretty jar or bowl and set it in a place where it will work its magic. Potpourri eventually loses its power due to a combination of releasing its energy and absorbing the ambient negative energy that encounters it. When the energy of the potpourri has faded or the goal you set for the spell has been achieved, bury the mixture outdoors or add it to your compost heap.

Incense

Incense has been used in many cultures in some shape or form, for purposes such as pleasing the gods, achieving trance states, and communicating with the otherworld. Essentially, incense is a blend of plant and tree matter burned in order to release the energy they contain for a purpose. Although most practitioners think of incense as an accompaniment to another spellcasting method, you can create and burn incense alone as a form of spell. Making stick incense can be tricky, but blending loose incense is a wonderful and simple form of green magic.

Loose incense is usually a blend of herbs, resins, and drops of oils, and it doesn't smell like the stick incense sold in New Age shops and drugstores; that kind of stick incense is usually soaked in oils. Loose incense usually smells like a fall bonfire where your neighbors burn grass clippings, dry leaves, and fallen branches. The more resin you use, the sweeter it will smell; the more herbal matter, the more it will smell like a grass fire. Loose incense is burned on a self-lighting charcoal tablet, available at religious and New Age shops, which, when lit, glows and produces heat for approximately an hour.

The trick to blending good incense is to use a balance of resins and herbal matter, and to reduce both to as fine a powder as possible. I like to put as much of my own energy into my incenses as possible, so I use a marble mortar and pestle more often than not, but if I'm making a large batch of loose incense I use an electric coffee grinder reserved for incense making. (Don't use your everyday coffee grinder—most resins should not be ingested, and are next to impossible to clean out of the blades.) Grinding resin can get a bit gummy, so try not to be too enthusiastic. I prefer to use my mortar and pestle to crush resins, by gently dropping the pestle down onto the resin from a height of about one inch. I find it crushes the resin enough to blend it in with the herbal powder evenly. Herbs, on the other hands, often require a lot of grinding to reduce them to a fine enough powder. For stiff or lumpy herbs like bay leaves or hops flowers, do yourself a favor and use a pair of clean scissors to snip them up; a mortar and pestle don't have much effect on them.

Remember that as you create the incense, you must visualize, in order to empower the components with the correct energies corresponding to the goal of the spell.

Success Incense

This is an excellent spell to perform in order to enhance your success in any situation. The incense is composed entirely of resins.

Timing: full moon; moon in second quarter; moon in Aries; moon in Leo; Sunday; midday; hour of the Sun; or your personal power time

Supplies:

1 part frankincense	¼ part copal
1 part myrrh	Censer
¼ part dragon's blood	Matches or a lighter

Steps:

1. Crush the resins gently in a mortar and pestle, concentrating on your intent of success. When the resins have been reduced to small grains or powder, transfer them to a clean glass container and cap tightly.
2. Hold the container between your hands and charge the incense with the energy of success.
3. Light a charcoal tablet carefully and place it in the censer. When the sparking has ceased and the charcoal glows red, it is ready. While you wait, concentrate on your success.

4. Sprinkle no more than a teaspoon of the incense on the glowing charcoal tablet. As you do so, say:

Incense sweet, rise to the heavens
And return to me my desire.

5. As the smoke rises, sit and visualize your success. When the smoke ceases, you may add more incense and meditate again, or consider the spell complete.
6. If there is incense left over, label the bottle as Success Incense, list the ingredients, and add the date. You may repeat the spell for the same goal until the incense is gone, or you may keep the incense and burn it all in thanks when your goal is achieved.

When you cast spells with incense, always keep a bowl of sand nearby to cover the charcoal if things get too smoky or out of hand. The spell isn't powered by billows of smoke; it's powered by the energy which is released, and your intention.

For more incense recipes and techniques, see Scott Cunningham's *Complete Book of Incense, Oils and Brews,* or *Wylundt's Book of Incense.*

Potted Plants

Spellwork with potted plants is a less common form of green spellwork, but just as effective. Charge your household plants to transform negative energy into positive energy, or to protect your home. Put a pot of daisies on your front porch to keep a cheerful guardian by the door.

I highly recommend Scott Cunningham's pair of herbal books, *Magical Herbalism* and *Encyclopedia of Magical Herbalism.* I also frequently use Paul Bayer's *Master Book of Herbalism,* and Mrs. Maud Grieve's *A Modern Herbal* for magical and botanical information.

GEM AND STONE SPELLS

While using herbs are undoubtedly one of my favorite forms of spellcrafting, I usually include stones somewhere in the process as well. Stone magic is a straightforward method of spellcrafting. Once empowered, a stone may be included in an amulet or talisman, carried with you to extend its magic to you, left somewhere to carry out your desire, or properly disposed of if your goal involves banishing something. Stones are also portable and nonorganic, which means they travel well with few problems. If you're on the road a lot, you know how tiring it can be. Stones are an excellent means of having portable power at your fingertips.

Create Magical Batteries

If you know you're going to need a lot of energy at some point, start stocking up early. These empowered stones also make an excellent addition to a traveler's personal spellkit. Not only do they provide a source of energy to replenish what you lose during travel, but they can also be used in spells. Quartz is known for its incredible powers of providing and holding energy, and they make ideal "batteries."

In this spell, you don't visualize anything; you have no specific goal except to empower the stones. In fact, it's important that you *don't* visualize a goal; otherwise you'll be empowering five quartz stones for that goal instead of just storing the energy you raise.

Timing: Sunday; moon's second quarter; first days of moon's third quarter; noon; hour of the sun; or your personal power time

Supplies:

1 clear quartz	1 citrine (yellow quartz)
1 rose quartz	1 amethyst (purple quartz)
1 smoky quartz	Small pouch

Steps:
1. Cleanse the stones.
2. Choose a method by which you will raise energy, and raise it.
3. Instead of sending the energy out to your goal, direct it into the stones.
4. Store the stones in the pouch.

You can place one stone at each cardinal point around you and hold the fifth in your hands while you meditate or spellcast, at home or on the road. If you have a particular affinity with a certain type of quartz, you can substitute that type for all five stones.

Another way to use this spell is to charge a clear quartz with a certain type of energy (full moon, dark moon, sunset, midnight, whatever you choose) and draw upon it later. If you have to do an emergency spell that would ideally be done at the full moon, but it's the new moon, you can include a stone you previously charged with full moon energy among your correspondences. In this way you can add full moon energy to your spell, further reinforcing the spell no matter what the current moon phase might be. This cannot replace the power of performing the spell at the ideal time, of course, but it does offset some of the less favorable aspects.

Elixirs

Whereas a potion is a blend of liquids, an elixir is a liquid form of the essential properties of something. Today it usually refers specifically to stones, although you can make color elixirs as well. An elixir is a method by which you can take in the properties of stones and gems. An elixir is a distillation of the essential energy of the stone.

Elixirs are prepared by placing a cleansed stone in a bowl or jar, then pouring pure water (well water or spring water) over it, leaving it to steep for a specific amount of time. Often the elixir is steeped in sunlight or moonlight. After a certain period, the stone is removed and the elixir is consumed with visualization, or transferred to a storage container and labeled. Storing elixirs requires sterilized opaque bottles of glass, so that no other energies are absorbed. The elixir does not need to be heated.

Color elixirs are prepared in a similar manner. The pure water is poured into a capped clear glass container, and a sheet of appropriately colored paper is wrapped around the container in a cylinder shape, and fastened. The water then absorbs the energy of the paper. If you can find a colored glass container in the color you require, so much the better. Storing color elixirs must be done either in containers of the color of the elixir, or in clear glass containers covered by appropriately colored paper cylinders to protect them and keep them pure.

Some practitioners like to add a single drop of food coloring in the appropriate color to stone and color elixirs to further reinforce the energy the elixir carries. This is not essential, and in fact can be difficult if you have to blend the food coloring to match the precise color of the stone.

Elixirs may be consumed, used as washes, or to anoint individuals or objects. Drops may be added to sachets or potpourris, and they may be used as oils are as well. Perhaps you might experiment with steeping a stone in a light massage oil and using it as an anointing oil, or to apply to the body to heal a particular ailment. Be creative!

Amulets and Talismans

Many practitioners mix these two forms of spellwork, and indeed, they are remarkably similar but for the method by which they function. An amulet is an object carried or worn which functions passively to protect the wearer or bearer; a talisman is consciously charged for a purpose and works actively, drawing or repelling something specific.

TALISMAN BAGS

In practices such as Voudoun and Hoodoo, a *gris-gris* bag is a small fabric pouch containing certain objects empowered for a purpose. These are also called charm bags, conjure bags, and mojo bags, among other things.

A Native American medicine pouch serves a similar purpose. Medicine is a term for the related energy of an object. An individual carries a variety of objects in the pouch, which reflect his own personal medicine or energy, as well as pouches of other objects designed to balance energy lacking in the individual.

Creating a Talisman for Protection

One of the most popular areas in spellcasting is for protection and safety. Talisman bags for protection are often hung over your front door, but you can also put the talisman in the glove compartment of your car, or carry it in your briefcase or gym bag, and use it wherever you feel protection is needed.

Timing: Sunday, Tuesday; moon's second quarter; noon; hour of the sun; hour of Mars; moon in sign of Leo; or your personal power time

Supplies:
Small square of red fabric
Snowflake obsidian
3 whole cloves
Pinch angelica
White ribbon or cord, measuring 1 foot

Steps:

1. Empower the materials for protection.
2. Spread the cloth flat on your work surface. Place your hands upon it and say,

   Red cloth, protect me from danger and evils; be active and vigilant.

3. While visualizing, place each component in the center of the fabric. As you do, say aloud what each is used for:

   Into this talisman I place angelica, to guard from evil.
   Into this talisman I place three cloves, to protect my spirit.
   Into this talisman I place snowflake obsidian, to warn me of danger.

4. Draw the sides of the fabric up and wrap the white ribbon around it, saying:

   White ribbon of purity, bind this talisman. About me shines the light of truth and love.

5. Tie the talisman shut with three knots, visualizing these knots as a barrier to negative energy.
6. Loop the ends of the ribbon, and use it to hang the talisman where you want it to work its magic.

EMPOWERING AMULETS

An amulet is a passive object that extends its power to the wearer. If you possess a cross, crucifix, pentacle, or favorite pendant or ring, the lack of which would make you feel naked, that piece of jewelry is already a sort of amulet. If you carry something you consider as a lucky piece, that is also an amulet. When you choose an amulet, think carefully about the correspondences traditionally carried by the symbol, your personal associations evoked by the symbol, and about the material in which the amulet has been formed.

Amulet for Health

This spell uses the symbol of the caduceus on a wax disk to create an amulet to guard your health. The caduceus is the symbol of a staff about which are entwined two serpents, crowned by two wings. It is used by physicians, and associated with Mercury.

Timing: Sunday; hour of the sun; noon; moon's second quarter; first days of moon's third quarter; moon in sign of Leo; or your personal power time

Supplies:
Candle in a color you associate with health
1 burin, nail, or dry ballpoint pen
1 small square of waxed paper or aluminum foil
    at least 4 x 4 inches

Steps:
1. Empower supplies for health.
2. Light the candle. Allow it to burn while you meditate upon the preservation of your health.
3. Pick up the candle and hold it horizontally. Allow the wax to drip onto a piece of waxed paper or aluminum foil in a roughly circular shape the size of a quarter. Make sure the wax is at least one-eighth of an inch thick, and try to keep it as even as possible.
4. Allow the wax to dry. Allow the candle to burn while you work.
5. Peel the wax off the aluminum foil and turn it over so that the smooth side is face up.
6. With the burin, lightly scratch a caduceus, representing health, into the wax. Do not carve too deeply, or you will snap the wax disk.
7. When you are satisfied with your symbol, carefully go over the lines again with your burin to provide more definition, but be careful not to snap the disk. If the disk snaps, simply drip more wax onto the foil in another circular shape and begin again.
8. Hold the wax amulet in your hands and envision yourself (or the individual for whom you are making the amulet) in perfect health. Say:

Essence of health
Walk with me each day,
Lie with me each night.
The caduceus guards my well being;
Health is my constant companion.
These are my words, this is my will.

9. Visualize healthy energy flowing to you, down your arms and into the wax amulet. When you feel it has been empowered adequately, leave it by the candle to further charge. (Don't leave it too close; if your candle melts and wax overflows, you will lose your amulet.)
10. Carry the amulet with you. If it breaks, some practitioners believe that it has deflected illness or disease. Melt the pieces, dispose of them with thanks, and make another amulet.

Recharging and Disposing of Amulets and Talismans

Every so often, a talisman or amulet goes missing; it appears to vanish. When this occurs, do not panic; this is simply the universe's way of telling you that you no longer need it.

Of course, the universe doesn't conveniently remove amulets and talismans every time they're no longer needed. If your talisman has done its work in the situation for which you created it, you may disenchant it by disassembling, burning, or burying it. If you think it requires a boost of energy, tuck it in a bowl of herbs and/or stones with correspondences sympathetic to the talisman's objective. For example, to revitalize a sluggish talisman bag for protection made from the instructions above, you might place it in a shallow dish of cloves and angelica. Or you might anoint the talisman bag with an oil corresponding to its purpose to add a bit more energy. Alternatively, you may remove the negative energy that has collected around the talisman by smudging it with sage or cedar, or by leaving it in sunlight all day or moonlight overnight. Think carefully about the objective of the talisman bag before choosing to cleanse it by sunlight or moonlight, and match it to the appropriate light energy. Under no circumstances, however, should you open a talisman bag, even to add more ingredients. This undoes the magic.

Amulets are a more permanent form of spell, and tend to endure over time. If you feel they need to be perked up, remove the negative energy which has collected around them by cleansing them with one of the methods described previously such as smudging, wiping it with a wash, covering it in salt or earth, or leaving it in running water or the light of sun or moon for a period of time. Then re-empower it with one of the charging techniques from Chapter 6. The symbol carries its own power and energy, which cannot be removed, but the act of re-empowering it confirms your connection to it, and your desired wishes concerning its function.

If you realize that you no longer need an amulet, you may set it aside and keep it, or you may pass it along to someone in need.

Petition Magic

Another simple spell, petition magic involves writing your need or desire on a surface and then burning it, burying it, or tossing it into a moving body of water. Write a letter to the universe, to your guardian angel, to a chosen saint, or to the Divine, and explain the situation and what you require. Then choose the method by which your goal would best be associated: if it is a spell for growth, bury it; if it is a spell requiring movement or communication, throw it into water; if it is to remove something from your life, burn it. Remember to visualize while you perform each action.

This is a marvelous method to use when you're at work. After a frustrating phone interview where I was deliberately misunderstood by a radio host in order to create a comic interview instead of the serious interview the producer had booked with me, I sat down at the computer and wrote a letter to my goddess regarding the poor taste displayed by the host and the lack of respect for my religion. I said exactly what I thought of the interview and the interviewer. Then I printed it out, tore it up, and flushed it down the toilet, willing the anger and hurt to vanish. I gave myself a few minutes to cool off and joined the world again.

Although simple and terrific for on-the-spot spells, petition magic can also be performed with great ceremony. Some practitioners like to have a special pen set aside for spellcraft alone, and many like to use dip pens or quills with little bottles of ink. Some occult and metaphysical shops sell magical inks with which you can write spells. These inks have usually been blended with herbal infusions or oils, which empower the ink with energies corresponding to its name and purpose. Like anything else you buy at a metaphysical store, you can make your own inks, and tailor them to your needs.

BASIC INK RECIPE

Pick up a small vial of ink at a craft store or art supply shop. (A dip pen will be required to use these inks; you can usually find inexpensive dip pens at both shops.) Choose a basic color such as black or brown, or a color associated with your goal. For example, many money-drawing inks are green; many attraction or love inks are red.

Make an herbal infusion of herbs chosen for their correspondences and associations with your goal. Allow it to cool. Add a drop or two of herbal infusion to the bottle of ink. Cap it and shake well. You can do this with herbal tinctures as well (infusions done with alcohol); again, add only a drop or two and shake well.

Alternatively, crush a couple of spoonfuls of herbs and put them into a small jar. Pour the ink over them and cap the jar. Place on a sunny windowsill and shake daily. Leave for one week, then strain and rebottle the ink in its original bottle.

If you wish to scent your ink as well, add a drop or two of oil chosen for its corresponding energies to the ink and shake well. Shake again before each use.

Whatever your method, be sure to label the bottle as magical ink, and use it only for spellwork, along with your dip pen or quill.

Paper

Petition magic often uses paper, naturally. As I've said about various other subjects, the purer the paper, the better. The size of the paper doesn't matter, so long as it's large enough to hold everything you need to write.

Grimoires and older spells often call for parchment paper, but most modern practitioners have no idea what it's made from. Traditional parchment is made from the skin of lambs, calves, or kid goats. It tends to be remarkably expensive for very small pieces.

I don't know about you, but using the skin of an innocent animal in my spellcraft simply for the implied purity of the product bothers me. I prefer to use vegetable parchment, which looks very similar to real parchment but is made of organic vegetable matter instead. This paper can be found at office supply shops as well as arts and crafts stores. If environmental concerns are high on your list of priorities, look for one that is unbleached and made of recycled materials.

There are such incredible varieties of paper available today that the type of paper you use in petition magic can be specifically chosen to reflect your goal. Explore stationery shops for small sheets of hand-made paper, complete with flowers pressed in it, or paper with cultural patterns which reflect the deities or angels you have chosen to work with, or make your own paper for a special spell in order to empower it from the very beginning with your goal and energy. Craft shops sell papermaking kits, or you can find simple directions online or in craft books at your local library.

One tip: don't use lined paper unless you absolutely have to. Lines tend to trap the images or words you put on the paper, and interfere with your visualization without your knowledge. Stick to blank paper, and fresh paper that hasn't been previously used.

Basic Petition Spell

Petition spells are simple. You can add energy in whatever way you like: burn corresponding incense while you write, choose paper and ink in the colors which correspond to your need, and so forth.

Timing: Variable according to your goal; or your personal power time

Supplies:
Vegetable parchment
Pen (if it's a dip pen, you will need ink)

Steps:
1. On the paper, write the following:

   I, [full name], ask my God, my angels, and my ancestors to help me obtain [goal]. I call upon your wisdom and your love to aid me in this task.
   Signed,
   [your full name].

2. Fold the paper up, and keep it in a secret place. When your petition has been granted, burn or bury the paper and give thanks.

Kitchen Spellcraft

The preparation and consumption of food is one of the central events in our lives. It is sustenance, it is comfort, and it is magic all its own. A kitchen witch is a spellcrafter whose magical tools are used in everyday life, and who sees every act as a magical act. Spells concerned with the hearth and home, with family and comfort, are usually the focus of kitchen spellcraft.

Many food correspondences can be found in a listing of herb or tree correspondences. Food can be charged or empowered and ingested to aid in gathering energy to achieve your goal, particularly for spells involving internal change or transformation. Simply prepare the food with focus and intent, visualizing your goal, and eat it with the same focus. Spellwork in the kitchen can introduce a whole new perception of tools: let your mixing bowl or cooking pot be a cauldron; let your wooden spoon be a wand; let your chef's knife be an agent of magic as well.

Think of the ingredients in your pantry and refrigerator as spell components, and empower them accordingly when you use them. When you cook, think of the ingredients as correspondences as well as nutritional fuel. Think of mixing ingredients as weaving their separate energies together to create something new. Cooking magic is a process whereby something completely new is created from different elements.

Another form of kitchen witchery is baking, my personal favorite form of kitchen spellcraft. I make a terrific soul-nurturing scone, for example, and I serve baked brie with sage and onion at afternoon gatherings, which encourages intellectual conversation. I choose ingredients for their correspondences as well as flavor.

What about the ethics of serving people spell-enhanced food? In my opinion, the spell is in the creation of the dish. It enhances the overall experience of consuming the food, but it isn't designed to manipulate or force anyone to do anything against her will. Everyone has the right to choose to accept the enhanced energy of food, or to reject it and simply enjoy the nutritional value and the flavor. In my experience, though, people tend to enjoy food prepared with awareness and visualization more than food prepared without it, even if they don't know it's been empowered.

Ash's Morning Coffee Spell

My husband is an animator and illustrator by training, but for the past three years he's been working with a landscaping firm while waiting for the local industry to pick up again. Whatever he does, he works hard and gives over one hundred percent to his tasks. However, even strong people like my husband need a special pick-me-up sometimes.

Not long after we married, I created this morning brew for him as a weekend treat. Now every once in a while I'll get up before he does, and make it for him as a special mid-week treat as well.

We use a drip coffee maker, but I have also successfully used a French coffee press to create Ash's special morning brew. The spice measurements flavor about four cups of coffee, so adjust according to your own requirements.

Timing: whenever necessary (although Sunday, Tuesday, Wednesday, Friday; moon's third quarter; moon in the sign of Aries; moon in the sign of Leo; hour of the sun; hour of Mars, hour of Venus, and hour of Mercury are all good as well)

Supplies:
Medium or fine ground coffee (caffeinated or decaffeinated)
3 pinches ground ginger
3 pinches cinnamon
Pinch nutmeg

Steps:
1. Empower the supplies for energy.
2. Add cinnamon to the ground coffee, saying:

   Cinnamon's for vision, money, and love.

3. Add the ginger, saying:

   Ginger's for strength when push comes to shove.

4. Add the nutmeg, saying:

   Nutmeg's for vision, good fortune, and wealth.

5. Kiss your fingers and hold them over the coffee and spices, visualizing your love flowing into the coffee, and say:

   A kiss keeps you happy and glowing with health.

6. Move your hand in a clockwise circle over the coffee and spices three times to blend the energies together, then proceed with brewing the coffee as per your usual process.
7. If you, or those to whom you're serving the coffee, take milk, cream, or sugar, add them with further visualization to support your spell.
8. If the brew is for you, then take at least ten minutes to sit down and enjoy the coffee, savoring the taste and the energies incorporated into it. Drink with visualization. If you're serving it to others, serve it with a smile and let them know you care about them.

Many of Trish Telesco's books are a treasure-trove of food-related spellcraft. Try *A Witch's Beverages and Brews*, *A Kitchen Witch's Cookbook*, or *Bubble, Bubble, Toil and Trouble* for wonderful ways of using food in spellwork. Scott Cunningham's *Cunningham's Encyclopedia of Wicca in the Kitchen* (formerly *The Magic of Food*) looks at food correspondences and the preparation of food as a magical method.

Final Words on Methods of Magic

Keep in mind that the form of the spell is in no way more or less powerful than the content. A candle spell is not necessarily more powerful than a spoken charm, or a talisman bag. In each case, your goal, your visualization, your focus, and your intent provide the raw substance of the spell; the spell method simply provides a context for them. There will be times when a simple cord spell will work for you; there will be other times when you want to create a long, formal spell involving lots of candles and gems scattered around you while you carve a wax talisman for healing. Only you can decide what methods will reflect the feeling of your goal. Follow your heart.

9

troubleshooting

What happens when a spell goes wrong? How did it get off track? If a spell

doesn't work, what happened? And what can you do to fix the situation?

⟡

Apart from the question of "Am I doing it right?" the fear of not succeeding is quite possibly the spellcasting subject which garners the most time in a question and answer session at the end of my workshops. As you've seen, your intent and belief in your goal are two of the major aspects of spellcrafting; it's highly unlikely, with these two points firmly established, that any combination of correspondences and raising of energy can send you wrong.

However, the fear of failure is a very real anxiety in the human psyche, and it is this fear that you must learn to conquer. Several aspects of fear can sabotage spellwork.

Practicing any new skill causes us anxiety, as we have no pool of experiences with which to compare our actions. As the new skill matures and you gather experience, it becomes easier to practice as confidence is gained and familiarity with the process is developed.

The fear of being punished for even attempting to change your life for the better is a fear you must also learn to filter. Our society tends to resent those who are happy and successful, while envy simultaneously drives us to wish that we could occupy the same niche. Seeking to better yourself and your life is not a bad thing. Each and every one of us deserves to live our life to the best of our ability, and allowing guilt, shame, or low self-esteem to hold us back from that is denying the very gift of life granted to us by the Divine.

What If I Make a Mistake?

If you took the time to think through your problem, and you crafted a spell carefully with appropriate correspondences and timing, casting it with focus, then a slip of a word is not going to shatter the energy you raise and direct toward your goal.

If you skip a step, the earth will not implode. If you notice it before the spell is complete, you may choose to include it, of course, but think carefully about where you are and how the introduction of an earlier step into the sequence will alter the energy level. A spell progresses, building action by action; more energy is raised with each word and act. If you forgot to light a candle or some incense, leave it out; it isn't important.

There's a saying that often comes up after a spell or ritual that reassures practitioners; it runs along the lines of "If it happened, it was supposed to happen; if it didn't happen, then it wasn't supposed to happen." Basically, this phrase tells you that if you forgot something, it evidently wasn't essential to the casting process. Likewise, if you were struck by inspiration in the middle of the spell and extemporized a charm or invocation, then it needed to be there for some reason.

Ultimately, if something doesn't go according to your plan, relax. Your intention is what counts. The universe also has certain checks and balances to make sure that nothing goes wildly out of balance.

I Forgot Something

It happens to everyone: you begin your spell, start focusing and slowly the energy builds until you reach for a tool or ingredient . . . and it isn't there.

There are two ways to deal with this. You can skip it and keep going (see above), or stop and go get it. If you're working within a circle, then you're going to have to cut a temporary door so that you can get out and return without popping it and having it collapse at your feet, necessitating a recasting of the circle before you continue. This isn't the end of the world; it's annoying and distracting, but, depending on what you're doing, you can usually get back into the swing of things.

Whatever you do, don't get down on yourself about it. That feeds into the feeling of fear and inadequacy that sabotages a spell. If you forget to put water in a cup, don't scold yourself, or tell yourself that you'll never get it right; it's just water.

If you forget *two* things, bring down the circle if you have one up, tidy away your ingredients and tools, and go for a walk or something. The universe is telling you that it's not the right time to do this spell. Again, don't get down on yourself; you can always try again later. This is also true of interruptions. If you're being distracted, whether it be by the doorbell or by your pets or family, simply postpone things. The timing might not be exactly precise when you settle down to do it again, but for some reason you're just not meant to perform the spell then and there.

It Didn't Work!

Often a spell succeeds in a manner we can't see right away. Remember, energy takes the path of least resistance, which means it might take the long way. Spells can take time.

We also tend to expect to see a certain proof of manifestation. For example, if you do a spell to help your chances of promotion at work, and you get fired, your first reaction will likely include thoughts about the complete and utter failure of your spell, and quite possibly the belief that it backfired. After three months of unemployment, however, you might land a much better position with another company where the pay is equal but you take more pleasure in the work, welcoming the challenges it presents and the subsequent growth and fulfillment you enjoy as a result. For those three months of unemployment, though, you'll see that spell as a failure. You might not even connect the new job and the spell for promotion. However, it's undeniable that you sent energy programmed for job changing out into the world. It took a while, and produced results that you hadn't expected, but in the end, you succeeded.

Sometimes we view a spell as a failure, but we learn valuable lessons in how we view the world from the experience. No spell is ever a complete failure, in my opinion; each is a learning experience in some way, shape, or form.

Why Didn't It Work?

Here's another common experience: you have all the tools and components, you follow the spell you've crafted to the letter, the energy you raise is high, and at the end of it you feel terrific. And yet . . . nothing happens.

There are a few reasons as to why this occurs. Sometimes you aren't focused enough, which means the energy didn't really go anywhere except out into the world aimlessly. That energy hasn't been wasted; it will go wherever it's needed. And you haven't completely wasted your time; you acquired more experience in handling energy and casting a spell.

A common error in spellcasting involves how visualization is used. If you cast a spell for money and visualize checking the mail every day for a check, you're visualizing the *process* by which the goal could be attained, not the actual goal. You're telling your subconscious that it will always be waiting for money, which is how the energy you send out will be programmed. Likewise, if you imagine buying a new car, for example, you're visualizing a use for that money, not possessing the money itself. Your current car could break down and be impossible to repair, necessitating a new vehicle (for which you won't have the funds). A strong imagination is an important element in spellcrafting and casting, but you have to be sure to imagine the positive outcome, not all the obstacles in the way. See the spell as having already succeeded, not in the process of working.

Spells can also fail because even though you have a clearly defined goal held firmly in your mind throughout the whole process, you don't really and truly *want* that goal. Deep emotion is what makes magic work, which is why spellcasting for others rarely works as well as it does for ourselves. Even if you clearly visualize, and truly want the outcome, sometimes the universe just has other plans for you. If you want something really badly and nothing you do works, either magically or in the physical world, the powers that be have a better idea that you haven't thought of yet. When this happens to me, I take a break from crafting and casting for the issue and try not to think about it for at least three days. Then I meditate around the subject, trying to remain open to points of view or information I might have overlooked or ignored. I'll do divination for myself or ask my husband or a friend to do some kind of reading for me. You can cast this spell for help.

Spell for Guidance

If inspiration or realization doesn't come my way to figure out why a spell failed, I'll do a simple spell for guidance such as this one.

Timing: whenever necessary; or your personal power time

Supplies:
Pale violet candle
Sandalwood incense
Your favorite oil
Matches or a lighter

Steps:
1. Take a few drops of the oil on your fingers and anoint the candle while focusing on your desire for guidance in this situation.
2. Light the candle, saying:

   As this light illuminates this room, may it illuminate my heart.
   Angels, guide me.

3. Light the sandalwood incense from the flame of the candle and close your eyes. Allow the scent of the incense to wreathe around you.
4. Clear your mind and focus on your breathing. Remain there in peace for at least five minutes.
5. Allow the incense and candle to burn out on their own, but make sure they are burning safely and under your supervision so as to not allow surrounding objects to catch fire. Then go about your day as usual. The answer will come to you somewhere within the next twenty-four hours.

Warning: The answer, solution, or action coming your way may not be the outcome you would have ideally chosen. What is important, however, is that the situation is moving again.

Will The Spell Really Make a Difference?

This question can arise during the crafting process when you're sorting through correspondences and various ingredients, working out what will enhance the energy of your spell. However, if you ask this question in these words, it means you already doubt the outcome. If you have to ask a question like this, phrase it differently and say, "What will work best?"

If the original question is posed in regard to the spell itself, and if the answer is a confident "Yes," then the spell will be successful to some degree. Conversely, if the answer is "No," then your subconscious has already decided that the spell won't succeed, and is already considering what your next plan will be to remedy the situation. You'll already have sabotaged your efforts.

Do I Really Need All This Stuff?

I know people who moan when caught in a tight situation, and say, "If only I had my wand! Then I could do something about this!"

That's a lousy excuse. The power that enables you to craft and cast spells does not reside in tools and components; it resides in you. Your will, your mind, and your ability to focus are the key tools. Even the energy residing in your components exists only to support the energy you raise and direct toward your goal.

So, no, you don't need all the props, costumes, and the set in order to act. There will be situations requiring you to act without a lot of time to prepare, or the resources, or the wherewithal to assemble your standard spellcasting gear. If you know all this, and you still use your wand as a symbolic trigger when you use nothing else, make sure you have it with you at all times, or train yourself to use a substitute in a crunch, like a pencil. Flexibility and the ability to improvise are two of a spellcaster's strongest virtues.

There's nothing wrong with using props, as I've said before. They're terrific aids to your concentration, and they can really help create a correct atmosphere. Just don't allow yourself to be shackled to them. Think about it: traveling with a full spell outfit can be cumbersome. Although, if you travel a lot and you like to use props, you can make yourself a travel spell arsenal. Buy or make a roll-up fabric case that ties shut, and slip various tools and components into the pockets. Roll it shut, tie it up, and keep it in your briefcase or in your carry-on luggage. As a general note to travelers, however, airport security and border crossing guards frown on things that are sharp and pointy. Use common sense. Remember, spells are supposed to make your life easier, not more difficult.

On the Road

If you do travel a lot, you might want to carry a mini spellkit with you. Here's a suggestion of what you might carry:

- Candle in tin
- Small packets of salt (pick a couple up from whatever take-out restaurant you pass through)
- Feather
- Stone
- Small cup or dish
- Small figure, picture, or icon of a saint, angel, or deity to whom you feel connected

These are all things that have power; they are potent objects from which you can draw energy. The feather is your connection to the element of air; the candle is your connection to the element of fire; the stone is your connection to the element of earth; the small cup or dish, when filled with water, is your connection to the element of water. The picture, figure, or icon is your connection to the Divine. The salt can be used for protection, purification, and a host of other purposes while you travel.

Naturally, these items will work better if you work with them at home a bit first, so that you establish a relationship with them and their energy. Dedicate the set by purifying and empowering each item separately.

If you're unsure about your ability to raise energy in a strange place, or are concerned about your safety in doing so, you might also want to review the spell in Chapter 8 on how to empower stones to serve as portable batteries for spells, and prepare a few to bring with you on your trip.

Record-Keeping and Troubleshooting

I stressed the importance of keeping detailed notes in Chapter 3, and it's not just for posterity or sentimental reasons. When something goes wrong, these detailed records are essential to the postmortem process. With clear records, you can go back and isolate problems in the crafting and casting process in order to avoid them in the future, or the successful elements in order to repeat them.

The basic questions you should ask yourself if you think something has gone wrong are:

1. Did I have a clearly defined, simple goal?
2. Did I empower my components with energy associated with my goal?
3. Did I visualize my goal as I performed the spell?

If you answered no to any of these questions, you've put your finger on the most obvious error you made. If you answered yes to all three questions, then it's time to sit down with your spell journal and start analyzing the spell itself.

Just as your notes can provide key information to help you figure out your power time, they can provide vital clues to the times when your abilities are at low ebb. Only by keeping detailed records was I able to discover that I can't cast a spell with any amount of solid energy when it's been hot and humid for more than three days. Living in Montreal, where a good part of our summer consists of heavy, energy-sucking humidity, this was a remarkably important revelation for me. When we finally have a thunderstorm something hits my reset button, and I can raise and direct power with accuracy, control, and zest. That dynamism slowly fades, however, the longer the humidity builds up.

The weather affects me deeply. For you, it might be a certain time of day, or a particular sign the moon travels through. Perhaps every time you use orange candles your spells veer off your intended course. These are crucial pieces of information that you will not be able to puzzle out and successfully work around unless you keep clear, detailed records, and review them when things go wrong.

Location, Location, Location

Where you choose to perform your spell can have great impact upon the spell itself. Explore the space thoroughly. What sounds are there? What does the energy of the area feel like? What kind of human and animal traffic does it see? Spend a bit of time there first to determine if the space will reflect the spell.

You can choose where to perform a spell in order to reflect what kind of change you are seeking to create. For example, if you are doing a spell to remove obstacles, you might chose to perform your spell by a river. If you are doing a spell for fertility, you might choose a field. If you are doing a spell for stability, you might choose to do it in a rocky area or in the foothills of a mountain or hill.

Privacy

Early on in their practice, many spellcasters fret about not having a place where they can cast spells. The common misconception is that you need a lot of space, billowing incense, and loud chanting. By now you've realized that this isn't true. Depending on the spellcasting method and the technique of raising energy that you decide upon, your casting could be very still and very quiet.

However, this doesn't necessarily ease the anxiety spellcasters experience regarding the proximity of other people. No matter how comfortable you might be with the act of spellcasting, there often remains a small nibble of doubt concerning what other people might think. What others think isn't an issue, however; the important point of view is, of course, yours. Valuable time and energy can be wasted fretting about what others might think if they discovered your practice, particularly if you are casting in a location where you do not feel secure.

There are ways of dealing with this. If you have a family, it might be a good idea to set some ground rules regarding privacy. If you will be casting in your home while other family members are present, you can tell them you need to be alone for a while, and agree on a time by which you'll emerge to rejoin them in regular activities. Perhaps you can agree that when a "Do Not Disturb" sign is hung on the door, nothing but fire, flood, or blood is to interrupt you. Many practitioners time their spellwork to the schedule of the family. For example, slip in some time to cast your spell after dinner when children are doing homework and your spouse is washing dishes, or on a Saturday afternoon when hockey practice, ballet, and yard work are occupying family members. Granted, these might not be the ideal times you would choose if you had complete freedom to schedule your spells: it might not be the hour of Jupiter, or a Monday.

Remember, we cast spells when we need to; precise timing isn't going to make or break your spell, it will just add more of a certain kind of energy. The time-honored practice of relaxing in the bath while burning candles is another excellent way around the privacy issue. You can also bring in herbal correspondences by tying herbs in a scrap of cloth, an old washcloth, or a small section of an old pair of pantyhose, and tossing them into the bath as the water is running. (This will stain the cloth, so be prepared to part with the whole bundle when you're finished, either by throwing it out or burying it.) Your techniques of raising energy might be a bit limited, but you are surrounded by water, after all; draw energy from it as you meditate, or whisper a mantra, or tighten and relax your fist rhythmically.

If you live alone or with people who are comfortable with your spells, then you're very fortunate. There are other obstacles which crop up, however. If you are an apartment dweller, dancing or drumming isn't always an option, and you can feel shy about using your voice. Sometimes burning herbs can create an odd smell along with releasing energy, which can drift into hallways and worry neighbors. Use discretion. Acceptable noise between 9 A.M. and 9 P.M. is usually not a problem. Think about how often you hear your neighbors playing loud music or watching films with subwoofers, and you will likely worry less about how people might react to soft chanting or incense.

There are ways to spellcast in your office as well. A collection of pretty stones in an earthenware dish, a vase of flowers, a bowl of potpourri—any of these combined with intention and a technique of raising energy such as deep breathing or meditation can successfully fuel a spell.

Spellcasting around others always does entertain the possibility of interruption, however. Working within a circle can reduce the possibility of interruption. A circle contains the energy you are working with and acts as a shield, which reduces the possibility of people drifting into your area, subconsciously drawn by the energy you are raising. The circle will also help screen out distractions, helping you focus. It also contains the energy and keeps it concentrated, which means your spell will take less time, which in turn reduces the chance that someone will wander up to you.

There are other concerns about the issue of privacy, however. If you don't particularly care what others think of your newly found ability to create positive change in your life, or if you have sympathetic friends, then you might be excited and want to share stories of your work with others. Traditionally this is not advised, because it "draws energy away from the goal." Working in secrecy was crucial for spellcasters in the past, partially due to a combination of circumstances including the inhospitable moral climate in Europe, but also due to the commonly held belief that if others knew about the spell their thoughts would interfere in its function. Keeping mum about your spell while it does its work is usually the best course of action. That doesn't mean you can't work on supporting it in other ways, of course, which includes talking to others about how the situation could be improved. Once the goal of the spell has been achieved (or it hasn't manifested in the period of time you've allowed it), sometimes sitting down and talking out the spell with a sympathetic friend can help you pinpoint how to successfully apply it in other areas, or how to improve it. You don't have to go into great detail; sometimes it's enough to say, "I did a spell to help my daughter stand up to the bullies at school, and it doesn't seem to have worked." Your friend might bring up options or suggestions regarding the circumstances that you might have overlooked or seen in a different light.

Discussing spells is a personal choice. If you have friends who also spellcraft, then you have a small community of people with whom you can knock ideas about. If not, then sometimes you can phrase it differently. Saying "I did a meditation about my career and I have the impression that it's about to take off" is a perfectly acceptable way of telling a nonspell sympathetic friend or family member that your spell for promotion is having an excellent effect.

I Can't Stay Focused

Does your mind wander when you cast spells? Do you find it difficult to concentrate on what you're doing? Are you getting caught up in the tools and the steps and the words you're supposed to say?

The first thing to do is to simplify your spells. You are likely attempting to cram in as much symbolism and visualization as possible. Reading a variety of authors and spellbooks can create a jumble of "ought tos" in your brain. In addition, sometimes practitioners get excited about a variety of techniques, ideas, and concepts, and try to use them all at once. Relax. Lighting a candle while visualizing an object or goal already in your possession is as equally valid as lists of invocations, drawing symbols, and lighting sequences of candles. If you must use a tool, use only one or two. Save some of those wonderful ideas for future spells. Record them in your spell journal.

Work within a circle to help screen out distractions and keep your energy focused. In addition, practice your meditation regularly to help improve your focus and to help reduce stress and anxiety which can intrude while spellcasting.

I'm Always Tired

Spellcasting can take a lot out of you. It's not uncommon to feel like you've just exercised afterwards, even though you might not necessarily have the aching muscles and the blisters on your feet to show for it. You've been exercising a different sort of muscle.

Many spellcasters make the error of drawing energy from themselves to power their spells. While everyone does this to a certain extent (your will and intention is a form of energy which binds the disparate energies together), some pour their life energy into their spells and then wonder why they can hardly stand afterwards, or why it takes a day or two to recover. If this happens to you, the most obvious explanation is that you're not grounding properly. Either that, or you're ignoring the energies in your components that you've assembled to lend their power to your spell, and using your own energy instead. Think of *channeling* the energies instead of pushing them, and you might find it easier.

Nothing's Happening

Are you so sure? Just because you don't see an immediate or drastic change doesn't mean that your spell isn't having some sort of effect. Take a careful look at what you asked for, and think about what you visualized during your spell. Remember that spell energy travels through the path of least resistance, which sometimes means a circuitous route. Spells won't temporarily stop the earth from rotating to give you more time to finish a project for a looming deadline; they're much more likely to find another way around the problem.

Think about your request, and think about how long it will reasonably take to achieve it. Patience is a necessary virtue when it comes to spellcasting. It can take a while for effects to become evident.

If you're positive that nothing has changed, pull out that record sheet and double-check your correspondences. Did you inadvertently choose two herbs whose other associations cancelled out the ones you were using? If you chose to do a fertility spell on a Monday during a waxing moon, did you verify that the moon wasn't void of course when you performed it?

Things Are Going Wrong!

Spells are a method of rebalancing the current energy of a situation. This means that yes, sometimes things will seem to go even further out of whack before they find that correct balance point and settle down. Energy takes time to move around and play with all the finicky little aspects of life, which are bound up in the situation you have targeted. Don't panic. Roll with it. Give it a chance before you declare it a failure.

Calling Back a Spell

If a spell obviously fizzles badly right off the mark—and I'm not so sure they truly do—then there are a few things you can do to save the situation. The best option requires that you've kept detailed notes on how you constructed the spell. Go back and undo the spell carefully. Some practitioners change a couple of words and in essence perform the spell in reverse: at the point where they sent out energy, they draw it back. (Note that this doesn't mean starting at the end of the spell and working back to the beginning; it means flipping the direction or the polarity.) In this scenario, use the same correspondences and colors and tools you used the first time; this is an instance of like attracting like, as employed in the first spell, but you're trying to attract the energy out there to you and the identical components.

To bypass all the previous steps, just call back the spell. When you call it back, however, be sure to ground it to avoid being flashed by its energy. Flashing is my term for energy backlash as a result of being in the line of backfire. Calling it back can be done: remember the analogy of the web of energy, which connects all things? The energy can travel back along those strands, the same way it traveled out.

This technique should only be used if you are secure in your grounding, because it can otherwise overload you. During this summons, I recommend holding a tool such as a wand or a knife, or whatever tool you use to direct energy (if you use one): you can channel the energy you summon into the tool, in order to use it later in spells. Or do this outside with your hands on the ground, and channel the returning energy into the earth to ground it directly. Under no circumstances should you call it back and attempt to contain it within yourself. That's a classic set-up for being flashed, creating migraine headaches, becoming physically ill, and being unbalanced for a day or more.

In order to call the spell back, ground, and say:

I command all energies released in the pursuit of [name the goal] on [name the day] at [name the time] to return to my hand this day, this hour, this minute. I recall you, I recall you, I recall you. Cease your activity, freeze your motion; as of this moment your purpose is null and void. Return to me, I command you now!

Visualize the energy you sent out stopping its flowing motion, then being sucked back along its path to you. Keep visualizing its movement through you to the earth, or the tool. If you created something during the spell, such as a sachet, knotted cord, or poppet, this is the time to undo it. Don't just destroy it; take the time to undo the knots, unpick the pouch, sort out the larger ingredients. Then dispose of them separately in running water, by burying them, or burning them.

I Was Wrong

Every now and then you acquire a new piece of information changing your understanding of a situation. If you've already cast a spell, it's a little difficult to say, "I'm sorry, I didn't mean it" and expect the universe to give you a gentle, understanding pat on the head and undo your work. In one respect, casting the spell was the lesson you needed to learn in this particular situation, because it brought the situation into sharp focus, enabling your new perception. Choosing to cast a spell means accepting the associated consequences. (For more on this, see Chapter 4 on ethics.) If you've chosen to exert your will on your environment, then you can't just take it back. The cosmos won't obligingly backtrack to where it was at the point of your spell. Too much water has passed under the bridge. It would take too much energy to tear down the new reality and reconstruct the old. It's much better to craft another spell to learn from your error, or to help you understand how this new situation is better than the old, or to help you accept the new adjustment to your environment.

Spell to Cancel a Spell

This is similar to calling back a spell, only you don't command the energy to return to you to be grounded and neutralized. Instead, you allow it to be released from its original goal to flow freely to wherever it can do the most good. The choice of method is up to you.

Timing: whenever necessary; your personal power time

Supplies:
1 foot of black thread
Sharp scissors

Steps:
1. To help your visualization for this spell, empower a foot of thread with your memory of the original spell. Tie a loop in the end of the thread, and slip it over your wrist. Allow the loose end to dangle straight down from the loop on your wrist. Have a pair of sharp scissors ready. Remember to purify both thread and scissors.
2. State:

   I command all energies released in the pursuit of [name the goal] on [name the day] at [name the time] to cease their motion this day, this hour, this minute. I release you, I release you, I release you. From this moment, you are free. Disperse and flow to where the universe desires, to do good in the way that the Divine commands. You are free, you are free, you are free!

3. Cut the dangling thread with the scissors. As you do so, visualize the energy you originally sent out being freed from its path toward the goal, and returning to the energy of the Universe to do the work of the Divine. You may choose to bury the thread and the loop, or burn them; it's up to you.

If you created something during the spell that you still possess, such as a poppet or talisman pouch, then take it apart and dispose of the ingredients separately.

It's a good idea to purify yourself after canceling or recalling a spell. Take a shower or a bath (add some salt), or at the very least wash your hands and let the water flow over them for a bit. Eat something grounding such as bread, crackers, or a rice cake, and go for a walk.

Final Words on Troubleshooting

You will make mistakes; everyone does. Consummate professionals still make mistakes. The mistakes can range from timing errors to errors in judgment. Some will be minor mishaps, and some will be major. From every spell that doesn't play out as you had intended, however, there is valuable information to be gained. Write all your thoughts and observations in your spell journal. If you have trouble reconciling yourself to a mistake, try this spell to help you deal with it.

"Help me learn from this" Herbal Pillow

Tuck this small herbal pillow under your bed pillows and sleep on it for at least one week. You may not consciously understand how your spell went wrong, but you will acquire understanding on a deeper level which will aid you in the future.

Timing: moon's third quarter; moon's fourth quarter; Wednesday; Saturday; hour of Mercury; hour of Saturn; moon in the sign of Pisces; your personal power time

Supplies:
2, 8 x 8 inch squares of cotton fabric in pale blue or pale yellow
Pins, needle and thread

2 tablespoons dried vervain
2 tablespoons dried sage
3 bay leaves
Sandalwood oil
Approximately ½ to ¾ cup flax seed
Glass bowl
1 sodalite
1 howlite
1 copy of the complete record sheet of the spell you performed

Steps:
1. Empower supplies for wisdom.
2. Lay the two pieces of fabric on top of one another, matching the edges, and pin. Sew the two pieces of fabric together on three sides with a small running stitch. Turn inside out.
3. In the bowl, combine the flax seed, the sage, the vervain, and the bay leaves. Pour half into the fabric square.
4. Fold the paper with the spell record on it into a small square or rectangle. Anoint it with the sandalwood oil. Place it in the fabric square. Add the sodalite and the howlite stones.
5. Fill the remaining space in the fabric square with the herbal mixture and pin it shut. Sew the edges closed and remove the pins.
6. Hold the small pillow in your hands and say:

   My spell is embraced with healing, wisdom, and love.
   Spirit, teach me; help me learn from this spell.
   Allow me to grow and understand.
   By the grace of the Divine,
   These are my words; this is my will.

7. Place the small herbal pillow under your bed pillows, or at the head of your bed, and sleep with it for at least one week.

Variations: Burn the spell record sheet and add the ashes to the herbal blend instead. Add a fluorite stone to enhance the action of the pillow.

10

solo spellcasting
and group spellcasting

This chapter looks at the benefits and drawbacks of working alone as compared to working with others. This chapter also examines some common myths regarding solo and group work, and provides valuable tips and tricks for both.

✺

Sooner or later it's probably going to occur to you to try spellcasting with others. The image of a group of people gathered around a cauldron or fire is as popular as the solitary magician in history. Contemporary media depictions of spellcasters suggest that a group of two or three can accomplish more than a solo spellcaster is able to achieve.

While working with others can be remarkably rewarding, the belief that more people automatically yields more power and better results is a myth.

As a solo spellcaster, you have complete freedom to choose a place in which to cast your spell, the components you wish to use, the goals you desire, and the methods you choose to employ. You can get up at dawn, or set your alarm for three in the morning to take advantage of the precise planetary hour. If you live with housemates, the only schedules you need to worry about are theirs. You know exactly what kind of energy you can raise, and the techniques by which you excel at doing so. As a solo spellworker, you are in complete and ultimate control of how you craft and cast your spells.

As a member of a group, you have a variety of resources to draw from. A support system is in place, with mentors from whom you can learn new spellcasting methods. A group also confirms your successes: if several people experience similar results, then data can be gathered to reinforce the spell record.

You do not have to be involved in a circle or coven to lend credibility to your spells. Simply because no one sees you work does not mean that your spells are any less important or potent.

FINESSE

This is where things get tricky. As a solo spellcaster, you can gauge the exact moment to perform certain actions in your spell, such as raising or releasing power. In a group, there is often a leader who handles the pacing of the spell, serving as the director for this particular production, handling and sensing the combined energies raised by the group and directing it toward the goal. This person is often the one who crafted the spell, or who requested the spell to be done.

Group work can be like handling a team of horses who aren't harnessed to one another, just to the stagecoach they're pulling.

You're constantly pouring your energy in the group spell, but at the same time you have to reserve a part of your mind and energy to watch how it's being done, to evaluate how much energy everyone else is pouring in, and to keep track so that you don't pull ahead of or fall behind the group.

Balancing Energy

If you're operating within an established group of people gathered to cast a spell, sometimes referred to as a circle or a coven, then you'll have at least some sort of energy connection to the people with whom you're working. The closer you are to one another, the easier it is to merge and balance energies. This comes with practice, of course; blending energy doesn't happen perfectly on the first try for anyone, no matter how experienced they are. Like a first date, there's a tentative fumbling where you wonder how far to reach out, how much to lower your defenses, what to reveal and to what degree. With practice, everyone finds the right balance of personal energy to put into the mix, and how to handle the energies extended in turn to them. In the meantime, spells might be clumsy.

Another issue a group often runs into is uneven energy. Some will contribute less than others, resulting in certain members being exhausted and others feeling like they weren't part of the experience. Sometimes someone unintentionally draws energy instead of providing it, feeding off the energy raised for the goal of the spell and reducing it.

Emotional Connections

When you're working with a group, there will be times when someone will bring a request for a spell to work on a problem for someone who is not a member of the group. Assuming that the target individual has given his or her assent to the spell, there can be a bit of a stumbling block involved in an operation like this. Depending on how well the group knows the target individual, the results can vary. In a situation such as this, the energy raised by the circle will often be gathered and directed by the member who knows the target individual best, or who has brought that individual's need to the circle.

Simply put, the closer you are to the individual, the fewer obstacles the energy you produce will have along its journey, and the better chance there will be of the spell succeeding. Think of it as degrees of separation: the web connects everyone, but some energy connections are stronger because of emotional reinforcement. A stronger connection ensures that the spell has more open roads along which to speed to its conclusion. This is one of the reasons why you yourself are the easiest person for whom to cast spells. It's also why successful spellcasters, occult store employees, and authors repeat patiently again and again that even if you've never cast a spell before in your life, if you want one performed, you're the best person for the job simply because you have the proper emotional connection to the goal. No one else feels exactly the same way about your goal, no matter how well you describe it. We can imagine, but in the end any reconstruction of your emotion will be an approximation at best, and will lack the depth of the original.

Mind Games

Every kind of group has its politics, and spellcasting circles are no different. Personality clashes, resentment, hidden agendas, and selfish motives are often intangible presences in a circle as well. Power games are just as common in circles as in any other environment.

When you sense something like this, you have two choices: you can bring the issue to the circle itself, expressing your concern; or you can leave.

It is essential to be as honest as possible with yourself and with your spellcasting circle. If your heart isn't really in it, then admit it and leave gracefully. If the spells being cast clash with your personal code of ethics, you owe it to yourself to address the situation.

Pros and Cons of Group and Solitary Spellcasting: An Overview

There are some advantages and disadvantages of working with a group to cast spells. Take a look at the following points and think about what is important to you to help you decide whether you'd prefer to work with a group or solo at this time. Some points, such as the group mind, appear as both pros and cons, as there are drawbacks and advantages involved.

Group Pros:
- A strong sense of connection similar to that of a family
- Emotional and magical support in times of need

- A pool of resources upon which to draw
- The sharing of responsibility and costs
- Commitment to others
- Guidance from others
- Belonging to, or creating, a tradition
- Amplification of energy
- Development of a group mind
- Opportunity for discourse, sharing, and mental stimulation
- Confirmation and validation from others
- Variety of skills
- New friends

Group Cons:
- Potential for too much, or too little, energy to handle
- Difficulty in synchronizing identical visualizations of a goal
- Difficulty in matching emotional investments in a goal
- Coordination of schedules
- Time management
- Personal conflicts
- Power struggles
- Dogma and rules
- The formation of a group mind
- Necessity of compromise
- Scarcity
- Need for discretion
- Intimacy issues

Solitary Pros:
- Individual freedom and choice
- No compromise or interference
- Personal growth
- One set of ethics
- Availability
- Self-reliance and complete responsibility
- Trusting yourself

Solitary Cons:

- Loneliness
- Uncertainty
- Lack of structure
- Can be costly
- Difficulty in self-evaluation
- Total responsibility for tasks and outcome

Establishing a Network

If you want to try working with others, the first place to look is among your own friends. If you're interested in this subject, chances are good that someone else is too. If there's no obvious person, try bringing up the subject casually in conversation one day. Don't jump right in with a bombshell like "So I've been casting spells for three years"; certain words, as you are doubtlessly well aware, are very sensitive. Instead, try certain phrases, which include words such as "meditation," or "I lit a candle," or "Oh look, the moon is waxing," and see what happens. A friend might notice books associated with spellcraft on your shelves, and ask questions. Chat with people about how good you feel about your life since you began implementing positive affirmations three times a day, or other New Age techniques. Gauge those who might be open to the idea. You might be very surprised.

The second place to look is your local occult or New Age store. If there are workshops offered, take one, and meet new people. Have coffee with them, and swap stories about your spellcasting experiences. Get to know them before you propose attempting a spell together.

The key, of course, is gathering with people you feel very comfortable with. Spellcasting with strangers can be dangerous: you never know what's going to happen, or what kind of energy you'll be involving in your spell.

That said, there will be times when your spellcasting circle might include a friend of a friend whom you've never met before. Casting a spell with someone is certainly a deep way of getting to know them quickly. If you wish to draw open-minded people to you in order to create the potential for a spellcasting circle, craft and cast a spell such as this one.

Create a Spellcasting Circle

Be as specific as you choose when you outline the invitation in this spell. If you wish to work only with men or women, be sure to say so. If you are open to working with an online spellcasting group, leave out the geographical conditions. If you wish to work with people of a specific religious path, then indicate that. Be aware, however, that the more conditions you stipulate, the fewer people will fill them. You have every right to be picky about the people you draw to yourself. And of course, you don't have to work with everyone whom you meet who happens to be a spellcaster. This spell is designed to increase your chances of meeting people open to working with other spellcasters, not to lock you into a partnership of any kind.

Timing: moon's first quarter; dawn; moon in Aries; moon in Pisces; Monday; Thursday; Wednesday; hour of the moon; hour of Jupiter; hour of Mercury; or your personal power time

Supplies:
Several little feathers (down is good; check your craft store)
Holy water (see the recipe in Chapter 12)
Vegetable parchment
Pen
Heatproof bowl or cauldron
Candle in the color you associate with community and family (brown is
    good)

Steps:
1. Empower supplies with your desire.
2. Anoint the candle with holy water.
3. Light it, visualizing the light growing and serving as a beacon for fellow like-minded spellcasters.
4. Write an invitation to your ideal future spellcasting partners on the parchment. You might phrase it as, "I, [your name], issue an invitation to honest, loyal, and true spellcasters of [your geographical area]. If you seek to meet new people with whom to work, let us find one another." Sign it.
5. Read the invitation aloud. Visualize your words flowing out into the world.
6. Touch the edge of the invitation to the candle flame. When the paper has caught fire, let it burn in the heatproof bowl or cauldron. As it burns, visualize the energy of your invitation being released to flow out into the world.

7. Allow the bowl or cauldron to cool. Place the small feathers into the bowl or cauldron, and sprinkle them with a few drops of holy water.
8. Take the bowl outside and hold it up so that the wind lifts and swirls the feathers and the ashes. If necessary, scoop the feathers and ashes out with a hand and toss them into the air. Watch the wind take and scatter the ashes and feathers, and know your request has been taken to travel by the elements.

The First Meeting

The first time you assemble with other practitioners, you'll probably feel nervous, and the butterflies in your stomach will be dancing. Spellcasting with others is a very intimate process, rather like undressing in front of someone for the first time. You're showing one another how you work with energy. On top of that, it's exciting.

To help everyone feel comfortable and settle in, discuss how you'd all like to approach the spellcasting process. You might decide to divide up the tasks: one person can purify the area however he or she does it, another can create the protective circle in the way he or she does it, and so forth. Establish ground rules such as a signal to release the energy, a sign to alert others to overload or difficulty, and so on. Establish if shouting or stomping is acceptable or not.

I've heard of small groups all invoking their personal gods or angels in a spell, instead of choosing one to focus on. More is not necessarily better. If you decide to invoke more than one entity, make sure the entities are compatible. The energy of an angel of healing will probably not work well with the energy of a god of war. There will be enough difficulty meshing your personal energies, let alone trying to handle the energies of three or more sets of invoked entities in your spell. Focusing on one entity will also help keep everyone focused as a unit, rather than individually.

Focus on One Spell At a Time

Everyone may have an issue to be addressed, but limit your issues to one spell per circle. Once you've raised energy to help make money at the street garage sale, don't move on to raising energy for healing your mother's broken ankle, then helping someone find a new job. Finish the circle, take a short break to ground and rebalance your energy, then start again. This signals to your subconscious mind that everything is separate, ensures everyone is completely focused on the goal, and allows everyone's goals to be addressed with equal importance. Otherwise, your mother is likely to be offered a new job, someone will show up at the garage sale and fix all the broken stuff, and the person looking for a new job will find themselves with really healthy ankles.

Group Strategy

If you and other spellcasters decide to try casting together on a regular basis, you'll encounter fewer obstacles and enhance your emotional affinity with one another if you establish a regular routine and set of preparations. A regular sequence of events both inside and outside the circle helps everyone get into the same frame of mind. As a group, then, you will need to come up with a set routine for:

- **Set up:** Does the group want representations of all the elements in the workspace? Is there an aspect of the Divine that the group considers a patron of the spellcasting circle?
- **Purify:** A standard purification of the area and the people involved will go a long way to getting people in the right frame of mind for spellcasting. Will it be smudging? Will it be anointing with a charged oil? Water with a pinch of salt? Passing a bundle of fresh herbs over people's hands? A group meditation? A combination of these?
- **Dedicate the space:** Some practitioners like to walk around the space to be used with each element to harmonize the energies of the area.
- **State your purpose:** A regular formula spoken to signal the beginning of the spell process will key everyone in right away. "Welcome, friends, to this gathering. We are here to [state the purpose of the spell]" is sufficient. If the circle has a patron deity or saint or angel, invoking its aid in the spell would happen here as well.
- **Raise and release energy:** Does the group have a favorite method of raising energy that works well? Does everyone like to drum? What

about a chant, such as "The Witches' Rune" by Doreen Valiente, or another poem that has good rhythm?

- **Ground:** Eating a certain food after every spell to ground will speed up the grounding effect due to a repeated association.
- **Release dedicated space:** Familiar words to thank and release the deity, saint, or angel would occur here, as would familiar words to release the circle.
- **Record experience:** Everyone might choose to record their experience together after the spell, or perhaps the circle might select a scribe to take notes and keep a record of the spells performed by the group. Regardless of whether there is someone acting as scribe or secretary, however, everyone should record their experience as soon as possible.
- **Reinforce spell with action:** The members of the circle should all support their work in the circle with work in the outside world. This can be done as a group or individually, depending on the goal of the spell.

Having a group with which to compare results and experiences can build your confidence. Bringing your observations and results back to the group and comparing notes on the success of the spell can also teach everyone about how magic moves and manifests.

If your group seems to be coalescing well after the first couple of meetings, why not seal the group with a talisman to signify your new commitment?

Talisman Spell to Bond a Spellcasting Circle

This spell is to help strengthen bonds between the members of a spellcasting circle, not to *bind* them. Binding is a form of imprisonment, and chaining members of a spellcasting group together is the wrong way to go about creating harmony.

Timing: New moon; moon's first quarter; moon in Aries; moon in Cancer; dawn; midday; spring; summer; Wednesday; Saturday; hour of Mercury; hour of Saturn

Supplies:
Ask each member of the circle to bring a small object that they feel
represents them. It might be a small figurine of an animal, a stone, a
twig of a tree they identify with, a feather, a brief poem, anything.

Steps:
1. Assemble the objects on a cloth in the center of the circle.
2. Raise energy with this chant:

We are one, our power flows,
We are one, our power grows.

3. Direct the energy you raise into the objects.
4. Put the objects into a pouch and keep it safe. If the group meets in
   someone's home regularly, keep it there. If the location changes, assign
   a different person each month to take it home and watch over it.

If the group would rather not create something physical, try a spell
such as this Chalice Spell to celebrate the new group instead.

Chalice Spell to Bond a Spellcasting Circle

This is a great spell for sealing the decision to form an official spellcasting
group, and launching it.

Timing: moon's first quarter; moon's second quarter; Monday; Wednesday;
Friday; hour of the moon; hour of Mercury; hour of Venus

Supplies:
Juice (see below)
Glass pitcher
Glasses (one for each participant)

Steps:
1. Have everyone bring one kind of juice to the meeting. Don't confer
   beforehand; let it be random. It doesn't have to be a large carton; a small
   single-serving size is fine. At the spellcasting site, have ready a clean,
   purified glass pitcher and one glass for each participant.
2. When all members are assembled, have them empower their personal
   juice with positive energy. Then, one by one, let them pour their juice
   into the pitcher. When all the juices have been poured into the pitcher,

pass it around so everyone can empower the potion with good wishes. These may be spoken aloud, or silently, as each person wishes. Then pour everyone a glass of your very own circle juice, toast one another and the successful future of your circle and your spells, and drink!

The juice is different every time. Sometimes it's terrific, sometimes it's a bit odd, but it's always a unique reflection of your circle. It's nice to do this spell again on each anniversary of the founding of the circle, when someone new joins the group, or whenever you feel that the bonds should be reaffirmed; the juices brought by each member may be different or the same. The wishes spoken each time will vary as well, as will the energy each person brings to it. This reflects the healthy evolution and development of the spellcasters and of the circle itself.

Groups as a Source of Energy

Sometimes a group doesn't physically meet to perform a spell together. Instead, the person requiring the spell will contact the others and indicate the need and the time his or her spell will be cast. The others will then send energy to the practitioner to work into the spell. This can be done in several ways; often the person sending energy will sit and meditate, or light a candle. Lots of spellcasters use the phrase "I'll light a candle for you" as shorthand to indicate that they will take the time and energy to focus on the practitioner in need, and send their goodwill to be used in the situation.

Lighting a candle or meditating isn't the only way this can be done, however. Are you good with herbs? Mix a small bowl of herbs sympathetic with the spellcaster's goal or need, and place it by a window. Do you have a regular exercise routine? You can perform it thinking of the practitioner, and as you build up energy, visualize sending it his or her way.

Solo and Group—Why Not?

If you have a regular group meeting to work spells, there isn't a rule anywhere stating that you're not allowed to do work on your own. In fact, most practitioners who work with a circle still work on their own, only bringing certain issues to the group.

There's nothing wrong with that. It doesn't mean that you don't trust the circle; it means that you consider some needs personal, or you're confident in your ability to handle them.

More Than One Group

Some groups focus on certain kinds of spells, such as prosperity or protection. This can be a benefit, as you can bring your need to a specific group with skill in the applicable area. It can also get you into trouble, however, if both groups need you at the same time (there's usually only one full moon per month, after all), or if certain people you work with become jealous of the fact that you split your focus between two or more circles. It's not your problem, of course, but when there's tension between spellcasters, the resulting atmosphere makes for poor spellcasting. If you work with more than one circle, keep them separate, and make it clear that what happens in one does not travel over to the other. Your loyalties are not divided; the circles serve different functions in your life.

Groups and Self-Expression

Sometimes it feels like you don't really get a chance to be yourself in a group. That's not unusual. The group itself takes on an identity and there's nothing wrong with a short break; in fact, time away from it might lead you to discover a new dedication to it. Alternatively, it might show you that the group no longer serves the purpose it once did in your life.

Leaving a spellcasting group can be a sad decision, as you're not only saying goodbye to the people in the circle as spellcasting partners, but to a small community of support as well. When it's time to move on, however, it's time to move on. Staying can often hold you back from further developing as a spellcrafter.

Cyber-Spellgroups

With the explosion of Internet use and access over the past decade, the increase in online spellcraft has increased proportionally. Before you dismiss the idea out of hand, think about the fact that electricity is a form of energy, just as friendship is. If you have friends in other states, provinces, or countries then you know that you don't have to be in someone's physical presence to share energy with them. A phone call, e-mail message, or online chat is often how we stay in touch with those we love who are far from us.

We meet many new friends online as well. There are several cyber-space spellcasting groups formed of people who have never met in the physical world. The sense of community, support, love, and communication between these people rivals that of many physical groups.

Where do you meet spellcasters from all over the world? Check out bulletin boards hosted by metaphysical and occult Web sites, join electronic mailing lists devoted to the subject of spellcraft or the practice of magic, or look at the personal ads in the back pages of metaphysical magazines. As with any other communication with strangers online, exercise prudence and judge carefully how much personal information to give out. Trust your intuition.

A cyber spellcasting group operates in a similar method as physical groups. There can be regular meeting nights, emergency meetings called by someone in need, topics of discussion, and spells shared ahead of time in order for all the members to simultaneously perform it physically in their own location, linked by intention and visualization. It can be a fascinating experience.

From Spells to . . . ?

Sometimes spellcasting groups morph into worship circles based on an aspect of the Divine. The spiritual aspect of spellcasting is a constant presence, and if the members of the group are all of a similar religious path, the circle might try a spiritual meeting of some kind. Perhaps some members of the group feel drawn to the nature-based Neo-Pagan paths of Wicca or Druidry, or if the group is of Judeo-Christian roots, magical techniques based in the Qabala might take place and lead the group in a new direction spiritually. As explored in Chapter 2, much spellcraft through the ages has been based on religious or spiritual practice.

Sometimes, however, a spellcasting group disagrees concerning what to do next, what steps to take in a specific situation, or regarding in which direction the circle should develop. In this case, try a guidance spell such as this one.

Guide a Spellcasting Circle

This is a lovely low-key spell allowing the members of a spellcasting circle to seek guidance in general, or on a particular subject.

Timing: midnight; moon's first quarter; moon's second quarter; moon in Pisces; moon in Aquarius; hour of Saturn; hour of Jupiter; Saturday; Thursday

Supplies:
Charcoal tablet
1 teaspoon each crushed sage, lavender, cedar, and copal resin
Large white pillar candle
Burin, needle, nail, or other object with which to carve the candle
Holy water
Bowl or deep saucer
Optional: If you have performed the talisman bag spell to bond the circle, have this in the center of the circle

Steps:
1. Grind and blend the herbs and resin into incense. (This incense may be prepared ahead of time.) Add three drops of the holy water.
2. Light the charcoal tablet in a heatproof dish, and sprinkle a pinch of the incense on it. Purify the space with this incense, wafting the smoke with your hands.
3. Purify each member of the spellcasting circle with the smoke as well. (You may have to add another pinch of the incense.)
4. Have the members assemble in a circle. Anoint each member's forehead with the holy water.
5. Have everyone focus on the group as whole for a few minutes. Begin a low hum to gently raise the energy.
6. While the hum continues, pass the pillar candle and the burin around the circle. Have each member carve his or her name into the candle, wherever they please. As they do so, have them empower it with energy.
7. When all members of the circle have carved their names into the pillar candle, anoint it with holy water.
8. Face east. Hold the candle up and say:

Angel Raphael, bless this circle with your guidance.
Help us to do right for those in need, and to work for good.

9. Face south. Hold up the candle and say:

   Angel Michael, bless this circle with your passion and strength.
   Help us to defend those in need, and to protect ourselves and our loved
   ones.

10. Face west. Hold up the candle and say:

    Angel Gabriel, bless this circle with your love and serenity.
    Help us to bring light and love to those in need.

11. Face north. Hold up the candle and say:

    Angel Uriel, bless this circle with your stability.
    Help us to provide for those in need.

12. In the center of the circle, place the pillar candle in the bowl or on the saucer, and carefully pour holy water around the base. With the circle focusing energy on the candle, light the wick, saying:

    Behold, we summon the light of Spirit to guide this circle.

Allow everyone to gaze at the candle as it burns and flickers, opening their minds to visions and guidance.

This spell may be accompanied by soft music, which allows for the circle to judge how much time has passed and to end the spell when a certain piece of music draws to a close. You may wish to elect someone to decide on when to signal the end of the meditation.

You may choose to burn the candle all the way down (beware—this will take hours and hours and you'll have to keep an eye on it as it burns), or to snuff or pinch it out at the end of the meditation and keep it for the next guidance-seeking session.

Afterward, all members should note their impressions and messages in their spell journals. A discussion concerning these visions and ideas can take place immediately, or at a later agreed-upon time.

11

the art of magical substitution

How do you amend, edit, personalize, or transform a spell into something else? Many existing spells use ethically questionable techniques to create change. With the knowledge in this chapter, you can rewrite negative spells to reflect a positive approach, replace missing ingredients, and encourage creation in your life instead of destruction.

❦

SPELLS IN BOOKS

Everyone dreams of coming across a huge, dusty, leather-bound volume in a second-hand bookstore, with curling yellowed pages of browned script where someone has entered the secrets of power and enchantment painstakingly by hand. Interspersed with the incantations and potion recipes are sketches of herbs, charts of codes, and above all, pages and pages of spells with assured results.

It's just that: a dream. Humanity's tendency toward nostalgia and romance has created the myth of the grimoire. In today's modern society, we assume that something new hasn't been proven, and something old is outdated. We swing erratically from one extreme to the other, now demanding old proven spells, or wanting the latest book incorporating modern tools and easily available ingredients. It's human nature, of course. It goes along with wanting immediate, tangible results of spellcasting.

The myth of the grimoire encompasses a few misconceptions about spellcraft. First, a spell doesn't have to be old in order to be valid. A spell's validity matters to one person, and one person only, who in this case is you. Second, a spell doesn't have to be published in order to be valid, either. Spells in books exist for one reason only, and that's to instruct and inspire you, the reader. By now you know that a spell is a set of symbolic actions, which trigger change on an inner level. Words on the page aren't what make the magic happen; you're the essential ingredient, you and your emotion.

I can't count the people who have come to me asking for a spell, then looked at me scornfully and said, "Don't you have something easier?" They're equaled only by the people asking, "That's a spell? Come on, where are your *real* spells?" A spell recorded in a book, published or not, is a spell which has worked for at least the author, or which has been constructed as a teaching device.

In fact, that hefty yellowing tome you dream of finding on a dusty shelf is nothing more than someone's personal collection of notes and information collected over a long period of time. Makes you think twice about your spell records and lists of correspondences, doesn't it?

An existing spell does not have more validity than a spell you make up on your own. The only difference is that you might trust a spell in print more than a spell you develop, and that's simply because you assume that the author has more experience than you do. However, you are not the author, and the components with which you have a strong connection are likely to be different. You probably live in a different climate, so the plants and terrain around you are different. Certain ingredients might not be available where you live. And above all else, the author is not you, and has different needs and desires.

There's nothing wrong with using a spell that you find in a book. There are a few questions that you should ask yourself before you do so, however.

Is It Ethical?

What does this spell aim to do, and how? Does it comply with your own personal system of ethics? For example, there are lots of spellbooks out there telling you how to manipulate others, or to get revenge. However, they operate in a moral void. Just because a spell exists doesn't mean it's safe, or recommended. Chapter 4 discusses the ethics of spellcasting.

Does It Make Sense?

Take the time to sit down and read through the spell thoroughly. Don't just look at the title, see that it's for attracting money, and start picking up the ingredients. Never follow a spell blindly without thinking it through carefully. What does it ask you to do? What does it ask you to visualize? How does it ask you to raise energy? Now that you have a handle on how spells work, you can analyze spells and see where they fall apart or if they go nowhere.

How Is It Put Together?

While it's gratifying to authors to know that readers trust them, it's more important for you to be able to understand how the author crafted the spell. Go through the spell step-by-step to figure out why the author chose the particular materials and actions. This will help you understand the deeper symbolism behind the spell, as well as sharpen your own spellcrafting skills.

If it all makes sense, flows well, and everything is fine, if you're comfortable with the spell as it is, then cast it if you so desire. Keep good notes, though. Copy out the spell into your spell record sheet, making sure to write down where it came from, and who the original author was.

Make It Yours

If the spell appeals to you but you don't like it as is, or if something in those three steps sets off a warning bell in your head, then use it as a template for your own spell. Instead of just reading the spell right from the book and performing it as is, why not use it as the basis for a spell of your own? It's more creative, and you'll have a better chance of capturing a way of addressing your own need and changing your life the way you want it to be changed.

Let's walk through an example. Here's a sample spell that you might find in a glossy little spellbook in your bookstore.

Spell for Health and Wealth

Sick and tired of being sick and tired? This spell will energize you and your finances, so you won't have to work yourself to death!

Timing: Moon's first quarter; moon's second quarter; midday; moon in Taurus; hour of Venus; hour of the sun; or your personal power time

Supplies:

Small wooden box	3 vitamin C tablets
Handful fresh mint leaves	Pay stub

Steps:

1. Line the inside of the box with the fresh mint leaves. Put your pay stub inside, and the three vitamin C tablets on top.
2. Close the box and say:

   Enough! Enough!
   From now, my life's no longer tough!
   Money and time come my way,
   Health and joy at work and play.

3. Keep the box by your bedside table and rap it once with your knuckles when you go to bed every night, and when you get up every morning.

All right. Let's deconstruct this spell.

Is it ethical? Well, I'm working on myself, so I'm not interfering with anyone else's life, or manipulating someone else. At first glance the goal appears a bit simplistic; no one gets anything for nothing. Then again, it's not claiming that I'll never have to work again and that everything will be handed to me on a silver platter; it says that it's designed to energize my finances. If your money energy is flowing better, you don't have to work as much overtime to make ends meet, and you'll sleep better and worry less. I'm okay with that.

Does the spell make sense? It asks me to collect certain items, to assemble them in a particular order, to speak certain words, then to keep them in a particular place where I'll see them when I wake up and when

I go to sleep. Seeing them will remind myself of the spell and the decision to improve my health and financial energy. I can understand how that would help keep the energy flowing. All the items are accounted for in the instructions. No new items are asked for in the instructions that weren't listed in the supply list.

How is it put together? Let's see: We have mint leaves, vitamin C tablets, a box, and a pay stub. Mint is associated with money, alertness, mental activity, healing, and action. Vitamin C tablets I definitely associate with healing, but I also associate them with prevention of illness. The box is a standard container to hold spell components. Made of wood, it has more energy than, say, a glass jar or a plastic container. The words state that I will no longer accept life as it is, and outlines concepts I wish to invite into my life: money, time, joy, and health. The pay stub represents my take-home pay, and likely has my total number of hours worked for that period on it, so it encompasses the reality I wish to change.

Now that I understand why the spell has been crafted the way it has, I would be comfortable with using this spell as it is. However, I would make certain decisions to code it to my particular use. For example, I would use fresh spearmint, because I find it a friendlier and less harsh herb than peppermint. I would paint the wooden box in shades of green, and I'd make sure not to paint it a solid color: I'd paint vines, which symbolize plenty and growth, or I'd paint swirls, to indicate action and movement. I'd paint the inside green too. I might add a bloodstone, which is mostly green, so it supports the idea of money, and it's also associated with protecting health. I'd choose to use chewable vitamin C tablets, because I associate them with childhood, when there was more time to play, and the idea of money worried me less. I'd certainly empower all my materials before beginning the spell. A pay stub would be difficult, as I'm a freelance writer and teacher and I rarely see one; so instead I'll make a short list of all the jobs I've worked in the past month, and the corresponding pay for each of them, and use that in place of the pay stub. I'd keep it in the kitchen, because I don't have a table by my bedside, and every morning when I get up to make my tea I'd knock the box, and knock it last thing at night when I feed my cats before bed. I'd also repeat the charm aloud again each time I knocked the box.

See? I didn't let the fact that I don't have a pay stub stop me from using the spell; I improvised. I deliberately chose to use spearmint instead of peppermint, because I've discovered over time and through experimentation that my personal energy responds better to spearmint.

Once you understand the reason behind everything, you can also change something if it doesn't suit you. Perhaps you're deathly allergic to oranges, so vitamin C tablets aren't a good symbol of health for you. Choose something different instead, something that has more meaning for you. For example, if a spell calls on Aphrodite as the goddess of love, and you're uncomfortable with calling on a deity you don't work with (or don't believe in), then don't dismiss the spell out of hand; this is your opportunity to tweak the spell to fit your personal system. Perhaps you're open to working with angels. If so, read up on what angels are associated with love, and take notes to expand your personal system of correspondences for future reference. Of the four archangels, Raphael is often associated with love and joy, so you might choose to invoke Raphael instead of Aphrodite. You might have to tweak the words a bit, too. If Aphrodite was invoked as "Blessed Aphrodite of the girdle," you might perhaps call upon Raphael as "Blessed Raphael, watcher over the spirits of men." Or, with a little more research, you might discover that the angel Anael is associated with the planet Venus, which in turn is associated with romantic love, and choose to invoke Anael instead.

The key to adjusting spells is to replace ingredients or energies that are associated with the same intent.

Reformatting Spells

Some spells are downright manipulative, and don't mesh with your ethical system. There's no need to go on a crusade about how people are misusing spellcraft; remember, energy is neutral, and your goal and intent are what make the spell a force for positive or negative change.

Despite the less than flattering light in which spellcraft has been depicted over the years, most people aren't out to control others or gain power. They just want to be happier, and have more positive energy in their lives. Every once in a while, though, you'll come across a spell that seeks to control others in order for the spellcaster to have his or her way.

How can you rescue a spell like this and turn it into a spell for positive change instead of a method of compelling others to do your will?

Here's an example. We'll deconstruct it as we did the previous spell for health and wealth.

Spell to Evict a Neighbor

Neighbor making too much noise, or making your life wretched by complaining about you? Evict them with this spell!

Timing: Moon's third quarter; sunset; autumn; Saturday; hour of Saturn; Wednesday; hour of Mercury; moon in Gemini; or your personal power time

Supplies:
Pinch chili powder
Pinch black pepper
Pinch paprika
Pinch mustard seed
Envelope or flyer with the person's name and address on it

Steps:
1. Crush the herbs together, visualizing the neighbor moving out.
2. Sprinkle one pinch of the herbs on the piece of mail.
3. Say:

   [Person's full name], I send you far away
   I take away your home
   I take away your comfort
   You have no place
   Be alone in this world
   By my word
   It is done!

4. Fold the mail with the herbs still inside it, and bury it outside the neighbor's front doorstep at midnight on a Saturday.
5. Sprinkle the rest of the herbs on the neighbor's front door handle and on their front doorstep.

Is this an ethical spell? Right away we know that it's not completely ethical, because it seeks to change someone else's life simply because we don't like them.

Does it make sense? If you look up correspondences for the ingredients, yes, they're all about inciting action. The general rule is that if it's hot, then active energy is associated with it. If you want someone to move, using ingredients like this makes sense. The use of mail with the current address and name also makes sense: they're associated directly with this individual at this address. Burying the mail and herbs keeps it in a location near the target without them knowing, and sprinkling the rest on the front doorstep means that everyone crossing it will be affected by the active energy. The door handle is touched by everyone who walk into the house.

How is it put together? It calls for blending certain herbs chosen for the active and aggressive correspondences, saying certain words, then burying part of the components near the neighbor's home so that it's in the very physical location, and applying the rest directly to their door to make sure they will encounter it.

Now that we've looked at the spell, and we know how and why it's assembled the way it is, what can you do to turn this into an ethical spell you feel comfortable using?

My first instinct would be to change the thrust of the spell from "evicting a neighbor" to "helping a neighbor move on to a better home." You might not want to do them any favors, but it gets the job done with a more positive spin. Remember, if you twitch the energy web with a heavy hand, you might not like the resulting vibrations. It's up to you to decide if you have the right to do this at all, and if you are willing to accept the consequences.

The herbs used are not unusual, but I might add a pinch of brown sugar to help make sure the move is something they want to do, so they won't fight it. I wouldn't steal their mail; not only is it a federal offense, I certainly wouldn't compromise the potential success of my spell by engaging in criminal activity. Instead, I'd draw a picture of the neighbor's house and write her name and address on it.

I'd change the words to something like,

You are called elsewhere, for another purpose. Go freely, to a better home.

It accomplishes a similar purpose, but doesn't stomp all over the ethical red flags that such spells trigger. Granted, you're still interfering in someone else's life, so you had better be sure about what you're doing, and why, and be willing to accept the consequences. Who knows what sort of new neighbors you'll get? You might choose to do a spell to improve your relations with this neighbor, which focuses the spell on you instead of them. As made clear in Chapter 4, it is important to consider all available options. Just because a particular spell would solve the problem doesn't mean it's the correct goal to work for.

The Real versus the Synthetic

In an earlier chapter I discussed how the further removed from nature a substance or object is, the weaker its energy. How does this apply to synthetic substances?

I used polyester as an example of a cloth with low energy, as it's manmade. Generally, if you have a choice, go with cotton, silk, or wool, as they're made from natural substances (plants, worms, and sheep, respectively; if you're vegan or have issues with using animal products in your spellwork, then this might affect your decision). However, as a spellcaster, you also know that there is more to a piece of cloth than the substance from which it's woven. The color is important, too. If you have a scrap of blue cotton, and a scrap of red polyester, you have to decide what is more important to the spell: the color, or the material used to make the fabric.

If a spell calls for an oil, then you'll probably have two choices: an essential oil, or a synthetic oil, which might be called a fragrance oil or a perfume oil. Synthetics are much less expensive, and they are often safe to use undiluted. However, they don't carry the same energy that an essential oil does, because they're far removed from natural sources. I used synthetics for years, and sometimes still do, and my spellcraft didn't suffer in the least. I must admit, however, that once I began using essential oils, I became a convert. The energy is clearer and brighter.

There are, of course, some substances which are no longer available or which are unethical to use in natural form, so you will have to use synthetics instead. Civet is one such component, as it was originally extracted from cats. Musk is another substance that is only used in synthetic form, as it is extracted from deer. Rare and expensive oils such as rose and jasmine are difficult to find, so a synthetic substitute is often used. The solution in cases such as this, however, is to make your own, which is easy and enjoyable. See below to learn more about obtaining supplies.

Spellcraft is an art. Sometimes you can spellcraft completely by intuition. Sometimes when you're baking you realize that you're out of cinnamon, so you think about what else is in the batter, and what the cookies are ultimately supposed to taste like. With that information, you can select another spice from the rack that will complement and enhance the flavor. Substituting ingredients in spellcraft functions on a similar principle. When you realize that you're missing an ingredient, think about the end result of the spell, think about the other ingredients and components you're using, and take a look at what else you have on hand. What has similar energy to the missing ingredient? What will complement the other components, and enhance the final outcome of the spell?

Sometimes, you can leave the missing ingredient out; it's not essential. (It's like the pinch of salt that every recipe calls for: it isn't necessary, but it somehow brings out the flavor of every other ingredient.) In order to ascertain whether or not the missing component is crucial, however, you have to do a bit of research. Examine the spell as above, and figure out what the ingredient's magical purpose is. If there are other components that serve this purpose, you're probably safe. If you're not sure, or if the missing ingredient carries another correspondence further enhancing the spell, find a replacement. If you can't find a replacement which carries the corresponding energies of both the primary and the secondary enhancing energy, then you have a choice: replace the single component with two components, or if there are other components which carry one of those correspondences, replace the missing ingredient with one that carries the missing energy.

And, of course, invaluable to developing your skills at magical substitution is your ever-expanding set of notes, records, and journals. Every time you substitute something, write it down for reference in order to have it at your fingertips. If it doesn't work, don't erase it; take note that you tried it and that it doesn't have the effect you sought. That way you won't waste time including it in other spells.

Component Forms

If a spell calls for a component in the form of a dried herb, and you have the oil, can you substitute it?

It depends. If the spell asks for the herb in order to make an herbal sachet or incense, then no; you'll need to find another dried herb carrying a similar energy. If you have a fresh herb when the spell asks for dried, then again, look at how it's being used. If you absolutely require the dried herb, spread some brown paper (cut a piece from a grocery bag) on a clean baking sheet, then spread your fresh herb out on it in a single layer. Slide it into the oven on very low heat (no higher than 100 degrees Fahrenheit), and check the herb often; you're not trying to bake them, just dry them out. The length of time to dry them will depend on the thickness of the herb. It usually takes between 1–2 hours to dry an herb. I don't recommend microwaving them, although other practitioners assure me it works well; I feel the energy changes in some sort of indescribable sense, although the technique might work for you. In *Bud, Blossom, & Leaf,* Dorothy Morrison recommends placing a layer of fresh herb leaves between two pieces of paper towel, and microwaving at high power for about forty-five seconds. If the herbs are crisp and crumble when touched, they're ready. If not, microwave them for a bit longer, and check at twenty-second intervals.

If you have dried herbs, and the spell calls for fresh, take a good look and try to figure out why fresh herbs are indicated. Perhaps the slow drying process is part of the spell. As an herb dries, it becomes more potent. If you're making a potion and the spell calls for fresh, you can often get away with substituting dry simply by using less, or by infusing them in some boiling water to reconstitute them. If the spell calls for fresh herbs and you have dried herbs plus some of the oil, then use the dry plus a drop or two of the oil to rev it up. *Never, never use oil if the mix is to be ingested!*

Obtaining Supplies

Not everyone has access to a metaphysical or occult shop, but there are plenty of other places you can pick up supplies for spellcrafting. It may come as a surprise or disappointment to some, but supplies purchased from an occult shop are no more or less powerful than those supplied anywhere else. It's fun to buy ingredients from people who understand what you are doing and who cast spells themselves, but it isn't essential.

Before you go anywhere else, check your local supermarket for herbs and spices. The cloves you buy in the grocery store work just as well as those sold in the occult shop, and they're likely to be cheaper, too. Supermarkets often sell items such as candles and flowers, too.

Natural food stores often sell herbs in bulk, and can often provide rare herbs; alternative health shops and even some drugstores sell essential oils. You can find paints, papers, clay, and other items at art supply shops. It might be a bit more of a challenge to find stones. If you don't have a lapidary shop in your city, try the occult store. When all else fails, there are dozens of excellent shops online. My personal favorite is The Magical Blend, which sells and ships internationally through their Web site at *www.themagicalblend.com*.

What do you do if you find what you're looking for, but it's too expensive? Your instinct might be to buy it, but take a moment to think about the ingredient. Can you use it in some other form? For example, rose essential oil is phenomenally expensive. Perhaps you could use fresh or dried rose petals instead. If a spell calls for dried orange peel, try adding a couple of drops of orange juice instead.

Alternatively, you can make your own oils or dry your own peels. To make a mild rose oil, find a glass jar with a lid. Fill it with fresh rose petals, any color. Don't pack them too loosely, but don't cram them in tightly, either. Then pour a light oil such as jojoba or olive oil over the petals, filling the jar. Fasten the lid tightly and leave it on a windowsill for a week, shaking it daily. When the week is up, open the jar and strain the oil through cheesecloth, wringing the petals out well. Put more fresh petals in the jar and pour the infused oil back in over them. Close the jar tightly again and leave it in the sun for a week, shaking daily. Continue this until the oil carries a delicate rose scent.

Oils that you make yourself often have a soft scent. Any rose oil you find on the market that's inexpensive and smells strongly of sweet rose is a synthetic oil. Any oil priced at under one hundred dollars that claims to be one hundred percent pure rose oil is also misleading you; expensive oils such as rose and jasmine are sold as *absolutes*, or a blend made of nine percent true oil and ninety-one percent base oil. If you use essential oils, you should dilute them in a base or carrier oil anyway; not only does it make them much safer to use, but they last longer.

To dry peels, slice the peel into strips about a quarter inch wide, and spread them out on a baking sheet. Heat them in a slow oven, at about 150 degrees Fahrenheit, and check on them frequently. You're not trying to bake them; you're trying to evaporate the water within them.

Collecting and drying your own herbs can also be a satisfying way to enhance your spellcraft. You can harvest them at a time of your choice, such as during the waxing or waning moon, at sunrise or midnight, on a certain day of the week, and so forth, which will add to the power of the correspondence you're aiming for. Making or harvesting your own components also means you have control over how much you have at any given time. When you buy ingredients, you often buy much more than you need, and the excess sits in a jar in a cupboard until you finally throw it out (as you should—if you use herbs in cooking or in teas to drink, a year is the limit; three years is the ultimate expiration date if you use them in spells).

Being in touch with your components from the ground up, so to speak, gives you a much deeper knowledge of their energy, which is a great advantage when you come to handle those energies later on in spellcraft.

Do I Really Need All This Stuff?

No, of course not. You know that you could sit down, close your eyes, and meditate on your goal, using nothing but your own energy to accomplish your goal. Sometimes you won't have the time, or the resources, or the inclination to use ingredients. Components and supplies are props, aids to your concentration, and an alternate source of energy to help power your spell. They can help create the right mental and emotional atmosphere. And face it, they're fun.

Ultimately, however, if you're missing something from a supply list, and you can't replace it, don't panic. In the end, your intent, your visualization, and your goal count for more than anything else. The rest of it is just icing on the metaphysical cake.

12

spells to inspire

Inspiration can help you develop your own spells for positive change. This chapter offers you a variety of spells designed for different situations to practice with, use as templates, and modify for your own use. Explore these spells for health, business, finance, protection, relationships, creativity, transformation, and more.

⁓

This chapter contains spells for you to attempt and to study. Feel free to tweak them to suit yourself once you've studied them and you fully understand what each element is for.

The times indicated for each spell are scheduling suggestions only. As elsewhere in this book, I've included a variety of times in order for you to see that scheduling can indeed be flexible, and suggested some variations to illustrate how flexible spellcrafting can be.

Increase Your Attractiveness

This is a terrific spell to use before you go out on a date. You can use this spell to enhance only your physical beauty, or to enhance your communication skills with a loved one as well.

Timing: moon's second quarter; first days of moon's third quarter; Friday; noon; hour of Venus; moon in Libra; or your personal power time

Supplies:
1 ripe strawberry
Small bowl or saucer
Fork

Steps:
1. Empower the strawberry for attraction.
2. In a small bowl or saucer, mash the strawberry gently with the fork while visualizing people looking twice at you, complimenting you on your appearance, approaching you and chatting.
3. Carefully anoint your lips with the strawberry juice. Say:

   The words I speak, the smiles I smile,
   Be made sweet.
   As bee to flower,
   As honey to fly,
   Draw near to me.

4. Eat the crushed strawberry sensually, enjoying the feeling of the pulp on your tongue, the seeds between your teeth, and the sweetness of the juice. Reserve the remaining juice to anoint your lips again before you go out or meet with your partner.

Self-Confidence Talisman Bag

Carrying a physical reminder of a spell we've cast to shore up our self-confidence can enhance the spell's effects. Create a powerful talisman bag with the following spell.

Timing: moon's third quarter; Sunday; noon; hour of the sun; moon in the sign of Leo; moon in the sign of Aries; moon in the sign of Taurus

SPELLS to INSPIRE

201

Supplies:
4 x 4 inch square of fabric in a color you associate with confidence and strength
Narrow white ribbon, at least six inches
Small rose quartz
Pinch eyebright herb
Pinch cinnamon (or a small piece of cinnamon stick)
Drop of orange oil

Steps:
1. Empower your supplies and charge them with self-confidence.
2. Anoint the rose quartz with the orange oil, visualizing happiness and confidence surrounding your heart.
3. Place the stone in the center of the fabric square.
4. Sprinkle the pinch of eyebright over the anointed stone, then sprinkle the cinnamon over it, saying:

   Clear vision of a strong heart:
   I am truth, I am strength, I am success.

5. Gather up the corners of the fabric square to create a small pouch with the stone and herbs at the center. Tie the white ribbon around the gathered fabric to secure it. Tie five knots in the ribbon, visualizing confidence being sealed into the talisman with each knot.
6. Hold the sachet between your hands and channel positive, confident energy and thoughts into it. Once the talisman is empowered, carry it with you.

Variations: Cast this spell during a waning moon, or on Saturday, or during the hour of Saturn to banish self-doubt instead.

Cleanse Your Aura

Negative energy collects in your aura simply by interacting with other energies in your everyday life. Give yourself or someone else a refreshing aura cleansing with this spell.

Timing: full moon

Supplies:
Spoonful vervain
Pulp from one lemon
3 crushed cloves

9 fresh white rose petals
Small glass bowl

Steps:

1. Empower supplies for cleansing.
2. Combine the components in the glass bowl. Sit or stand, and hold the bowl up. Say:

   Gracious Luna, queen of the night sky,
   Bless this blend with your serenity and love.
   Grant me harmony and balance.

3. Visualize the light of the moon filling the bowl and overflowing, flowing down your arms and into your heart and spirit.
4. Slowly and carefully move the bowl up and down over the surface of your body, approximately one to three inches above your skin. Visualize the blend in the bowl erasing a dull coating on your body, leaving behind fresh glowing energy. Don't forget to visualize the areas behind your back, your head, and the soles of your feet.
5. When you are finished, take the blend outside and bury it.

Variations: Add a small clear quartz to the blend to enhance the potency of the spell.

Milk of Human Kindness Spell

This is a spell to give energy back to the earth. It's a wonderfully balancing spell, and can be done once a month, or whenever you have had a wish granted or a particularly important spell succeed. Perform this spell whenever you are grateful for something, or in thanks for a successful spell. You may sit under a tree to meditate before or after the libation, if you like.

Timing: Monday; Thursday; hour of the moon; hour of Jupiter; dawn; sunset; midnight; moon in the sign of Pisces

Supplies:

1 cup milk	Pinch lavender
1 teaspoon honey	Small moonstone

Steps:

1. Empower all supplies for peace and gratitude.
2. In a small pot, warm the milk, the honey, and the lavender over low heat until the honey has dissolved. Remove from the heat and pour into a jar.
3. Touch the moonstone to your forehead, to your lips, then to your heart, and add the stone gently to the liquid.

4. Dip your finger into the warm milk, touch your heart with it, then dip it back into the liquid. Visualize the peace and gratitude in your heart being transferred to the milk.
5. Allow the milk to cool slightly. Cap the jar and carry it outside to a tree near your home, or a tree that is special to you.
6. Bow to the tree, uncap the jar, and pour the milk and the stone out at the base of the tree on the roots, saying:

   I give to the earth
   As the earth gives to me.
   Bless all those who live in this place.

7. Bow again to the tree, and return home.

Spell for Romance

This spell increases your sparkle in an intimate situation.

Timing: Friday; hour of Venus; moon's first quarter; moon's second quarter; dawn; sunset; moon in Libra

Supplies:
1 glass champagne
3 drops rose water

Steps:
1. Empower components for romance.
2. Add the first drop of rose water to the glass of champagne, saying:

   I dazzle.

3. Add the second drop of rose water to the glass of champagne, saying,

   I sparkle.

4. Add the third and final drop of rose water to the glass of champagne, saying,

   Romance me!

5. Swirl the champagne in the glass gently to blend the rose water. Drink the champagne, visualizing exactly how you wish to be attractive, and what sort of night you'd like to experience. Remember not to visualize anyone specifically, or this spell becomes manipulative.

Variations: Float an empowered fresh red rose petal on the surface of the champagne. Modify the amount of ingredients to serve two people, and drink it with your partner. Serve empowered strawberries to further enhance the atmosphere for love. Add a whole empowered clove to each glass to add spice to the experience. For a nonalcoholic version, use sparkling water, but be sure to still serve it in champagne flutes or elegant wine glasses.

Spell for Protection

Who doesn't need extra protection? Feeling safe and secure is one of our basic needs. Carry this spell bottle with you for added protection in your daily life.

Timing: Sunday; Tuesday; Thursday; noon; moon's third quarter; hour of the sun; hour of Mars; hour of Jupiter; whenever necessary; your personal power time

Supplies:

Small vial or bottle with a tight sealing lid   Pinch salt
Olive oil (enough to fill the bottle)   Small hematite stone
3 cloves

Steps:
1. Empower the components for your protection.
2. Place the cloves in the bottle one by one, visualizing the bottle filling with green light.
3. Add the hematite, visualizing the silver color of the stone weaving and swirling through the green light.
4. Add the salt, and visualize the silver and green light growing brighter.
5. Carefully pour the olive oil into the bottle over the contents, and fill it almost to the brim.
6. Cap the bottle tightly. Shake it gently to further blend the ingredients.
7. Hold the bottle between your hands and channel the idea of protection into it.
8. Carry the bottle with you in a pocket when you are in need of protection. The bottle is fully active, but stir it when you feel the need for added strength. Shake it gently and visualize the silver and green energy swirling in the bottle to surround you, defending you from harm.

Variations: You can make this bottle and leave it in a place you wish to be defended, or bury it outside your door. If you're concerned about the oil leaking while you carry it, seal the bottle in a Ziplock bag; or, fill the bottle with more cloves and salt, and add only three drops of olive oil before sealing it.

SPELLS TO INSPIRE

205

Refreshing Wealth

Mint is traditionally associated with prosperity, and lemon is associated with cleansing. Use them together for a powerful spell to refresh your finances.

Timing: Thursday; Friday; hour of Venus; hour of Jupiter; moon in Taurus; moon in Capricorn; moon's second quarter; first days of moon's third quarter; your personal power time

Supplies:

Handful fresh mint leaves	Small aventurine
3 peppercorns	Small tiger's eye
3 bay leaves	1 lemon

Steps:
1. Empower the components for wealth.
2. Slice the lemon into thin slices and dry them in the oven at a low temperature.
3. Sprinkle the mint leaves over the bottom of a glass bowl. Lay the dry lemon slices over it. Place the three bay leaves on top of the lemons. In the center, place the three peppercorns. Rest the aventurine and the tiger's eye over the peppercorns.
4. Hold your hands over the bowl and close your eyes. Empower the spell bowl for wealth. Place it in the physical or social center of your home.

Variations: Replace the peppercorns with ground pepper, and sprinkle it over the bowl's contents. Carry the aventurine and the tiger's eye stones with you every day, and return them to the bowl at night for further charging. Use an orange instead of a lemon, or use both.

Mint Melody

This is a good spell for those gloomy days when you're down for no apparent reason.

Timing: Sunday; Friday; hour of the sun; hour of Venus; moon's first quarter; moon's second quarter; or whenever necessary

Supplies:
Fresh mint leaves (any kind of mint will do, but it must be fresh)
Honey (any kind)
Boiling water

Steps:

1. Bruise the fresh mint leaves in a glass with the back of a spoon (this is also called muddling).
2. Pour boiling water over them.
3. Add a touch of honey.
4. Allow this potion to sit in the sun for at least three hours.
5. Strain and drink, while visualizing joy and happiness. Allow your mood to change.

Variations: Use peppermint, spearmint, or a flavored mint to fine-tune your mood. (Yes, the wonderful world of agriculture has bred flavors into mint plants. Chocolate mint, apple mint, and orange mint all have slightly different energies, for example. Look for different varieties at your local nursery or garden center and experiment.) This is also a great potion for mental activity, or to drink hot in mid-winter. To create a hot version, strain the potion into a coffee mug after the potion has rested for three hours, and heat it up in the microwave. Add a drop or two of lemon juice to add joy to your heart.

Spell to Release Sorrow

Exercise is often recommended to help fight depression, while flying a kite helps your heart remember the more carefree days of childhood.

Timing: moon's fourth quarter; sunset; midnight; Monday; Friday; hour of the moon; hour of Venus; or your personal power time

Supplies:
Kite (check your dollar store—this is a one-time use)
Kite string

Steps:

1. Empower the kite with your sorrow.
2. Take the kite to an open area.
3. Feel the wind flow around you. Feel the sorrow in your heart, and channel it down your arms into the kite.
4. Allow the wind to catch the kite and lift it up into the air. If you've never flown a kite before, abandon yourself to the experience. It takes focus, and intuition, and patience—just as healing grief does.
5. As you fly the kite, visualize the wind stroking the kite and lifting your sorrow gently away.

6. Fly the kite for as long as you choose. When you are done, reel it in and cleanse it of any residual energy by your preferred method, then take it to your nearest Goodwill or Salvation Army shop, or donate it to a children's group.

Variations: If kite-flying appeals to you, you might want to invest in a sturdier kite which you can reuse. Empower as per the directions, and when you fly it, visualize the sorrow being transformed by the wind into happiness. Fly it for as long as it takes for the transformation to be complete.

Color Spell for Reinterpreting Your Life

This spell is useful when you know you want your life to get better, but you can't put your finger on precisely as to why or how.

Timing: moon's first quarter; moon's second quarter; dawn; noon; moon in the sign of Aries; moon in the sign of Virgo; moon in the sign of Pisces; Monday; hour of the moon; or your personal power time

Supplies:
1 piece of white paper, 8 x 10 inches
1 new box of crayons (there must be at least eight colors in the box)

Steps:
1. Empower your supplies for positive change.
2. Draw a big circle on the paper. This circle represents your life.
3. Look at the colors in the new box of crayons and compare them to your own personal color correspondences. (See Chapter 6 for an exercise on creating your own color correspondences.)
4. Visualize the ideal balance of emotions, ideals, and energies in your life. Divide the circle into pie-slice shapes, the size of each corresponding to one of the emotions, ideals, or energies.
5. Color in each slice of the life chart with the appropriate color, visualizing your life rebalancing to reflect it. For example, if you associate stress with the color red, in your new life it would color a slice equal to the slice you associate with relaxation, which you might color blue. Empower each slice with the associated energy as you color.
6. Put your spell up on the fridge with magnets. Each time you go to open the fridge, pause and look at it, and reaffirm your commitment to the ideal balance of energy in your life.

When you color the slices, don't be concerned about staying in the lines. Life isn't neatly compartmentalized. It's messy. Emotion cannot be contained. Recognize that, accept it, and embrace it. You can further decorate your color chart with stickers, glitter, cut-out photos, words, or whatever you like to personalize it. It's your life; play with it and have fun!

Spell for Comfort

Sometimes the world just gets to be too much for you, and you need a time-out.

Timing: Monday; hour of the moon; moon's third quarter; moon in the sign of Cancer; sunset; your personal power time; or whenever necessary

Supplies:
1 new bath towel in the color you associate with comfort and reassurance
Heating pad

Steps:
1. Empower the towel with comfort.
2. Fold the towel around a heating pad set on low.
3. Have a bath.
4. When you get out, unfold the towel from around the heating pad, and wrap it around yourself. Absorb the warmth and comfort.

Variations: Add comforting stuff to the bath such as bubbles, salts, oils. Bring a glass of wine or a cup of tea into the bath with you. Light candles in colors which relax and reassure you. You can also use the towel without taking a bath. Whenever you need reassurance and affection, wrap it around your shoulders and absorb the energy.

Spell for Creative Energy

Search through your correspondences for angels or deities associated with creativity. Use one to represent your creative catalyst.

Timing: Monday; Sunday; Wednesday; Tuesday; Thursday; hour of the sun; hour of the moon; hour of Mercury; hour of Mars; hour of Jupiter; moon's first quarter; moon's second quarter; dawn; noon; your personal power time

Supplies:
Small statue, icon, or stone

Steps:

1. Empower the item with creativity.
2. Hold it in your hands, visualizing creative activity. Say:

   Spirits of Air, fill me with inspiration.
   Spirits of Fire, fill me with passion.
   Spirits of Water, fill me with transformation.
   Spirits of Earth, fill me with patience.

3. Place the item near your workspace. When you feel the need for a creative boost, touch the object and repeat the charm.

Simple Spell for Encouraging Good

This simple spell helps you recognize the areas in your life which are rich and fulfilled. If we perceive ourselves as in need, we will lack things. By counting blessings and being grateful, you attract more of the same. The result is positive energy flowing through your life.

Timing: Sunday; Monday; Thursday; Friday; hour of the sun; hour of the moon; hour of Jupiter; hour of Venus; moon's second quarter; noon; moon in the sign of Taurus; or your personal power time

Supplies:
Recipe card and a pen

Steps:

1. Empower the recipe card with abundance.
2. Write "thank you" on it.
3. Put it where you will see it often, such as on your refrigerator, on the frame of your mirror, pinned to the inside of your front door. Each time you see it, pause and say, "Thank you for [name a blessing]."

Say thanks for the little things. Lots of people think that it's only the big things which count. We often forget that the big things are made up of the little things. Say thanks for the song that you heard on the radio which made you remember a special day from your childhood. Say thanks for the pouring rain which is nourishing your garden. Say thanks for the crossing guard who works near your child's school.

Spell to Release Perfection

Yes, you read that right. By clinging to the belief that you have to be perfect, you automatically fall short. Release perfection and appreciate the freedom!

Timing: moon's third quarter; moon's fourth quarter; sunset; midnight; Monday; Friday; Saturday; hour of the moon; hour of Venus; hour of Saturn; or your personal power time

Supplies:
Piece of vegetable parchment and a pen

Steps:
1. Design an official-looking certificate. On it, write the following:

   I hereby authorize [your name] to be imperfect.

2. Sign your name.
3. Keep the certificate somewhere safe. Take it out and look at it when you feel guilty of not being a superhero in your daily life.

Ongoing Affirmation

Although saying an affirmation aloud creates change over time, writing it out brings it into the physical realm in a different way.

Timing: moon's second quarter; dawn; noon; your personal power time

Supplies:
Recipe card and a pen

Steps:
1. Empower the recipe card with the energy associated with your affirmation.
2. Write your affirmation out on the card.
3. Put it up on your fridge, slide it into the frame of your mirror, pin it next to your computer—wherever it will be seen often, or where it will reinforce the object of your affirmation. For example, if your affirmation is designed to reflect a lower ideal weight, put it on the refrigerator door, or tape it to your scales.
4. Each time you see it, pause, and repeat the affirmation with awareness and intent while visualizing your objective.

Spell to Release Anger

In order to release something, you must first acknowledge it.

Timing: Saturday; Tuesday; hour of Saturn; hour of Mars; sunset; midnight; moon's third quarter; moon's fourth quarter; or your personal power time

Supplies:
Sheet of paper and a pen

Steps:
1. Write a letter to the person with whom (or the situation with which) you are enraged, furious, or infuriated. Use profanity, excess exclamation points, capital letters, and bad grammar. Tell them (or it) exactly what you think of them, of their actions, of how it makes you feel.
2. When you are done, reread your letter. Allow yourself to feel as emotional as you like.
3. Take three deep breaths and exhale all your tension and stress.
4. At the bottom of your letter, write *I release my anger. You no longer hold any power over me.*
5. Burn the letter in a fireproof container or fireplace.

Variations: Adapt this spell to celebrate your appreciation of someone, or to say thank you for a situation in your life. Perform it on a Monday, Sunday, or Wednesday, in the hour of the moon, in the hour of the sun, or the hour of Mercury. Rephrase the final sentences to read *I send you my joy (or thanks). May the universe bless you.* You may burn this letter of appreciation, or address and mail it if it has been written to a person. You don't have to sign it.

Spell to Protect a Home

This spell uses modern technology to protect your home and possessions in a unique way.

Timing: Monday; Sunday; Thursday; moon's first quarter; moon's second quarter; hour of the sun; hour of the moon; hour of Jupiter; noon; your personal power time

Supplies:
Computer disk (3.5 inch or a CD-RW)
Computer
Image of your house (scan a photograph or use an already existing
   electronic image)

Steps:

1. Empower supplies with protection.
2. Save the image of the house to the disk.
3. Visualize a white light surrounding the entire home.
4. Remove the disk and keep it in a safe deposit box off the site of the house.
5. As long as the disk is safe, your house will be safe. Update this enchanted computer disk regularly; once per season is a good idea. Erase the old image before uploading the new image.

Variations: This spell can be applied to anything you wish to keep safe, such as valuables. Of course, this spell enhances work you do in the physical world, so be sure to lock your doors, engage your alarm system, and replace the batteries in your smoke and heat detectors regularly.

Spell to Heal a Wound or Illness

This is a more complex spell, which creates a focus for the ill individual, which can be reused for further healing and positive spellwork. Remember to obtain the permission of the ill individual before you perform this spell.

Timing: Monday; Sunday; Wednesday; hour of the sun; hour of the moon; hour of Mercury; morning; noon; moon's second quarter; moon's third quarter; your personal power time

Supplies:
1 square foot plain cotton cloth (use white, or choose the color to match the skin color of the individual requiring healing)
Yarn or doll hair (match to the hair color of the individual)
Needle and thread to match the cloth
Pins
Scissors
Cotton fiberfill or batting to stuff the poppet
Various herbs corresponding to illness or wound (comfrey is good)
Small piece of vegetable parchment
Pencil or colored chalk; pen; colored markers; embroidery thread
Cloth in a color you associate with healing

Steps:

1. Empower supplies with healing energy.
2. Fold the cloth in half and pin it together. With the pencil or the colored chalk, trace a basic human shape on the top layer of the cloth. Don't make it too small; use as much space as you can on the cloth.

3. Cut the human shape out, cutting through both layers of cloth at the same time. You will have two flat human shapes.
4. Match the edges and pin the two shapes together. Sew them together with a small running stitch. Leave one side of the body open between the hip and the arm.
5. Stuff the poppet gently with the cotton batting or fiberfill. Pin the hole shut temporarily.
6. With the markers or embroidery thread, personalize the poppet to look like the individual who will be healed. Add yarn for hair, or sew on the doll hair and style it to match the individual's hairstyle. Add any physical markings such as birthmarks or tattoos.
7. Write the person's full name and birthdate on the slip of paper, and fold it up. Unpin the hole and tuck the folded paper inside doll. Pin it shut again.
8. Hold the doll in your hands and look it in the eyes. State aloud the name of who it is with confidence and awareness. For example: "You are Lorraine Pearson."
9. Visualize the person whole and well. Unpin the hole, and as you visualize, gather up pinches of the herbs you have selected to correspond with healing the illness or wound, and tuck them into the doll.
10. Sew the hole up, saying:

Needle and thread, blood red,
Knit bone to bone,
Flesh to flesh,
Cell to cell.
[Name], you are well.

11. Hold the poppet in your hands and hum a single note. As you hum, visualize healing energy flowing down your arms and into the doll.
12. When you feel as if the doll holds as much energy as it can handle for the moment, wrap it gently in cloth of a color you associate with healing (green or blue is good, or white), and keep it in a safe place.
13. You may repeat the healing hum once a day if the individual requires it.
14. When the person has recovered and is well again, thank the doll for its help. Then hold it in your hands and look it in the eyes, and state with confidence and awareness: "This is no longer [name]."
15. Reverently disassemble the doll and dispose of it. You may bury the cloth and cotton filling, so long as you are certain that they are natural materials.

Variations: You can further strengthen the connection between the doll and the individual who requires healing by including a *taglock*, or something connected to them, such as a bit of hair, a piece of jewelry, a scrap of material from a piece of clothing, and so forth. If the individual is chronically ill, do not destroy the doll, but keep it as a focus for ongoing healing work. You may ask if they would allow you to leave it with them for a day or overnight in order to strengthen the connection.

Some practitioners make a doll of themselves as a focus for their own magic. If you do this, you may sever the connection at any time by stating your intention to do so and undoing the doll, as above. Other practitioners choose to be buried with their dolls. Do not shut the doll away in the back of a drawer or a closet and forget about it, as the doll is connected to the individual it represents; keep it loosely wrapped in a place where it will be safe and undisturbed but also not forgotten.

Amulet to Enhance a Quality

For this spell, you will need to consider and choose one animal whose corresponding qualities you wish to emulate (for example, an owl for wisdom, a rabbit for fertility).

Timing: This depends on the quality you desire; in general, moon's second quarter; morning; or your personal power time

Supplies:
1 candle (color: your choice)
1 burin, nail, or dry ballpoint pen
1 small square of waxed paper or aluminum foil, 4 x 4 inches

Steps:
1. Empower supplies for the quality you seek (for example, wisdom).
2. Light the candle. Allow it to burn while you meditate upon the animal whom you have chosen to represent this quality (for example, the owl to represent wisdom).
3. Carefully pick up the candle and hold it horizontally. Allow the wax to drip onto a piece of waxed paper or aluminum foil in a roughly circular shape the size of a quarter. Make sure the wax is at least one-eighth of an inch thick, and try to keep it as even as possible.
4. Allow the wax to dry. Leave the candle to burn while you work.

5. Peel the wax off the waxed paper or aluminum foil and turn it over so that the smooth side is facing up.
6. With the burin, lightly scratch a simple symbol into the wax representing the animal you have chosen to represent the qualities you desire. Do not carve too deeply, or you will snap the wax disk.
7. When you are satisfied with your symbol, carefully go over the lines again with your burin to provide more definition, but be careful not to snap the disk. If the disk does snap, simply drip more wax onto the foil in another circular shape and begin again.
8. Hold the wax amulet in your hands and envision the animal whom you have chosen. Say:

   O [animal], be my [quality]
   [Quality] flow to me night and day, day and night.
   These are my words, this is my will.

9. Visualize the quality you seek flowing to you, down your arms and into the wax amulet.
10. Carry the amulet with you.

Variations: Carve a word on the wax disk, such as "love" or "patience." Carve an astrological symbol to align yourself with the energies associated with that astrological sign.

Charm to Bless a New Business Venture

This spell was commissioned to bless the launch of a new publishing imprint. You can use it to bless the launch of anything new, business or otherwise.

Timing: moon's first quarter; moon's second quarter; dawn; morning; Thursday; Wednesday; hour of Jupiter; hour of Mercury; or your personal power time

Supplies:
1 candle in a color you associate with new beginnings

Steps:
1. Face north. Stand quietly and take three deep breaths, inhaling peace, and exhaling stress and tension. Say:
   Power of Earth, mountains and plains,
   Bless this new venture with stability and prosperity.

2. Turn to face east. Say:
Power of Air, winds and laughter,
Bless this new venture with clear communication.
3. Turn to face south. Say:
Power of Fire, flame of enthusiasm and glow of passion,
Bless this new venture with joy and success.
4. Turn to face the west. Say:
Power of Water, rain and seas,
Bless this new venture with transformation and positive growth.
5. Turn to face north again and say:
We honor your many gifts, and thank you for our continued success in the field.
Powers of Earth, Air, Fire, and Water: blessed be!
6. Light the candle, visualizing the gifts from the four elements radiating from the flame and energizing your new project with their gifts. Allow it to burn down completely.

Variations: This spell can be performed without the candle. For a more formal ceremony, have a representation of each element set up around the candle or around you, such as a stone or a potted plant to the north side of the candle, a feather or incense on the east side, a smaller candle such as a tea light to the south side, and a cup or small bowl of water to the west side. This spell can also be adapted to bless anything, including people.

Banish Negative Energy

This is a great spell to perform on a regular basis, such as once a month, or at the beginning of every season.

Timing: moon's third quarter; moon's fourth quarter; Saturday; hour of Saturn; moon in Cancer; sunset; midnight; or your personal power time

Supplies:

Holy water (see recipe later in this chapter)
Salt
Charcoal tablet
Heatproof dish or censer
I tablespoon dried sage leaves

I tablespoon dried cedar
I white candle
Matches or a lighter
Tray

Steps:

1. Empower supplies for banishing negativity.
2. Begin at the back door of your home. If you do not have a back door, use a balcony door, or the front door. Light the charcoal tablet carefully and place it in the censer or dish. Place the dish and the herbs on the tray. Sprinkle a pinch of the dried herbs on the charcoal and, carrying the tray, begin to walk counterclockwise through the house. (Counterclockwise is the direction traditionally associated with banishing.)
3. In each room, walk counterclockwise and waft the smoke of the herbs around the perimeter. Open the closet and wardrobe doors to allow the smoke inside. As you waft the smoke, visualize the energy of the herbs filling the room and pushing out any negativity there. Open the windows to allow the negativity to escape. You will have to continually add pinches of the herbs as they burn away.
4. Continue throughout the house until you reach the back door again. Open the back door and visualize all the negativity you've been chasing out escaping into the great outdoors. Close the door.
5. Dip your finger in the holy water. Draw a symbol you associate with protection above the door. This symbol may be a cross, a pentacle, an X, a circle, a rune, or a symbol of your own design.
6. Remove the censer and the herbs from the tray, and replace them with the candle, the holy water, and the salt. Beginning at the back door, walk *clockwise* through your house with the tray.
7. In each room, close the windows and draw a protective symbol over each door and window with the holy water. Take a pinch of salt and sprinkle it around the perimeter of the room in a clockwise direction. (The salt does not need to form an unbroken line; sprinkle sparingly.) Hold the candle up in the center of the room and visualize the light filling the room with positive energy.
8. Continue clockwise around the house until you reach the back door once again. Over every door and window, draw the protective symbol with the holy water. Draw it over every mirror as well.
9. Take the candle and place it in the center of your home to burn down, and to continue radiating the positive energy. This may be the physical center of your home, or the spiritual center.

Variations: You may replace the dried herbs and charcoal with sage incense in cone or stick form, or purification incense. Leave a white candle burning in each room. If you have a two-story house, begin on the top floor: move counterclockwise around the top floor, descend the stairs, move to the back door, and move counterclockwise around the ground floor. If you have a basement, begin there and move up to the main floor. If you have both an upper floor and a basement, do the top floor, descend to the basement, and then ascend to the ground floor. If you have an attic and store things in it, begin there, then do your living floors in descending order.

Petition Spell to Banish Faults

Use this spell to systematically eliminate weaknesses from your life.

Timing: moon's third quarter; moon's fourth quarter; Saturday; hour of Saturn; sunset; midnight; autumn; winter; or your personal power time

Supplies:
2 pieces vegetable parchment (one small, one larger)
I pen
Cauldron or heatproof dish
White candle
Matches or a lighter

Steps:
1. Empower the supplies for success.
2. On the larger piece of vegetable parchment, write down five faults that you would like to banish from your life. Choose one from this list and write it on the smaller piece of parchment.
3. Light the candle.
4. Fold the small paper up and touch the corner of the paper to the candle's flame until it ignites. Drop the paper in the cauldron or heatproof dish.
5. Watch the paper redden, whiten, then blacken, and visualize your fault losing substance and vanishing from your life. With intent and awareness, cross that fault off the list on the larger piece of parchment.
6. When the ashes of the paper have cooled, bury them outdoors off your property.
7. Choose the next appropriate time to banish another fault from your list and proceed as above. Repeat weekly or over the next series of moon cycles until your list is done. After the final repetition of the spell, burn the larger list as well.

Holy Water

Holy water is, in essence, water that is sacred to you in some way. For some, this might be water blessed by a member of the clergy of their chosen religious path; for others, this may be rainwater; spring water personally collected from a natural site; well water; or water empowered through a method such as this.

Timing: Monday; hour of the moon; moon in the sign of Pisces; dark, full, or new moon; dawn; noon; sunset; midnight; blue moon; or your personal power time

Supplies:
1 cup nonsparkling bottled water
3 drops rose water
Glass bowl
Small clear quartz, cleansed (scrub it physically in addition to purifying it)
Sterilized bottle and cap

Steps:
1. Pour the bottled water into the glass bowl. Hold your hands over it and empower it with positive energy.
2. Add the rose water drop by drop. As each drop lands in the water, visualize the mixture sparkling and glowing.
3. Hold your hands over the mixture again, and empower it, saying:

   The blessings of love and light upon this water.

4. Pour the empowered water into the sterilized bottle.
5. Empower the small quartz stone with love and positive energy, then gently add it to the water in the bottle. Cap it.

Variations: Holy water makes a lovely offering to the Divine, as well as a good addition to wash water, bath water, and water for your houseplants. You can bury small vials of it outside your door to protect the home, carry it with you, add a drop or two to oils, potpourris, potions, incenses, and elixirs. I store my holy water in the refrigerator, so it lasts longer. Although holy water can last some time, I recommend making fresh holy water approximately once a month. If you have older holy water left over, pour it outside as an offering.

Simple Blessing Oil

The act of creating a tool such as an oil, incense, talisman, and so forth is in itself a spell. Your goal is to combine the disparate energies into one unit, programmed or charged for a certain purpose. This blessing oil can be used to anoint candles and stones to be used in any spell, or to purify objects and people.

Timing: moon's second quarter; first days of moon's third quarter; dawn; noon; Monday; hour of the moon; moon in Pisces; blue moon; your personal power time

Supplies:
9 drops frankincense oil
1 teaspoon olive oil
Small glass bottle and cap

Steps:
1. Empower the supplies for positive energy and blessing.
2. In the glass bottle, combine the olive oil and the frankincense oil. Cap and shake to blend.

13

beyond spellcasting

When you have mastered spellcasting by the traditional method, challenge yourself with these advanced techniques. Established spellcasters often discover that experience offers wisdom which can inform their lives on various levels, leading them to integrate magical acts into the flow of daily life instead of doing extensive spellwork to transform their lives for the better.

࿋

After a few years of spellcrafting you're likely to discover that you need spells less frequently. The more you handle positive energy, the more calm and serene your life will become, reflecting the energy with which you work. Eventually, the energy will flow throughout your life and actions.

It's easy to forget, but the ultimate goal of spellcasting isn't to have more or to be able to work less. It can be a nice bonus once the positive energy is free to flow through your life, but it's not the object of the practice. Using spells to achieve balance and positive change in your life theoretically leads you to live your life in a positive fashion.

The Witches' Pyramid

The Witches' Pyramid is a concept which some spellcasters never hear about, but it's a valuable meditative device. It lists four key actions: To Know; To Dare; To Will; To Be Silent. These four concepts bear much fruit upon meditation, and mean different things in every individual spellcaster's life, but here are some concepts associated with each action for you to start thinking about.

To Know

Every spellcaster has the right and the responsibility to gather as much knowledge as possible, by experiencing as much as you can, by reading as much as you can, by thinking, by discussing with others, and by being open to new ideas. It means amassing experience upon which to base future decisions and judgments.

To Will

A spellcaster's most valuable personal tool is his or her will. Your will is what creates change in the world around you. Your desire might begin it, but your will forces it to happen. By focusing your willpower you direct your determination to act upon your environment, your circumstances, and your life. Your will is what drives your desire to improve and excel. It is the key to your success.

To Dare

A spellcaster has to dare to take action and change his or her circumstances. To dare means to apply the knowledge you have gathered. It also means that you have to take risks, push your boundaries, and challenge yourself. Dare to go beyond what you are already familiar with, and beyond who you are today in order to make a better tomorrow for yourself and for your loved ones.

To Be Silent

The value of keeping quiet is often overlooked in today's society where everyone is jockeying to have their own say and to be heard. There's a wonderful adage that illustrates this concept: "Better to be thought a fool than to open one's mouth and prove it to be true." Judge carefully as to whom you should discuss your accomplishments, your spellwork, and your beliefs with. There are those who believe that to speak of something draws power away from it, rendering it weak. Keeping silent also avoids the needless waste of energy.

BE CAREFUL OF WHAT YOU WISH FOR

As you work with natural energy and refine your abilities to effect change upon your environment, you will begin to recognize that idle wishes and spoken thoughts will seem to have more power invested in them.

Over the course of this book, you have discovered that anything spoken with awareness and intent can be powerful. The more you learn, the more knowledge and experience you acquire as a spellcaster, the more power you bring to bear on your everyday life. Spellcasting trains you to create change at will, using the energy available to you. If you are careless, then the change you have not thought through can occur in response to your words and actions. As you've read, the spoken word is an important element in the "as above, so below" relationship, representing bringing a thought or desire, which exists on the mental plane, into manifestation on the material plane. In Chapters 7 and 8, I discussed how the spoken word alone carries great power as a spell or as a technique to raise energy. The more experience you gain in this sort of application of energy, the more you will develop your abilities, and your words will carry greater and greater significance.

It may sound like a cliché, but with greater power comes greater responsibility. Be aware of what you say, and how you say it. Make every word count, both in spellcasting and in your daily life.

WORKING ON THE ASTRAL PLANE

The astral plane is a spiritual reflection of the material world. Technically, every time you physically perform a spell, you are also working on the astral level. A physical action in a spell is performed specifically for the equivalent and associated energy where it moves on the astral plane. Once you have become adept at handling energies gathered in the physical world, then you might find yourself using fewer and fewer props and components. The web of energy, which connects everything, also extends to the astral level. It's perfectly possible to do an entire spell on the astral plane, which is where most change occurs anyway, initiated by your symbolic actions on the physical plane. It takes a lot of focus, and the establishing of a personal place of power on the astral plane.

You're most likely familiar with the astral plane due to the concept of astral projection. The art of astral projection involves sending your consciousness elsewhere. It takes a lot of energy and concentration to do it, and it's usually prefaced by meditation. Basically, spellcasting on the astral plane is rather like doing the spell in your head, but with all the awareness and intention of performing the spell in the physical world.

MEDITATION

Meditation is an excellent method of refining your awareness and your ability to sense and control energy. It's a method of managing stress, which can interfere with your ability to channel energy. It smoothes the rough energy flowing through our lives into calmer, positive energy.

Most people think of meditation as sitting cross-legged with their eyes closed, trying to think of nothing. While this is certainly a valid interpretation, there are actually many different kinds of meditation. Most practices may be classified as one of two kinds of meditation:

- **Active Meditation:** This is when you allow an object to evoke associations in your mind as you focus on it. Associations can include such things as sounds, dialogue, memories, and even interaction with images.
- **Passive Meditation:** This is when you don't allow your mind to wander, focusing your visualization upon only the object of your meditation.

There are several reasons to meditate. The opportunity to quiet our minds allows self-discovery, healing, insight, the re-establishment of emotional balance, and it encourages positive change. Meditation provides the opportunity to listen to our souls and bodies without the distraction of mental chatter, or stream of consciousness. It can be a very spiritual practice. Edgar Cayce once said, "Prayer is talking to God. Meditation is listening to God."

The benefits of meditation are legion. It creates increased awareness of the self and the environment; it provides a time of inner silence, which is important for physical, mental, and emotional health; it creates a better energy flow for easier and more efficient living; it enhances personal energy for use in spiritual practice; and it conditions the mind through mental exercise.

Why exercise your mind through meditation? Everything begins with mind power. Even physical action originates with a thought. You've already discovered the importance of visualization and a clearly defined goal in spellcasting. Meditation helps hone these skills.

There are four basic requirements for meditation: a quiet environment to eliminate distractions; a comfortable position allowing complete relaxation of the physical body; a few moments spent relaxing to start; and a "mental device" to help block stream of consciousness generated by the waking mind, often called a mantra. That mental chatter, known as the stream of consciousness, is always present; you just notice it more when you try to meditate.

When is the best time for you to meditate? Take a moment to think about what the quietest time of your day is, or when you're least likely to be disturbed. That's an ideal time. Make sure the phone is off the hook, and that the TV and radio are turned off. Make sure you leave yourself enough time for preparation, for meditating, and for slowly coming out of the relaxed state. Create your ideal relaxed environment by selecting gentle music, soft lighting, and scents that calm you.

How often should you meditate? Remember that meditation is exercise, just like going to a gym, except this is a mental workout. Don't overdo it. And have patience: we frequently become frustrated with a practice such as meditation, because we expect instant change in the twenty-first century. Meditation is a slow process by which the mind is trained. It's better to meditate for ten minutes per day than for one hour per week. Like physical exercise, regular workouts are more effective than longer, fewer sessions.

Posture is important in any exercise, and being aware of your body is part of the work of meditation. Your physical state reflects your emotional state, so logically, your emotional state is also capable of influencing your physical state. While you may be tempted to lie down to meditate, be aware that your mind associates this position with sleep.

- When sitting, keep your spine erect by imagining a string running all the way up your spine and out of the crown of your head, pulling you taut. This allows your energy to flow unimpeded throughout your body.
- Relax your jaw; allow your head to float over your neck. Don't strain your head forward or force it backwards.
- Allow your arms to rest gently at your side or on your lap. Do not cross your arms or fold your hands.
- Let your feet contact the ground, preferably flat.

If something happens during your meditation, accept it; look at your response objectively, and don't leap to judge yourself. You have the ability to choose how to respond to things like annoying little itches, thoughts of inadequacy, and physical discomfort.

Exercise: Sacred Breathing Meditation

For each of these exercises, breathe as instructed for several cycles. If at any time you feel dizzy or ill, stop and try again later.

- **Version One:** Breathe in for four heartbeats; hold for a count of four heartbeats; exhale for four heartbeats; pause for four heartbeats. Don't catch and hold your breath aggressively; be gentle and allow this rhythm to flow. Focus only on your breath as it flows into your lungs, infuses them with oxygen, and flows out.
- **Version Two:** Repeat the breathing cycle from Version One. This time, imagine pure white energy being drawn up your core from your feet, rising to your nose; as you exhale, see the energy flow out with your breath and flow down to join your feet once again, forming a cycle.

CREATIVE VISUALIZATION

Imagination is a key player in your spellwork. It is a tool used by the rational mind to create alternate solutions, or to run "what-if" scenarios for problem solving. Using your imagination does not mean that you are pretending; done with intent and awareness, it is a deliberate creation of another reality. To pretend means that you know it's not real, which defeats the purpose of creating an alternate possibility. The human mind is a powerful tool. The trick is to know what you want so that you can work on changing things; hence the importance of determining a clear and simple goal in spellcasting.

Like meditation, working on creative visualization can help refine your spellcasting abilities.

THE ALPHA STATE

To help you understand how your thoughts can affect reality, here's a basic breakdown of the four main levels of brainwave activity.

- **Beta** (everyday), which is our everyday level of functioning
- **Alpha** (light trance), which we settle into when we get lost in a good book or film, and suspend our disbelief
- **Theta** (deep trance/light sleep)
- **Delta** (deep sleep REM)

Most spellwork occurs in the alpha state. Author and witch Laurie Cabot says that in the alpha state, the brain "receive[s] mystical, visionary information that does not come through the five senses. In alpha the rational filters that process ordinary reality are weakened or removed, and the mind is receptive to nonordinary realities" (Cabot, 1989, pp. 173).

Dreams are a form of unconscious visualization; daydreams are conscious visualization. Remember always that thoughts are energy, and that like attracts like. If you constantly think negative thoughts, you will attract negative energy. This is a classic example of creating a self-fulfilling prophecy.

Creative visualization is a skill like any other, which requires practice and time to improve the skill. Like meditation, creative visualization requires determination, concentration, and, of course, practice.

Exercise: Creative Visualization: The Screen

This is the visualization exercise I teach to students, based on Laurie Cabot's alpha meditation found in *Power of the Witch*.

1. Close your eyes and visualize a white screen—just a white screen—in front and above your eyes. This would put it in front of your forehead. You may have heard the term "the third eye": when you close your eyes they naturally focus a bit out and up. This is where your third eye would be, if you had one. This is also the place known as the brow chakra.
2. See a couple of static images, like slides, on this imaginary screen. Run a little film or a scene on it. Play with it until you're comfortable.
3. Now project/imagine a static image of a specific object on this screen: for example, an apple.
4. Slowly add other senses to this flat picture: the smell; the sense of mass, weight, and volume, making it three-dimensional. Touch the apple or image you have pictured on your screen.
5. Add emotion: How does the apple make you feel?
6. Add action: Taste the apple. Imagine the feel of your teeth breaking through the skin, the faint bitterness of the peel, the cellular structure of the flesh, the juice, the rush of saliva in your mouth, and so forth.

When you practice your creative visualization, remember to relax: don't squint, don't hunch, and don't tense. You're using mental muscles, not physical ones. As occultists Melita Denning and Osborne Phillips say, "Visualization is something that you do with your mind, not something you do with your eyes."

Practice creative visualization frequently and you will notice your ability to maintain a visualization of improving your desire or goal. The more emotion you can pour into that visualization the better, as emotion helps fuel the spell.

The Importance of Instinct

In Chapter 4, I talked about trusting your instincts when it comes to ethics, and also in Chapter 9 in conjunction with substituting components. Now I'm going to talk about it in relation to not consciously casting spells at all.

Sometimes, you will have a certain response to a situation that doesn't seem like a spell at first. A friend might show up on your doorstep in tears, because her significant other walked out on her. You might make her a cup of tea to help comfort her. While most of the time you might not consider brewing a cup of ordinary tea a spell, if you do it with awareness and intent, your action will carry more power with it. As you brew it, you might visualize your friend drinking the tea and calming down, feeling loved and secure. What was likely a part of your original unconscious desire which led you to brew the tea can be reinforced and further empowered simply by performing the everyday action with awareness.

The more you work with spells, and the more accustomed you become to handling natural energy, the more attuned you will become to the ways things work. Fundamentally, you will have trained your mind and instincts to define your goal and channel your will toward that goal, and you will apply the same method in what appear to be nonmagical situations.

Your instinct might direct you to make a certain choice, and intellectually you might not be able to explain why you made that decision. Without being consciously aware of it, you will have sensed the energy of the situation and responded to it in the way that you decided was best. Likewise, you might not consciously be able to explain why you feel drawn to use an herb, a color, or a symbol in a spell, but instinctively you will be connecting the cure with the problem. Trust your gut instinct at all times. You might not be able to find the proof in a book, but if you're strongly pulled to it, do it, use it.

Living the Magic

One of the wonderful results of spellcrafting is how your everyday life begins to reflect your magic. Not only do your daily choices and actions support your spellwork, they reinforce your feeling of control over your personal path, and your expression of personal power and capability within your sphere.

By using spellcraft to enhance and improve your life, you draw positive energy your way. You do the work of the Divine, improving your life so that your capability to help others is also enriched. By learning to channel your desires through the spellcrafting and spellcasting process, you manifest abundance and joy in your life. The more positive energy that you channel in your spellcraft, the more beneficial energy flows your way on its own, attracted by the changes you have wrought and the signs that positive energy leaves in your life.

Everyone deserves to have their basic needs met so that they may look to self-actualization and transcendence. The art of spellcraft not only fulfills you on those basic levels of shelter, food, clothing, and other needs dependent on financial security; it also opens up a world of celebration. The resplendent world that the Divine has created for us to live in possesses wondrous energy, and our lives possess so much potential. Spellcraft is one of the many ways that we may reach out and share in the energy of Nature, and I do mean share: we borrow, but we also give back. Live your life to the fullest, and rejoice in the glory that surrounds you.

template and worksheet

BASIC SPELL TEMPLATE

Crafting the Spell
- Identify your goal or desire
- Examine the context of the situation
- Evaluate the repercussions
- Refine the specifics of your need or desire
- Decide on a time
- Decide on a method
- Choose correspondences and components
- Create central symbolic action
- Write the text of the spell
- Write the complete list of required materials

Casting the Spell
- Set up
- Purify
- Dedicate the space
- State your purpose
- Raise and release energy
- Ground
- Release the dedicated space
- Record the experience
- Reinforce the spell with action

Recording Spell Notes

- Name of spell:

- Date and time performed:

- Moon phase:

- Location:

- How long it took to cast the spell:

- Weather:

- Your state of health:

- Purpose of the spell:

- Deities/Elementals invoked:

- Tools and ingredients required:

- The full text of the spell or ritual:

- Your immediate reaction:

- Short-term results:

- Long-term results:

correspondences by component

I have assembled these tables of popular correspondences of commonly found components for quick reference. This appendix does not absolve you of the responsibility of developing your own sets of correspondences! No book can dictate how you can or cannot use a substance's energies. These are guidelines only.

COLORS

Red: life, passion, action, energy

Pink: affection, friendship

Orange: success, speed, career, action

Yellow: intellectual matters, communication

Light green: healing, wishes

Dark green: prosperity, money, nature

Light blue: truth, spirituality, tranquility, peace

Dark blue: healing, justice

Violet: mysticism, meditation, spirituality

Purple: occult power, spirituality

Black: protection, fertility, mystery

Brown: stability, home, career

White: purity, psychic development

Grey: calm, spirit work, gentle closure, neutralizing energy or situations

Silver: purity, divination, psychic work, feminine energy, spirit, lunar energy

Gold: health, prosperity, solar energy, masculine energy

Stones

Agate: strength, courage, healing, protection

Agate, blue lace: peace, soothes stress, spirituality, inspiration, tranquility

Agate, moss: healing, strength, the plant world, agriculture

Amber: energy, healing, creativity, life, beauty, love, attraction

Amethyst: truth, protection, peaceful sleep, spirituality, soothes stress, courage, travel, meditation, psychic awareness, justice, beauty

Aquamarine: peace, joy, happiness, psychic powers

Aventurine: luck, fortune, money, mental powers, healing

Bloodstone (also known as heliotrope): healing, money, courage, strength, fertility

Carnelian: career, success, hunting, courage, confidence, eases nightmares

Citrine: eases nightmares, creativity, digestion

Fluorite: meditation, enhances energy, study, mental ability, amplifies other stones

Garnet: happiness, fidelity, strength, protection, healing

Hematite: grounding, protection from negative energy, healing

Howlite: communication, perception, intellectual pursuits, action

Jade: wealth, abundance, prosperity, money, business, love, friendship, healing, wisdom, protection

Jasper: energy, courage, strength, protection

Lapis lazuli: healing, wisdom, mental powers, joy, stress-reliever, spirituality, peace, fidelity, psychic awareness, protection

Malachite: fertility, protection, travel, love, soothes stress, sleep, money

Moonstone: love, compassion, friendship, psychic powers, sleep

Obsidian: protection, divination, grounding

Onyx: protection

Pearl: lunar energy, water, love, luck

Rhodochrosite: energy, peace, love

Quartz, clear: energy, meditation, healing, psychic abilities

Quartz, rose: peace, love, affection, beauty, children, comfort, fidelity

Sodalite: soothes stress, wisdom, emotional balance, meditation, peace

Tiger's eye: luck, wealth, honesty, protection, courage, confidence

Turquoise: eloquence, health, happiness, protects children, travel, money, beauty, luck

Metals

Aluminum: This metal is associated with mental abilities and travel.

Brass: An alloy of copper and zinc (communication, prosperity), brass can be used as a magical substitute for gold. Brass is associated with solar energy, healing, protection, and money.

Copper: This metal is associated with Venus, love, attraction, feminine energy, conducting energy, luck, energy, healing, and money.

Gold: Associated with solar energy, purity, wealth, prosperity, success, and energy, gold is also known for healing, protection, wisdom, and male fertility.

Iron: This metal is associated with Mars, defense, protection from evil fairies and spirits, power, strength, and grounding.

Lead: This metal is associated with Saturn, the underworld, protection, defensive spells, divination, strength, community, and leadership.

Mercury: Also known as quicksilver, mercury is very rarely found, as it has been declared toxic. It used to be used in thermometers. For the sake of reference, I have included the information here. It is associated with Mercury, communication, links, mental agility.

Pewter: An alloy of mostly tin, pewter has a small amount of antimony (advancement, determination, success), and traces of copper.

Platinum: This metal is associated with harmony, health, and relaxation.

Silver: Associated with lunar energy, the Goddess, purity, love, psychic abilities, silver is also known for peace, protection, money, and travel.

Steel: This metal is an alloy of iron and small amounts of carbon. It is associated with protection, healing, and protection from nightmares.

Tin: This metal is associated with Jupiter, divination, luck, intellectual pursuits, and new beginnings.

Herbs, Trees, and Plants

NOTE: I have included poisonous herbs in this list of correspondences and note them as "toxic." I do not recommend using them, especially since there are several other components you can substitute with similar energy. However, you may run across references to them in other spellbooks, and so I have listed them here.

Aconite (toxic) (also known as wolfsbane and monkshood): consecration, purification

Allspice: prosperity, luck, healing, purification, protection, money

Almond: love, money, healing, wisdom

Angelica: protection, hex-breaker, healing, psychic abilities, house blessing, purification

Anise: psychic abilities, lust, luck, purification, love

Apple: love, healing, peace

Ash: protection, strength, healing, prosperity

Basil: discipline, protection, marriage, purification, prosperity, love, luck, mental abilities

Bay: healing, purification, protection, wisdom, psychic abilities, strength

Bayberry: abundance, prosperity

Benzoin: purification, healing, prosperity

Birch: protection, purification, new beginnings, children

Calendula: protection, psychic abilities, dreams, success with legal issues, fidelity, healing, love, animals, comfort

Camphor: chastity, sleep, healing

Catnip: love, cats, beauty, happiness, tranquility, luck

Cedar: healing, purification, protection, prosperity

Chamomile: money, love, sleep, meditation, purification, protection, tranquility

Chickweed: animals, love, fidelity, healing, weight loss

Cinnamon: healing, love, lust, success, purification, protection, money, psychic awareness

Cinquefoil (five-finger grass): eloquence, cunning, money, protection, sleep, prophetic dreams, purification, love

Clove: protection, mental abilities, attraction, purification, comfort

Clover: lust, hex-breaking, prosperity, purification, love, luck, protection, success, fidelity, comfort

Coffee: energy, grounding

Comfrey (boneset): healing, prosperity, protection, travel

Coriander: healing, love, lust

Cumin: protection, anti-theft, love, fidelity

Cypress: protection, comfort, healing

Daisy: nature spirits, love, children

Damiana: lust, love, psychic abilities

Dandelion: enhances psychic abilities, divination

Dill: protection, love, attraction, money, strength, luck, eases sleep, mental abilities, weight loss

Dragon's blood: energy, protection, purification, strengthens spells

Echinacea (purple coneflower): healing

Elder, Elderflower: protection from lightning, beauty, divination, prosperity, purification, house blessing, healing, sleep

Elm: love, protection,

Eucalyptus: protection, healing

Eyebright: mental abilities, psychic abilities, clairvoyance, memory

Gardenia: love, attraction, peace, meditation

Garlic: healing, house blessing, protection, lust, anti-theft

Geranium: love, healing, protection, fertility

Ginger: healing, love, money, energy

Feverfew: love, fidelity, protection, healing

Flax: money, protection, beauty, healing

Frankincense: protection, purification, meditation

Hawthorn: protection, fertility, happiness

Hazel: mental abilities, fertility, protection, wisdom, luck

Heather: protection, rain, luck

Heliotrope: clairvoyance, psychic abilities, health, money

Hibiscus: love, lust, divination, harmony, peace

High John: prosperity, success, happiness, hex-breaker, removes obstacles

Honeysuckle: prosperity, psychic abilities, money

Hops: healing, sleep

Hyacinth: love, comfort, protection

Hyssop: purification, protection

Jasmine: love, attraction, prosperity, tranquility

Juniper: purification, love, protection, health, anti-theft, fertility, psychic abilities

Lavender: love, protection, healing, purification, peace, house blessing, wisdom, children, marriage

Lemon: purification, love, protection, happiness

Licorice: love, lust, protection, fidelity

Lilac: protection, beauty, love, psychic abilities, purification, prosperity

Lily: protection, love antidote, truth

Lime: love, purification, luck, sleep

Lotus: blessing, meditation, protection

Maple: sweetness, prosperity, marriage, love, money

Marjoram: love, marriage, protection, healing, happiness, money, comfort

Mint (see also Peppermint and Spearmint): money, healing, travel, purification, lust

Mistletoe: healing, protection, love, fertility, sleep, luck

Mugwort: travel, divination, psychic abilities, protection, healing, strength, lust

Myrrh: protection, purification, healing, meditation

Neroli (orange blossom): love, marriage

Nettle: protection, healing, lust, hex-breaking

Nightshade (toxic) (belladonna): protection

Nutmeg: clairvoyance, health, luck, fidelity

Oak: purification, protection, prosperity, health and healing, money, fertility, luck, strength

Onion: healing, protection, purification

Orange: love, joy, purification, prosperity

Oregano: peace

Orris root: inspiration, purity, love, divination, wisdom, purification, faith, courage

Parsley: healing, lust, fertility, protection, hex-breaker, prosperity

Patchouli: money, fertility, lust, clairvoyance, divination, love, attraction

Pepper: protection, purification

Peppermint: healing, love, purification, sleep, psychic abilities, lust

Pine: prosperity, healing, purification, fertility

Poppy: fertility, abundance, sleep, love

Rose: love, fertility, psychic abilities, healing, marriage, luck, protection

Rosemary: mental abilities, memory, anti-theft, purification, healing, sleep, love, lust, protection

Rowan (mountain ash): purification, house blessing, protection, healing, psychic abilities, strengthens spells, wisdom

Rue: protection, mental abilities, purification, health, comfort

Sage: longevity, wisdom, healing, purification, prosperity, business, wishes

Salt: protection, purification, grounding, courage

Sandalwood: protection, healing, meditation, purification

Spearmint: lust, healing, mental abilities, protection at night

St. John's Wort: protection, health, strength, happiness

Strawberry: love, beauty, luck

Sugar: love, sweetness, attraction, friendship

Tea, Black: mental abilities, money, courage, strength

Tea, Green: healing, longevity

Thyme: love, healing, psychic abilities, sleep, purification, courage

Valerian (all-heal): purification, protection, healing, love, sleep, attraction

Vanilla: love, prosperity, lust, energy, mental abilities, creativity

Vervain: creativity, inspiration, purification, healing, divination, protection, prosperity, love, sleep, tranquility

Vetivert: money, love, hex-breaking, luck

Violet: tranquillity, love, luck, protection, healing

Walnut: healing, mental abilities

Willow: communication, eloquence, protection, healing, love, dreams

Wintergreen: protection for children, hex-breaker, healing

Wormwood: removes negative energy, soothes anger, psychic abilities, divination, protection, purification, love

Yarrow: marriage, courage, love and friendship, psychic abilities, hex-breaking

Deities

Again, I caution you against simply inserting the name and energy of a deity into your spellcraft. Take the time to research the culture from which they derive, and the methods of spellcraft and worship to which they are accustomed, in order to ascertain the correct and respectful approach, or to determine if it is indeed appropriate to work with them.

Most deities have name variations, as well as cultural and/or regional variations; I have not included all of this information simply because to do so would create another book in its own right. Nor is this by any means an exhaustive list; these deities are commonly found in myth and spellwork.

For further research on deities, I recommend reading *The Witches' God* and *The Witches' Goddess* by Janet and Stewart Farrar, as well as *The New Book of Goddesses and Heroines* by Patricia Monaghan.

Amaterasu: (Japanese) the sun, ancestor of humanity, the seasons

Anubis: (Egyptian) the underworld, otherworld guide, protection

Aphrodite: (Greek) love, romance, sex, passion, women, lust, beauty

Apollo: (Greek) sun, arts, light, prophecy, logic, knowledge

Aradia: (Italian) spellcraft, magic

Arianrhod: (Welsh) magic, female independence, virginity, the moon

Artemis: (Greek) celibacy, fertility, hunting, protector of animals, the moon, birth, bees, bears

Athena: (Greek) wisdom, the arts, crafts, negotiation, olives, virginity, community, owls, serpents, protection

Bast: (Egyptian) love, the arts, luxury, cats, lioness, pleasure, dancing, music, joy, health

Brighid: (Pan-Celtic) inspiration, creativity, animals, children, women, hearth and home, healing, smithcraft, metalwork, defense, fire, water, cattle, milk

Cernunnos: (Pan-Celtic) forests, sovereignty, wildlife

Cerridwen: (Welsh) inspiration, transformation, initiation, death and rebirth, wisdom

Danu: (Irish) sovereignty, fertility

Demeter: (Greek) the earth, agriculture, crops, motherhood

Diana: (Roman) light, fertility, childbirth, the moon, hunting

Epona: (Gaulish) horses, fertility, sovereignty

Eros: (Greek) romance, passion, lust, physical love

Freyja: (Norse) love, passion, death, shapeshifting, prophecy, fertility, lust, battle, falcons

Frigga: (Norse) domestic balance, prophecy, herons

Ganesha: (Hindu) wisdom, luck, study, prosperity, abundance

Gwydion: (Welsh) spellcraft, shapeshifting

Hecate: (Greco-Roman) mysteries, the underworld, spellcraft, spellcasters, justice, dogs, horses, serpents, the moon, wisdom

Hera: (Greek) marriage, women, cuckoos, the three phases of womanhood: maiden, mother, crone

Hermes: (Greek) intellect, communication, commerce, messages, travel

Herne: (British) hunting, forests, wild animals

Hestia: (Greek) domestic balance, hearth, home, fire, community, family, hospitality

Horus the Elder: (Egyptian) falcons, balance, solar and lunar energy, healing, moon, sun

Horus the Younger: (Egyptian) humanity, rulership

Hygeia: (Greek) healing, health

Inanna: (Sumerian) fertility, sky, love

Isis: (Egyptian) magic, women, the moon, culture, healing

Jupiter: (Roman) business, career, leadership

Kuan Yin: (Chinese) compassion, peace, mercy, rainbow, willow, generosity

Lakshmi: (Hindu) wealth, abundance, cows, lotus, jewels

Lugh: (Pan-Celtic) success, excellence, competition, adoption

Ma'at: (Egyptian) justice, order, truth

Mercury: (Roman) communication, commerce, travel, theft

Odhinn: (Norse) wisdom, ravens, wolves, travel, poetry, sacrifice, mysteries

Osiris: (Egyptian) resurrection, agriculture, the underworld, afterlife

Pan: (Greek) lust, nature, wilderness, passion

Poseidon: (Greek) sea, horses, dolphins

Rhiannon: (Welsh) underworld, birds, journeying to the otherworld, horses, joy

Sarasvati: (Hindu) water, eloquence, study, arts and sciences, writing, music, speech, genius, inspiration

Sulis: (British) healing, water

Thor: (Norse) weather, agriculture, working class, soldiers, thunder, sky, farmers, sailors

Thoth: (Egyptian) wisdom, time, architecture, language, mathematics, moon, science

Tyr: (Norse) law, justice, leadership

correspondences by need •

Knowing how frustrating it is to page through reference books for a correspondence matching your need, I've prepared this appendix to help you locate ingredients and components by subject. Once again, these are not exhaustive correspondences; they are suggestions.

Action: cinnamon, clove, allspice, ginger; jasper, carnelian

Anger management: catnip, vervain, lavender, chamomile; amethyst, sodalite

Animals: catnip, chickweed; turquoise, pearl; Bast, Diana, Artemis, Cernunnos, Herne, Rhiannon

Beauty: rose, elderflower; amber, opal, rose quartz; Aphrodite

Career: basil, bayberry; aventurine, jade; Athena, Jupiter

Children: catnip, chamomile, lavender; moonstone, malachite, turquoise, coral; Brighid, Demeter, Hera, Horus

Communication: lapis lazuli; Brighid, Mercury, Sarasvati

Courage: ginger, bay, thyme; agate, amethyst, bloodstone, carnelian, hematite, jasper, tiger's eye; Mars, Artemis, Athena

Creativity: amber, vanilla; citrine, lapis lazuli, carnelian; Apollo, Athena, Brighid, Odhinn, the Muses

Defense (see also Protection): hematite, obsidian, onyx

Depression management: catnip, rose, St John's Wort; rose quartz, sodalite

Family: malachite, moonstone; Demeter, Horus, Frigga

Fertility: motherwort, nuts, seeds; malachite, moonstone; Hera, Inanna, Demeter, Isis

Happiness: rose, lemon, orange; Amaterasu, Bast

Health and Healing: apple, bay, cinnamon, comfrey, feverfew, eucalyptus, echinacea, ginger, garlic, hyssop, horehound, mint, rosemary, thyme, willow; amber, green agate, aventurine, bloodstone, hematite, carnelian, lapis lazuli, jasper, citrine; Apollo, Mercury, Brighid, Hygeia, Isis, Sulis

Hearth and Home: fire, earth; Hestia, Brighid, Vesta, Frigga

Justice: High John; lapis lazuli, amethyst; Apollo, Athena, Hecate, Isis, Tyr

Legal issues: High John, calendula; Ma'at

Love: apple, basil, catnip, cinnamon, ginger, damiana, gardenia, jasmine, lavender, maple, rose, passionflower, mint, strawberry, vanilla, vervain; amber, jade, lapis lazuli, moonstone, pearl, rose quartz; Aphrodite, Isis, Venus

Luck: allspice, heather; aventurine, jade, tiger's eye; Lakshmi, Ganesha

Lust: allspice, damiana, clove, vanilla; carnelian; Aphrodite, Venus, Eros, Pan

Mental activity: bay, mint, rosemary, camphor; hematite, quartz, sodalite; Apollo, Cerridwen, Hecate, Mercury, Lugh, Ganesha, Athena

Peace: chamomile, rose, lavender; amethyst, obsidian, malachite, sodalite, rose quartz

Prosperity: cinquefoil, clove, orange, nutmeg, cinnamon, nuts, clover; green agate, jade, pyrite, tiger's eye; Lakshmi, Ganesha

Protection: angelica, clove, salt, rosemary, sage, oak, ash, rowan, hawthorn, bay, frankincense, myrrh, lavender, mugwort, pepper, rose; carnelian, hematite, jade, jasper, onyx, obsidian, tiger's eye; Mars, Thor, Athena

Psychic abilities: mugwort, eyebright, nutmeg; amethyst, citrine, quartz; Apollo, Hecate, Odhinn

Purification: sandalwood, lotus, frankincense, cedar; Kuan Yin

Sleep: chamomile, valerian, verbena, lavender, jasmine, hops; amethyst, citrine

Stress management: valerian, lavender, rose, chamomile, calendula, St. John's Wort; amethyst, rose quartz, sodalite, jade; Kuan Yin

Study: eyebright, mint, rosemary; sodalite, fluorite, citrine; Thoth, Ganesha, Sarasvati

Success: cinnamon, High John, orange, clover, bay; carnelian; Apollo, Diana

Transformation: Cerridwen, Persephone

Wisdom: rowan, hazel, sage; amethyst, jade, sodalite; Athena, Thoth, Odhinn

appendix 4

exercise, spell, and technique index

Suggested Answers for Exercises

Exercise: Lunar and Solar Phases

1. When would you work a spell for a pregnant cat to have a successful delivery?
Possible answers: Moon's first quarter (animals, children); moon's second quarter (family); moon in the sign of Taurus (manifestation); moon in sign of Cancer (family and children).

2. When would you work a spell to bless a baby?
Possible answers: Dawn; moon's first quarter (children, new beginnings); moon's second quarter (family); moon in sign of Cancer (family); spring (new beginnings).

3. In what season would you choose to cast a spell for academic success?
Possible answers: Summer (energy, activity); fall (beginning of the academic year, concept of harvest); moon in sign of Sagittarius (study); moon in sign of Leo (success); moon in sign of Gemini (intellectual pursuits).

4. What moon phase would you choose to cast a spell to honor a newly deceased elderly relative? What moon sign? What season?
Possible answers: Moon's third quarter; moon's fourth quarter; moon in sign of Cancer (family); moon in sign of Pisces (spirituality); autumn (farewells and endings).

5. When would you choose to cast a spell to deepen spiritual awareness?
Possible answers: Dawn; moon in sign of Pisces (spirituality).

Exercise: Planetary Hours

1. What kind of spell could be cast on a Monday in the hour of the sun?
Possible answer: women's health issues.

2. You've decided to study for an M.B.A. What planetary hour on what day would be a good time to cast a spell to support this?

Possible answers: Wednesday; Saturday; hour of Mercury; hour of Saturn.

3. Your relationship with a hopeful new significant other just isn't working out. What planetary hour on what day of the week would be best to break the news that you think you should just be friends? (Okay, there's never a good time for something like this, but what time might minimize the potential fallout, maximize understanding, and a cordial return to being single?)

Possible answers: Wednesday; hour of Mercury; Friday; hour of Venus.

4. Your daughter is being pestered by someone at school. What planetary hour on what day would be a good time to create a talisman for her to carry to help keep her safe?

Possible answers: Sunday; Tuesday; hour of the sun; hour of Mars.

5. You and your partner have just planned your first vacation in years. You've made reservations, bought tickets, and now your partner's boss is threatening to cancel the vacation time in order to keep your partner working on a project. What planetary hour on what day would you choose to work a spell to protect your vacation plans from being ruined?

Possible answers: Wednesday; Monday; Thursday; Sunday; hour of Mercury; hour of the moon; hour of Jupiter; hour of the sun.

bibliography

Agrippa, Henry Cornelius. *Three Books of Occult Philosophy.* Translated by James Freake. Edited and annotated by Donald Tyson. St. Paul: Llewellyn Publications, 2000.

Aswynn, Freya. *Northern Mysteries and Magic: Runes & Feminine Powers.* Second edition. St. Paul: Llewellyn Publications, 1998.

Badonsky, Jill. *The Nine Modern Day Muses (and a Bodyguard).* New York: Gotham Press, 2003.

Beith, Mary. *Healing Threads.* Edinburgh: Polygon, 1997.

Beyerl, Paul. *Compendium of Herbal Magick.* Custer: Phoenix Publishing, 1998.

———. *Master Book of Herbalism.* Custer: Phoenix Publishing, 1984.

Budge, E. A. Wallis. *Egyptian Magic.* New York: Dover Publications, 1971.

———. *Egyptian Book of the Dead: The Papyrus of Ani in the British Museum.* New York: Dover Publications, 1961.

Cabot, Laurie and Tom Cowan. *Power of the Witch: The Earth, the Moon, and the Magical Path to Enlightenment.* New York: Delta, 1989.

Carmichael, Alexander. *Carmina Gadelica: Hymns and Incantations from the Gaelic.* Great Barrington: Lindisfarne Books, 1992.

Cicero, Chic and Sandra Tabitha. *Self-Initiation into the Golden Dawn Tradition.* St. Paul: Llewellyn Publications, 1998.

Cunningham, Scott. *Cunningham's Encyclopedia of Crystal, Gem, and Metal Magic.* St. Paul: Llewellyn Publications, 1988.

———. *Cunningham's Encyclopedia of Magical Herbs.* Second edition. St. Paul: Llewellyn Publications, 2000.

———. *Cunningham's Encyclopedia of Wicca in the Kitchen.* Third edition. St. Paul: Llewellyn Publications, 2003.

———. *Earth, Air, Fire, Water: More Techniques of Natural Magic.* St. Paul: Llewellyn Publications, 1991.

———. *Earth Power: Techniques of Natural Magic.* St. Paul: Llewellyn Publications, 1983.

———. *Magical Herbalism: The Secret Craft of the Wise.* St. Paul: Llewellyn Publications, 1983.

Denning, Melita and Osborne Phillips. *Practical Guide to Creative Visualization: Manifest Your Desires.* Third edition. St. Paul: Llewellyn Publications, 2001.

Farrar, Janet and Stewart. *The Witches' Goddess: The Feminine Principle of Divinity.* Blaine: Phoenix Publishing, 1987.

———. *The Witches' God: Lord of the Dance.* Blaine: Phoenix Publishing, 1989.

Fortune, Dion. *The Mystical Qabalah.* Revised edition. York Beach: Red Wheel/Weiser, 2000.

Frazer, James George. *The Golden Bough: A Study in Magic and Religion.* Abridged edition. New York: Macmillan, 1951.

Gamache, Henri. *The Mystery of the Long Lost 8th, 9th, and 10th Books of Moses.* Bronx: Original Publications, 1986.

Gardner, Gerald B. *The Meaning of Witchcraft.* Lake Toxaway: Mercury Publishing, 1959.

———. *Witchcraft Today.* Lake Toxaway: Mercury Publishing, 1954.

Gawain, Shakti. *Creative Visualization: Use the Power of Your Imagination to Create What You Want In Your Life.* San Rafael: New World Library, 1978.

Gonzalez-Wippler, Migene. *The New Revised Sixth and Seventh Books of Moses.* Bronx: Original Publications, 1982.

Grieve, Mrs. Maud. *A Modern Herbal in Two Volumes: The Medicinal, Culinary, Cosmetic and Economic Properties, Cultivation and Folk-Lore of Herbs, Grasses, Fungi, Shrubs & Trees with Their Modern Scientific Uses.* New York: Dover Publications, 1982.

Herr, Karl. *Hex and Spellwork: The Magical Practices of the Pennsylvania Dutch.* Boston: Red Wheel/Weiser, 2002.

Hohman, John George. *Pow-Wows or Long-Lost Friend: A Collection of Mysterious and Invaluable Arts and Remedies.* Pomeroy, WA: Health Research, 1971.

Holland, Eileen. *The Wicca Handbook.* York Beach: Weiser, 2000.

Jones, Leslie Ellen. *From Witch to Wicca.* Cold Spring Harbor: Cold Spring Press, 2004.

K, Amber. *True Magick: A Beginner's Guide.* St. Paul: Llewellyn Publications, 2000.

Kraig, Donald Michael. *Modern Magick: Eleven Lessons in the High Magickal Arts.* St. Paul: Llewellyn Publications, 1988.

Leland, Charles. *Etruscan Roman Remains.* Blaine: Phoenix, 1999.

———. *Aradia: Gospel of the Witches.* Expanded edition. Blaine: Phoenix, 1999.

Lindholm, Lars L. *Pilgrims of the Night: Pathfinders of the Magical Way.* St. Paul: Llewellyn Publications, 1993.

Lipp, Frank J. *Healing Herbs.* London: Duncan Baird Publishers, 1996.

Lust, John. *The Herb Book.* New York: Beneficial Books, 2001.

Malbrough, Ray T. *Charms, Spells, and Formulas for the Making and Use of Gris-Gris, Herb Candles, Doll Magic, Incenses, Oils, and Powders to Gain Love, Protection, Prosperity, Luck, and Prophetic Dreams*. St. Paul: Llewellyn Publications, 1986.

———. *Hoodoo Mysteries: Folk Magic, Mysticism, & Rituals*. St. Paul: Llewellyn Publications, 2003.

———. *Magical Power of the Saints: Evocation and Candle Rituals*. St. Paul: Llewellyn Publications, 1998.

Mathers, S. Liddell MacGregor. *The Key of Solomon the King (Clavicula Salomonis)*. York Beach: Red Wheel/Weiser, 2002.

McColman, Carl. *Before You Cast a Spell: Understanding the Power of Magic*. Franklin Lakes: New Page Books, 2004.

McLelland, Lilith. *Spellcraft: A Primer for the Young Magician*. Chicago: Eschaton, 1997.

Melody. *Love Is in the Earth: A Kaleidoscope of Crystals, Updated*. Wheat Ridge: Earth-Love Publishing House, 1995.

Meyer, Marvin W. and Richard Smith. *Ancient Christian Magic: Coptic Texts of Ritual Power*. Princeton: Princeton University Press, 1999.

Morrison, Dorothy. *Bud, Blossom, & Leaf: The Magical Herb Gardener's Handbook*. St. Paul: Llewellyn Publications, 2001.

Nichols, Ross. *Book of Druidry*. Toronto: HarperCollins Canada, 1992.

Oribello, William A. *Candle Burning Magic With the Psalms*. New Brunswick: Inner Light, 1988.

Paracelsus, Theoprastus. *Archidoxes of Magic*. Kessinger Publications, 1992.

Pliny (C. Plinius Secondus). *The History of the World, commonly called The Natural History*. Translated by Philemon Holland; selected and introduced by Paul Turner. New York: McGraw Hill, 1964.

RavenWolf, Silver. *American Folk Magic: Charms, Spells, and Herbals.* Second Edition. St. Paul: Llewellyn Publications, 1998.

———. *Angels: Companions in Magick.* St. Paul: Llewellyn Publications, 1996.

———. *Solitary Witch: The Ultimate Book of Shadows for the New Generation.* St. Paul: Llewellyn Publications, 2003.

Schueler, Betty and Gerald. *Egyptian Magick: Enter the Body of Light & Travel the Magickal Universe.* Second edition. St. Paul: Llewellyn Publications, 1994.

Shelley, Mary. *Frankenstein* (1818 text). Oxford: Oxford University Press, 1994.

Smith, Steven R. *Wylundt's Book of Incense.* York Beach: Weiser, 1996.

Teish, Luisah. *Jambalaya: The Natural Woman's Book of Personal Charms and Practical Rituals.* New York: HarperSanFrancisco, 1985.

Telesco, Trish. *Bubble, Bubble, Toil and Trouble: Mystical Munchies, Prophetic Potions, Sexy Servings and Other Witchy Dishes.* Toronto: HarperCollins Canada, 2002.

———. *A Kitchen Witch's Cookbook.* St. Paul: Llewellyn Publications, 1994.

———. *A Witch's Beverages and Brews: Magic Potions Made Easy.* Franklin Lakes: New Page Books, 2000.

Thorsson, Edred. *Northern Magic: Rune Mysteries and Shamanism.* Second edition. St. Paul: Llewellyn Publications, 1998.

Valiente, Doreen. *Natural Magic.* Custer: Phoenix Publishing, 1975.

———. *The Rebirth of Witchcraft.* Custer: Phoenix Publishing, 1989.

Wade, Carole & Carol Tavris. *Psychology.* New York: Harper & Row, 1987.

index

POWER SPELLCRAFT FOR LIFE